A Compass Pointing Home

A Compass Pointing Home

*The Adventurous Life of William Bratton
of the Lewis and Clark Expedition*

Amie Kunkle Cox

Copyright © 2022 Amie Kunkle Cox
All rights reserved.

ISBN 13: 979-8-9857383-0-8 (paperback)
ISBN 13: 979-8-9857383-1-5 (hardcover)

No part of this book may be reproduced, or stored
in a retrieval system, or transmitted in any form or by
any means, electronic, mechanical, photocopying, recording,
or otherwise, without express written permission of the author.

Printed in the United States of America

To the keeper of my heart,
you are my compass straight and true.
To my own sweet Gemini, you are the wind beneath me.
To my two chickadees, you always make me smile.
To my maternal sun, you encourage me to always reach.
To all the other stars in my sky, you light my path.

CONTENTS

Author's Note
The Bratton-Dunlap Family Tree
The James Maxwell Family Tree
The James Berry Family Tree
Chapter One – Augusta County, Virginia   1
Chapter Two – Settling in Kentucky   17
Chapter Three – Franklin Co., Ky.   37
Chapter Four – Lewis and Clark Expedition   55
Chapter Five – Franklin Co., Ky, 1807-1812   89
Chapter Six – The War of 1812   121
Chapter Seven – Warren County, Kentucky   149
Chapter Eight – Terre Haute, Indiana   167
Chapter Nine – Montgomery Co., Indiana   185
Chapter Ten – Montgomery Co., 1825-1841   201
Chapter Eleven – Real William Bratton?   221
Chapter Twelve – The End of an Adventure   241
Pictures   255
Appendix A – William Bratton's Account Book   263
Appendix B – Montgomery Co. Petition, Fields   273
Acknowledgements   277
Bibliography   279
Index   287

AUTHOR'S NOTE

Either in preparation for the Lewis and Clark Expedition, or in admiration of the compass owned by Meriwether Lewis, William Bratton bought his own pocket compass for the journey. His compass might not have been as fancy but it too was nestled in a block of wood. The block was two and a half inches long by one and three quarters inches wide. A depression dominated the center of the block where a needle rested upon a paper dial to make the compass. A round glass covered the compass and was held by a spring that was fixed inside the depression. The other half of the block, a hinged wooden cover, when clasped with its other half, stalwartly protected the compass against jostles or falls. If William needed to calculate the time, he could also use the compass as a sundial. While William's compass was probably just a useful but ordinary item to him, to me, it is a specific and tangible possession of his that most symbolized his greatest adventure.

I first initiated research on William Bratton to help my husband write a grant. Like many, he wanted to follow in the legendary footsteps of Lewis and Clark, and if he was successful in securing the grant, I was willing to trot along beside him. I am a history buff too but I was more enamored at the time with exploring hidey-holes from the Underground Railroad and reading tombstones in 17th century cemeteries. This was even after I coincidentally at age thirty-one read Stephen Ambrose's Undaunted Courage and discovered a thoughtful reflection by Meriwether Lewis upon his own 31st birthday. He was very much unimpressed with his own contributions towards society and mankind. I remember being incredulous about the lofty expectations he set for himself but was also inspired to write down my own reflection of my life's journey up to age thirty-one. Ultimately, it was my research about William Bratton that amped my rampant interest for the early 1800s era into an obsessive enthusiasm.

    William Bratton is a local hero in the county where I live. He settled in Indiana during the latter half of his life. Such documents as early county commissioner records, his account book, and his probate papers were as close as a trip to the local library and courthouse. As a former journalist, current librarian, a part-time archives assistant, and an uncertified amateur genealogist, I began to dig. At the Crawfordsville District Public Library in Montgomery County, Indiana, I delicately worked my way through an archival document container of Bratton material. Some of it pertained to William and some of it did not. However, after uncovering details of this man's life that were so fascinating, I soon realized this was not just grant material, it was more.

    Imagine moving to the Kentucky frontier at around age ten and taking your life into your own hands every time you opened your front door. Frontier pioneers not only had to watch for wolves and bears but for Native Americans who violently opposed their presence on their hunting grounds. As a boy moving from a civilized society to a verdant forest full of predators, William Bratton honed his observation skills, his survival skills, and his hunting skills. He practiced swiftly loading a gun and firing it; he learned to swim; and he learned to walk as quietly as he could through the forest. He also learned to write, to read, and to do arithmetic. In that frontier setting, he learned that to live to be a man, a good man, one needed to be smart, courageous, loyal, strong, and reliable. For whatever reason, at age twenty-six, he was romantically unattached, and the necessary skills he learned in his boyhood coupled with the skills he learned when apprenticed as a gunsmith made him the perfect candidate for the Lewis and Clark Expedition.

During his epic journey, when William and the rest of the Expedition members began making their way back from the Pacific Ocean, their journey was more than halfway over. The winter had been a trial for many and especially for William who suffered from back problems; many thought he was lucky to be alive. At that point and for the rest of the way, William's compass was pointing his way home. I can only imagine how joyful he was to be reunited with family and friends. The Expedition was not the only adventure in which the compass served him well. He worked on keelboats for a time. He served in the War of 1812, and as a prisoner of war, he marched across Canada. He moved to Indiana but made several trips back to Kentucky. For any of his journeys in which he carried his compass, once he rounded the halfway mark, it led him home. William kept the compass his whole life, and it given to his grandson James T. Fields who lived in Illinois in the 1920s. Hopefully today, one of his descendants still has it. Regardless, William Bratton's compass inspired the title of this book, A Compass Pointing Home: the Adventurous Life of William Bratton of the Lewis and Clark Expedition. I hope you enjoy his story.

Sincerely,
Amie Kunkle Cox

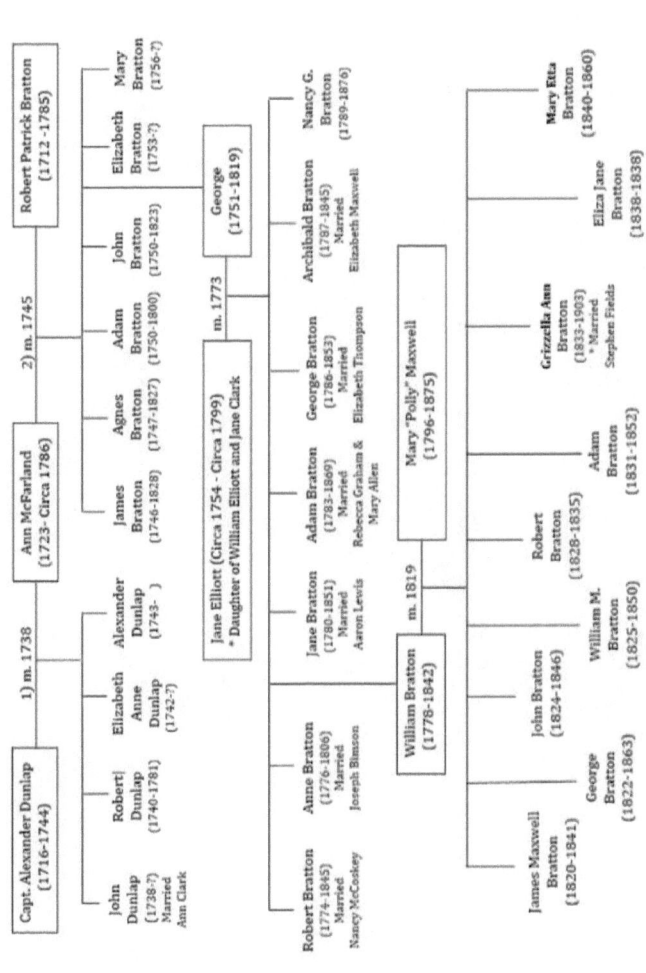

The Bratton-Dunlap Family of Augusta County, Virginia

The James Maxwell family of Washington County, Virginia and Warren County, Kentucky

James Maxwell - Grizella/Grisal Berry

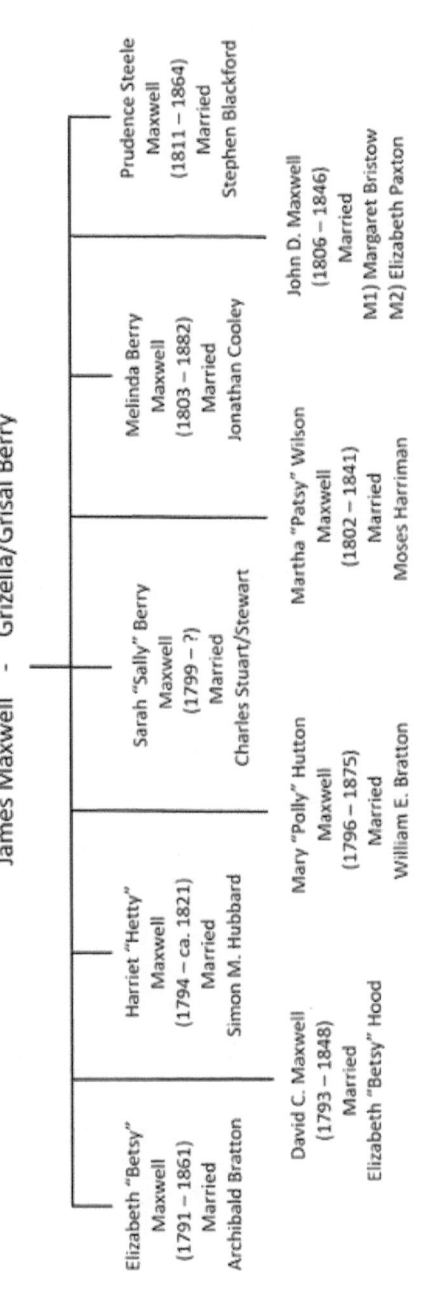

- Elizabeth "Betsy" Maxwell (1791 – 1861) Married Archibald Bratton
- David C. Maxwell (1793 – 1848) Married Elizabeth "Betsy" Hood
- Harriet "Hetty" Maxwell (1794 – ca. 1821) Married Simon M. Hubbard
- Mary "Polly" Hutton Maxwell (1796 – 1875) Married William E. Bratton
- Sarah "Sally" Berry Maxwell (1799 – ?) Married Charles Stuart/Stewart
- Martha "Patsy" Wilson Maxwell (1802 – 1841) Married Moses Harriman
- Melinda Berry Maxwell (1803 – 1882) Married Jonathan Cooley
- John D. Maxwell (1806 – 1846) Married
  M1) Margaret Bristow
  M2) Elizabeth Paxton
- Prudence Steele Maxwell (1811 – 1864) Married Stephen Blackford

The James Berry family of Washington County, Virginia

James Berry - Elizabeth McCutchen

- **Thomas Berry** (1763 – 1805) Married Elizabeth Walker
- **William Berry** (ca. 1768 – ?)
- **Grizella Ann Berry** (1770 – ca. 1821) Married James Maxwell
- **Prudence Berry** (1772 – 1810) Married William Steele
- **James Berry** (1773 – 1842) Married Rebecca Reagan
- **Mary Berry** (ca. 1775 – ?) Married Leonard Hutton
- **Samuel Berry** (1780 – 1855) Married Jane Anne Weir
- **Jonathan Berry** (ca. 1783 – aft. 1806) Married
- **Sarah Berry** (1785 – 1846) Married Joseph Williams
- **Rev. John McCutchen Berry** (1788-1857) Married Frances Williams

* After Elizabeth McCutchen Berry died, James Berry married again in 1791 to Martha Wilson in Washington Co, Va.

CHAPTER ONE
Augusta County, Virginia

On the sweltering day of Monday, July 27, 1778, a revolution was raging across America. Yet, the number one nemesis that day in George Bratton's house was the heat. His home was a middle-class farm in Augusta County, Virginia near Jackson's River, a branch of the James River. Although he was the patriarch of the household, he was most likely shooed away by female relatives as his wife Jean Elliott Bratton gave birth to their third child and son, William E(lliott) Bratton. Their eldest son Robert was almost four-years-old, and their daughter Anne was about two-years-old and the two young children were probably very interested in the new arrival. If they were present in the house at the time of the birth, they were just two of many people there that day. Besides their parents and any relatives helping with the birth, there were three enslaved people, Jack, Sal and Mose, who completed household chores like cooking, chopping firewood, washing clothes and bedsheets, and doing the various outside tasks needed to take care of numerous livestock. If Robert and Anne were not there that day because of the impending birth, they might have been sent to one of the nearby homes of their grandparents, Robert and Ann McFarland Bratton or Jane Clark Elliott. Their grandmother Jane Clark Elliott was a widow, and the Bratton children never knew their maternal grandfather William Elliott who died in 1771. It was most likely he whom William was named after though this is not proven. William Bratton's middle initial was definitely an E, and Elliott is the most logical suggestion for a Scots-Irish family that followed the Scottish Onomastic naming tradition of naming a first-born son after the paternal grandfather and a second-born son after the maternal grandfather, and so forth for daughters after grandmothers.[1] Then children were named for aunts and uncles. With the addition of William's name, it is clear that George and Jean were following this naming tradition as their son Robert was named after his paternal grandfather Robert Bratton, and their daughter Anne was named for her paternal grandmother Ann McFarland Bratton. This naming pattern continued as each of their children was born.

William became a member of a large, extended network of relatives. On his father's side, he had three uncles and an aunt with the last name of Dunlap – John, Robert, Alexander and Elizabeth – they were the children from the first marriage of William's grandmother Ann McFarland to Alexander Dunlap (1716-1744).[2] William also had several aunts and uncles from Ann McFarland's second marriage to his grandfather Robert Bratton – James, John and Adam, and Agnes, Elizabeth, and Mary.[3] On his mother's Elliott side, William had four aunts and four uncles. Additionally, William also visited his Clark relatives who were siblings, nieces and nephews of his grandmother Jane Clark Elliott. She was the daughter of James and Elizabeth Clark. William's family lines were further enmeshed when his great-aunt Sarah Clark married his great-uncle Archibald Elliot, and his great-aunt Anne Clark married his uncle John Dunlap.[4] This Clark family has been credited to be cousins of the renowned Clark family of General George Rogers Clark and his brother William Clark of Lewis and Clark fame. Both of these men visited many times with John and Anne Clark Dunlap in their home, a three-story brick mansion near the town of Goshen that today would be

---

[1] William E. Bratton, grave marker, Old Pioneer Cemetery, Waynetown, Montgomery County, Indiana.
[2] Herndon, John Goodwin. "Colonel Alexander Dunlap (1743-1828): The Correction of an Identification." The Virginia Magazine of History and Biography 54, no. 4, (October 1946): 321.
[3] Cleek, George W. and Catherine Cleek Mann. 1957. *Early Western Augusta Pioneers*. Staunton, Virginia: Genealogical Publishing Company: 302.
[4] McAdams, Mrs. Harry Kennett. 2007. *Kentucky Pioneer and Court Records: Abstracts of Early Wills, Deeds and Marriages from Courthouses and Records of Old Bibles, Churches, Graveyards, and Cemeteries*. Berwyn Heights, Maryland: Heritage Press: 78.

located in Rockbridge County, Virginia.[5]

Not only was William's family large, but they were very involved in public service in their community in Augusta County, Virginia. On May 18, 1780, when William was almost three-years-old, his father George Bratton was appointed road surveyor for a stretch of public road. In August of the same year, three weeks after William's third birthday, George was appointed Constable.[6] The other exciting event at this time was the birth of William's sister Jane on August 11, 1780 whom the family nicknamed Jenny. The wonderful news might have been shared the following Sunday with members of their community if the family attended the Tinkling Spring Presbyterian Church in Augusta County where George himself was christened as an infant.

In 1782, a larger picture of the George Bratton household emerged. According to the 1782 tax list for Augusta County, Virginia, George was taxed as the only tithable male (only free white male over 21 years) in his household. He was also taxed for three enslaved people, Jack, Sal and Mose, as well as nine horses and twelve cattle. Some of his neighbors were Duncan McFarland, David Gwin, William Slevin, Thomas Nail, Richard Elliott, Ephraim Bates, James Ellis, Elizabeth Wright, and Tabby Jewell. The tax list for this area was executed by George Poage on April 20, 1782 and designated as a list of tithables under David Gwin's militia company.[7]

Just a month later, on May 22, 1782, the civil government in Augusta County appointed George as a qualified lieutenant.[8] It is likely that he earned this rank from his previous service and experience in Captain John Lewis' company in Dunmore's War. His company was part of a militia formed by Colonel Andrew

---

[5] Morton, Oren Frederic. 1920. *A History of Rockbridge County, Virginia.* Staunton, Virginia: McClure Company, Incorporated: 250.

[6] Chalkley, Lyman. 1912. *Chronicles of the Scotch-Irish Settlement in Virginia: extracted from the Original Court Records of Augusta County, 1745-1800.* Vol. 1. Rosslyn, Virginia: Commonwealth Printing Company: 215-216.

[7] Virginia. Augusta County. Tax List. 1782. Database with images. "Personal Property Tax Lists." Entry for George Bratton: p. 53. *FamilySearch*.com.

[8] Chalkley, Lyman. 1912. *Chronicles of the Scotch-Irish Settlement in Virginia: extracted from the Original Court Records of Augusta County, 1745-1800.* Vol. 1. Rosslyn, Virginia: Commonwealth Printing Company: 225.

Lewis (also father of Captain John Lewis) in the fall of 1774 by command of Lord Dunmore, the Governor of Virginia, to retaliate towards Native Americans for their previous attacks on settlers. The Virginia militia raised by Colonel Lewis came from the counties of Augusta, Bedford, Botetourt, Culpeper and Fincastle, and their orders were to march to Fort Pitt and meet Lord Dunmore's other forces. When Colonel Lewis' militia arrived at Fort Pitt, they battled the Native Americans led by Shawnee chief Cornstalk alone because Dunmore's other forces did not arrive until the end of the battle, which became known as the Battle of Point Pleasant. Colonel Lewis later accused Dunmore of restraining his troops from aiding the Virginians on purpose so it would result in a high loss of men as recompense for previous defiance towards the British government. Though the Virginians fought as British subjects at the Battle of Point Pleasant in October 1774 and Lord Dunmore was their governor and ally, tensions were high between government officials and the common people due to high taxes. In the battle, over seventy-five Virginians were killed and over 140 were wounded.[9] Many of the remaining Virginian militia spent those winter months returning home by foot after the battle, and mere weeks later the Battles of Lexington and Concord occurred. Lord Dunmore maintained his British loyalty and began leading British forces against many of these same men, now American patriots. For his service in Dunmore's War, George Bratton received two pounds, three shillings and two pence for twenty-nine days of service. He received his pay in 1775.[10]

    Another reason why George Bratton might have received his new post as a qualified lieutenant on May 22, 1782 was due to his service in local militia duty in 1780 and 1781. As part of a community infrastructure, any able-bodied free man between the ages of sixteen and fifty in Virginia was enrolled in the militia. George, like so many other men in the community, would have left his wife and children at home for short stints of time. His

---

[9] Atkinson, George W. 1876. *History of Kanawha County.* Charleston: Printed at the Office of the West Virginia Journal. (doi: 31735054780584.)

[10] *Augusta, Bedford, Botetourt, Culpeper, and Fincastle payrolls and public service claims, 1775.* 2004. Fort Wayne, Indiana: Allen County Public Library: 104-106.

family and the enslaved people on his farm would have shouldered the responsibility of tending crops in the field and seeing to livestock while he was gone. Despite his obligations at home, the colonial government was insistent about his assistance. Specifically, a legislative session in Virginia on October 16, 1780 issued a summons for 3000 men of which eighty were to be furnished by Augusta County. An act in the same session requested that residents of Augusta County provide forty-six suits of clothes for soldiers.[11] Due to scant documentation of George's Revolutionary War service, it is unclear in which company he served. If he served in the company from Augusta County raised after the Battle of Cowpens, and who fought in the Battle of Guilford Courthouse, then he was part of the militia who heard a parting address by the Reverend James Waddell of Tinkling Spring Presbyterian Church. The troops left for Guilford, North Carolina in February 1781.[12]

If George was at home instead of fighting on one particular Sunday in June 1781, he would have been alarmed with the rest of the community when a strange man was arrested for his suspicious appearance near their homes. The man was dragged into the Tinkling Spring Presbyterian Church during the church service. He was the only one left of a group of four that had been captured after the other three men had escaped. Because the stranger was dressed in remnants of a British uniform, the congregation speculated that the man was a spy and that General Banastre Tarleton's army was approaching within days. With the pastor's encouragement, the men in the congregation left church immediately to hasten home, grab their firearms, and rendezvous at nearby Rockfish Gap. A few days later when the stranger tried to escape too, he was shot, and while dying confessed that the congregation was correct, that he was a British soldier sent ahead of Tarleton's troops.[13] The Revolutionary War was on their doorstep.

---

[11] Waddell, Joseph A. 1886. *Annals of Augusta County, Virginia*. Richmond, Virginia. Wm. Ellis Jones, printer: 174.
[12] Ibid: 179.
[13] Waddell, Joseph A. 1886. *Annals of Augusta County, Virginia*. Richmond, Virginia. Wm. Ellis Jones, printer: 183.

In addition to George Bratton's Revolutionary War service, his older brother James Bratton served as well. James worked his way up in rank from a private in Captain William Kinkead's company of Virginia militia to the position of captain in the Battle of Guilford Courthouse.[14] It is also possible that George's brother John Bratton served too. A John Bratton served in Captain Thompson's company but deserted his unit while marching to Fort Pitt. He was tried for this desertion but was acquitted due to "bodily infirmity" and was exempted from further military duty.[15] George was definitely home at times because he and Jean continued to grow their family. On May 20, 1783, they welcomed a son named Adam. It is probable that Adam was named for his uncle Adam Bratton, another brother of his father's. After Adam's birth, George was home to stay after September 1783 when the United States and England signed the Treaty of Paris. British troops left New York City by Thanksgiving and by Christmas, General Washington resigned as Commander. William Bratton, his father George, and the rest of his family were no longer just patriots but officially Americans.

Life resumed to a quieter pace for William and the rest of the family after the Revolutionary War. The issue and reality of war had been present for William since his birth through his fourth year. Now at age five, William learned what life could be like in a country mostly at peace, and men in the area could refocus on the industry of their livelihoods. In William's community in the colony of Virginia, the numerous farms in the county produced oats, barley, rye, wheat, Indian corn and broomcorn, pumpkins, parsnips, carrots, turnips, potatoes and groundnuts.[16] Orchards on the farms produced apricots, nectarines, peaches, plums, quinces, apples and pears while women grew okra, figs, pomegranates, watermelons, tomatoes and muskmelons in their

---

[14] "U.S., Sons of the American Revolution Membership Applications, 1889-1970," s. v. "William Arthur Porter, Sr." (membership 48358) *Ancestry.com*.

[15] Waddell, Joseph A. 1886. *Annals of Augusta County, Virginia*. Richmond, Virginia. Wm. Ellis Jones, printer: 166.

[16] Jefferson, Thomas. 1825. *Notes on the State of Virginia*. Philadelphia, Pennsylvania: H.C. Carey and I. Lea, printers: 57-58.

gardens.[17] Staple commodities that were in great demand were cotton, flax, hemp and tobacco and during the growing season, a farmer could yield two cuttings of indigo.[18] William might have helped his mother in the garden or with chores about the house. He might have helped his father George clean and oil his gun and no doubt followed his eldest siblings Robert and Anne around the farm. It is at this time too that he could have begun learning his ABCs as the beginning of his education of reading, writing and math or what used to be referred to be called ciphering.

As spring approached in 1785, the month of May proved to be an exciting one for the Bratton household. On May 17, 1785, Margaret Elliott, William's aunt, married Robert Givens. George Bratton served as surety for the marriage.[19] However, by fall, sadness also arose for the family. William's grandfather and Bratton patriarch Robert Bratton Sr. died in October 1785. He might have been sick for a while because he wrote his will on May 10, 1783 and it was proved and probated only six months later on October 18, 1785. In the will, George Bratton inherited a 240-acre tract of land on Jackson's River and the 100 pounds that his father had already given him. George's mother Ann received one enslaved man named Bob and one enslaved woman named Daphne as well as half of the household and kitchen furniture and half of the livestock. George's siblings received the following – big brother James Bratton received the land he lived on and the 100 pounds that his father had already given him; brother John Bratton received 700 acres on a branch of the Little River; brother Adam Bratton received the home plantation where Ann was living and would also receive the enslaved people Bob and Daphne after his mother died; sister Agnes and her husband William Givens received ten pounds and the previous provisions already made to them. Additionally, John was given 200 pounds in trust for their sister Mary whom Robert Bratton Sr. stated as

---

[17] Jefferson, Thomas. 1825. *Notes on the State of Virginia*. Philadelphia, Pennsylvania: H.C. Carey and I. Lea, printers: 57-58.

[18] Ibid.

[19] Chalkley, Lyman. 1912. *Chronicles of the Scotch-Irish Settlement in Virginia: extracted from the Original Court Records of Augusta County, 1745-1800*. Vol. 2. Rosslyn, Virginia: Commonwealth Printing Company: 270-279.

having infirmities of the mind and body that made her ineligible for marriage or to even support herself. His wish was that the interest of the 200 pounds would support and maintain her and that if she died, the 200 pounds was to be split equally between her siblings, Adam, George, John and Agnes.[20]

There is no doubt that Robert Bratton Sr. was quite wealthy after examining the amount of acreage and property he left to his children. In addition to land, he was taxed in 1782 for five enslaved people, ten horses and forty-five cattle. (George's siblings were also listed on the tax list. His brother Adam was taxed for one enslaved person and six horses; his brother John was taxed for eight horses; and his brother James was taxed for three enslaved people, fourteen horses and nineteen cattle.)[21] Additionally, Robert Bratton Sr. employed Irish indentured servants at one time. In September 1747, he and neighbor James Kirk were called into the Augusta County court for a case involving two of Robert Bratton's indentured servants, Patrick Burk and Bridget O'Dowland, who were caught, arrested, and convicted for horse-stealing.[22] It is unclear whether they stole one of his horses or a neighbor's or both but they stole four horses - two blacks ones, a sorrel mare with a star on her forehead, and a yearling colt.[23] Patrick Burk was described by Will Jameson, a Justice of the Peace of Augusta County, as pockmarked with black curly hair, and scars on the right side of his face and on his jawbone. Bridget O'Dowland was described by Jameson as tall, also pockmarked and with curly hair. Besides the horses, they also made off with "one orange-colored sitting gown, a pale china gown, one striped blue and white cotton gown, one single petticoat, one light-colored broadcloth coat, two beaver hats, one black velvet cap, one old hunting saddle, one woman's saddle of buckskin, one blue jacket of homemade cloth, one hat of Bermuda

---

[20] Snyder, Marion Bratton. n. d. *History of William H. Bratton Family.* n. p.:31.
[21] Virginia. Augusta County. Tax List. 1782. Database w/ images. "Personal Property Tax Lists." Entry for Robert Bratton: 3. *FamilySearch*.com.
[22] Chalkley, Lyman. 1912. *Chronicles of the Scotch-Irish Settlement in Virginia: extracted from the Original Court Records of Augusta County, 1745-1800.* Vol. 1. Rosslyn, Virginia: Commonwealth Printing Company: 286.
[23] Ibid: 529.

platt with a red ribbon band, shifts, shirts, table linen, sheets, women's head cloths, four pairs of men's shoes, three pairs of women's shoes, two bridles and a halter accompanied by a curb and snaffle, an ornamental rifle gun, and a plaid gown." For the capture of the two servants and the recovery of their belongings, Robert Bratton and James Kirk each paid a reward of three Spanish gold coins.[24] It is clear that besides land, livestock, and servants, Robert Bratton's home must have boasted of the finer things of life. Though the exact items of his estate that were appraised on September 1, 1786 are unknown to the author, other items are known to have been in his possession or that of his wife's in his lifetime besides those listed in the criminal case. They owned several pairs of silver buckles, and a silk gown according to his business associate William Preston.[25] Since Robert Bratton Sr. distributed his notable wealth among his children, George was able to provide fairly well for his family.

George and Jean Bratton continued to have children. A son, George Jr. was born into the family on August 2, 1786 and another son, Archibald, was born on April 9, 1787. (The time between the births of both sons was close in proximity but not impossible. Tombstone information for Archibald could be a bit erroneous.) Several months later, the household was represented on the 1787 Virginia tax list for Augusta County.[26] George Bratton was listed as having no males in his household between the ages of sixteen to twenty-one which makes sense since Robert, his eldest son, was around age thirteen. George was listed as having one enslaved person above the age of sixteen and four enslaved children under age sixteen. He had eleven horses and twenty-four cattle.

It was probably about this time that George began seriously considering a move to Kentucky. His older brother Alexander

---

[24] The Bratton Historian, Vol. II, No. 1, Muskogee, Oklahoma, 1979; p. 106. Bratton Association.

[25] Tillson, Albert H. 1991. *Gentry and Common Folk: Political Culture on a Virginia Frontier, 1740-1780.* Lexington, Kentucky: University Press of Kentucky: 29.

[26] Virginia. Augusta County. Tax List. 1787. Database with images. "Personal Property Tax Lists." Entry for George Bratton: p. 235. *FamilySearch*.com.

Dunlap and his wife Agnes Gay had already moved to Kentucky to McConnell's Station, one mile from Lexington, in September 1783. Dunlap and his family made the journey with Dunlap's brother-in-law John Gay and his wife Sarah Lockridge.[27] They joined Dunlap's brother-in-law Samuel Stevenson and his wife Jane Gay, and several Stevenson brothers who had undertaken their own journey to Kentucky in 1779. Maybe Alexander Dunlap was sending letters home to tell his family about their experience and overall good fortune. Maybe he was urging the Brattons to join them. Regardless, the following accounts were probably some of the news that George Bratton received about family members and their kin in Kentucky.

According to Jane Gay Stevenson who was interviewed by Reverend John Dabney Shane in the elderly era of her life, the Stevenson family and the James Gay family traveled to Kentucky with another family and schoolmaster John McKinney. They began in Greenbrier County, Virginia and traversed along the Wilderness Road via Powell's Valley, the Cumberland Gap, Clinch's Ford and Blackmore's Station. It took them about two weeks to reach Blackmore's Station, and they did not travel on Sundays. When approaching Blackmore's Station, the group witnessed the aftermath of a family massacre. This could have been the slaying of the German woman Fanny Alley Napper and her young children. Jane described the scene to Shane:

"The morning before we came to the ford of Clinch, these murders were committed…a mother and four children; in sight of the fort too. The husband was in the field, but escaped. A girl about half-grown, and three little boys tomahawked and scalped, who were talking while their brains were boiling out. The grandmother asked them if they saw their little brother. What had become of him? Said they didn't know. These were Dutch people. We stayed there good part of the day. Their Aunt sat on a stump, in sight of the fort, and cried all day."

Although Jane Stevenson's family did not see any Native Americans themselves, another group within three quarters of a

---

[27] Railey, William E. 1928. *History of Woodford County*. Frankfort, Kentucky: Roberts Printing Company: 152.

mile ahead of them had their horses stolen and they had no choice but to leave their feather beds behind with no way to transport them. Besides the threat of Native Americans, the Wilderness Road itself posed numerous challenges for travelers because it was no more than a crude trail. In addition, the Cumberland Gap was very fierce because of many steep ascents, five major river crossings and other small streams to ford, and rolling terrain.[28] Jane was very fearful in crossing the Gap. "I was most afraid coming down Cumberland Mountain. The place was narrow and rocky. (It) stood up on either side, not broader than a house," she recalled.[29] After the Stevenson family successfully crossed the Gap, they took the northern fork on the Wilderness Road when it split into two parts. They turned onto the eastern spur to Boonesborough and then to Lexington. They arrived there in October 1779 just in time to hunker down in the Lexington blockhouse or fort for an exceptionally rough winter.[30] According to one source, Jane Gay Stevenson was one of the first four white women at Lexington.[31] The following spring, Samuel and Jane Stevenson were anxious to move out of the Lexington blockhouse. The other blockhouse occupants were a varied lot and supposedly, they were not the sort of people the Stevensons wanted around their children for an extended period of time. In April, they moved out to McConnell's Station, just over a mile away, which Jane stated was established on the day they arrived. It was named for its new occupant Francis McConnell whom Jane knew from her days as a very young child in Pennsylvania.[32] Though Samuel Stevenson had erected a crude cabin on land nearby in 1776, they could not live there due to danger from

---

[28] Eslinger, Ellen, ed. 2004. *Running Mad for Kentucky: Frontier Travel Accounts*. Lexington, Kentucky: The University Press of Kentucky: 8-11.

[29] Jane Gay Stevenson Interview by Rev. John Dabney Shane. Draper Collection: Kentucky Papers, 1768-1892, 13CC:135-143, (microfilm) Wisconsin Historical Society, Madison, WI.

[30] Ibid.

[31] Kentucky Historical Society, 1981. *Genealogies of Kentucky families: from the Register of the Kentucky Historical Society*. Frankfort, Kentucky: Kentucky: Genealogical Publishing Company: 765.

[32] Jane Gay Stevenson Interview by Rev. John Dabney Shane. Draper Collection: Kentucky Papers, 1768-1892, 13CC:135-143, (microfilm) Wisconsin Historical Society, Madison, WI.

antagonistic Native American activities. McConnell's Station was home to the Stevensons until the arrival of Alexander Dunlap and his family in 1783.

Alexander Dunlap and his family along with John Gay and his family arrived at McConnell's Station after their own journey along the Wilderness Road in September 1783. On their journey, Reverend Adam Rankin, a fellow citizen of Augusta County, Virginia passed them on the road. He was traveling to Lexington as well.[33] Stations or non-military forts such as McConnell's Station were essential to frontier settlers as waypoints connected by trails that created a web of spatial orientation for them in a landscape devoid of any other manmade towns, fences or roads. Stations or forts served as communal bases for habitation in hopes that a higher number of frontier folk in one exact area provided a united front to intimidate any hostile outside forces, namely Native Americans in the area.[34] It was a safety in numbers mentality. The Dunlaps lived in McConnell's Station over the winter and then moved out nine miles west with their kin and other families in March 1784.[35] At this time, this area was still Fayette County, but when county lines changed in 1788, it became Woodford County. Samuel Stevenson acquired and claimed the grant of land where they moved and their settlement was established as the community of Pisgah.[36] Alexander Dunlap, along with his brother-in-laws Samuel Stevenson, John Gay and friend Moses McIllvain, tamed the area by clearing canebrakes and dense woodlands and then erecting log cabins.

---

[33] Railey, William E. 1928. *History of Woodford County*. Frankfort, Kentucky: Roberts Printing Company: 152.

[34] Perkins, Elizabeth A. 1998. *Border Life: Experience and Memory in the Revolutionary Ohio Valley*. Chapel Hill, North Carolina: The University of North Carolina Press.

[35] Herndon, John Goodwin. "Colonel Alexander Dunlap (1743-1828): The Correction of an Identification." *The Virginia Magazine of History and Biography* 54, no. 4, (October 1946): 325.

[36] Kentucky Historical Society. 1981. *Genealogies of Kentucky families: from the Register of the Kentucky Historical Society*. Vol. 2. Lexington, Kentucky: Genealogical Publishing Company: 770.

John and Sarah Gay built a saddlebag-style log cabin.[37] This was a log cabin with two rooms with a double chimney in the middle. Sometimes the two rooms would share a wall or there might be a boxed-in passageway between the two rooms. This kind of log cabin also usually had two front doors.[38] John and Sarah's saddlebag log cabin was a single story with a loft. Their two rooms measured roughly 16 ft. x 17ft. with the boxed-passageway actually serving as a central hall, five feet across from inside wall to inside wall. The logs to construct the cabin were square-hewn, 8 in. x 16 in., and chinked with "diagonally placed rock held with various mortars of mud, cement, and sand, and joined with a rough half dovetail and saddle notching."[39] John and Sarah Gay's land contained a "natural amphitheater" with a spring at its base. They built their log cabin upon a random-laid, un-chinked, limestone foundation on the top curve of this amphitheater facing south. Because of the acoustics of the amphitheater, their home was known as Mt. Echo.[40]

On Alexander Dunlap's farm, which was known as The Pastures, he built a log cabin at the base of a hill and then built a springhouse nearby. He used field and outcrop limestone to construct the springhouse, and dry laid the walls to the dimensions of 15 ft. x 14 ft. After the spring house was completed, he began building a stone wall using field and ledge rock that extended "north and south from the corners of the spring house" to act "as a barrier between the hill above and the flat road bed to the east." He again used a method of dry laying the rock with diagonally laid coping.[41] Samuel and Jane Stevenson built their cabin on a wooded point of land. One source stated that in

---

[37] Amos, Christine, "Pisgah Rural Historic District," National Register of Historic Places Nomination Form (Washington, DC: U.S. Department of the Interior, National Park Service, 1989), Section 7.

[38] McRaven, Charles. 2005. *The Classic Hewn Log House: a Step-by-Step Guide to Building and Restoring.* East Peoria, Illinois: Versa Press: 9.

[39] Amos, Christine, "Pisgah Rural Historic District," National Register of Historic Places Nomination Form (Washington, DC: U.S. Department of the Interior, National Park Service, 1989), Section 7.

[40] Ibid.

[41] Amos, Christine, "Pisgah Rural Historic District," National Register of Historic Places Nomination Form (Washington, DC: U.S. Department of the Interior, National Park Service, 1989), Section 7.

addition to Samuel and his family building his cabin, enslaved people worked hard alongside them. Jane did not mention the presence of enslaved people traveling with them to Kentucky in her narrative but that does not mean that enslaved people did not accompany them.[42]

By fall of 1784, the log cabins were erected all within a mile of each other, all near a spring of water. The community of Pisgah invited Rev. Adam Rankin to preach in their cabins. As Scotch-Irish families, they welcomed religious instruction following the Presbyterian denomination. According to Jane Gay Stevenson, Rev. Rankin preached in her home, and in those of Captain McConnell, Moses McIlvain and Samuel Kelly.[43] In 1785, Samuel Stevenson donated ten acres of ground to the congregation and an additional two acres for a meetinghouse and graveyard. The church was named Mt. Pisgah but later, it was also referred to as the Pisgah Presbyterian Church.[44]

Besides Alexander Dunlap and his family, kin to Jean Elliott Bratton also lived in Kentucky. Several members of the Elliott family lived in Lexington. William Elliot, Jr., Jean Elliott Bratton's older brother, moved to Lexington in 1787 with his wife Mildred "Millie" Cleveland and several of their children.[45] Robert Elliott, Jean's uncle, also lived there. He arrived in 1787 also and could have traveled along the Wilderness trail with his nephew William.[46] As families like the Elliotts settled in Lexington, and other families like the Dunlaps and Stevensons moved out of stations or forts and created neighborhoods like the Pisgah community in Woodford County, Kentucky's population began to boom. At the beginning of 1788, George and Jean Bratton

---

[42] Kentucky Historical Society. 1981. *Genealogies of Kentucky families: from the Register of the Kentucky Historical Society.* Vol. 2. Lexington, Kentucky: Genealogical Publishing Company: 770.

[43] Shewmaker, William O. 1935. *Pisgah and her People: 1784-1934.* Woodford County, Kentucky: Pisgah Presbyterian Church: 3.

[44] Ibid.

[45] Kentucky. Fayette County. William Elliott entry. 1788 Tax Lists. Allen County Public Library, Fort Wayne, Indiana. Microfilm, #0100, 1781-1797, 1799 – 1804.

[46] Kentucky. Fayette County. William Elliott entry. 1788 Tax Lists. Allen County Public Library, Fort Wayne, Indiana. Microfilm, #0100, 1781-1797, 1799 – 1804.

probably debated long and hard weighing the advantages and disadvantages of moving their household. By spring, they made up their minds. On May 10, 1788, in anticipation of joining the mass migration westward to Kentucky, George Bratton sold his land in Augusta County, Virginia to his brother Adam Bratton. His specific destination was Lexington and then beyond to Pisgah to join his brother Alexander Dunlap. William E(lliott) Bratton, was nine years of age when his first real adventure began.[47]

---

[47] Virginia. Augusta County. Deed Book 26. George Bratton to Adam Bratton: 235.

CHAPTER TWO
Settling In Kentucky

While there is no known account about the Bratton family's journey along the Wilderness Road in that early spring or summer of 1788, George and Jean Bratton had to determine how best to transport their family. Their eldest son Robert was around age fourteen and had probably already proved himself valuable as essential help to his parents on their Virginia farm. He might have even been considered as one of the men on this journey. William was almost age ten and he too was probably given much responsibility. Their daughters Anne, about age twelve, and Jenny, age eight, would have been their mother's little helpers with the younger children, Adam, age five; George, age three; and baby Archibald, age two. An enslaved boy, about age thirteen, also traveled with the family. The family also took several horses.[48] Furthermore, it is likely that John Elliott, another brother of Jean's, and his family traveled with them.[49]

Like other families before them, they probably used quite creative and effective ways of transporting their youngest children over the challenging terrain. The Thomas Little family who made their journey to Kentucky just a few years before, and whose granddaughter would be the future bride of William's brother Robert Bratton, described how they situated their young children in this manner - "They had no wagons, so they crossed over the mountains on pack horses. All their goods were strapped

---

[48] Kentucky. Fayette County. George Bratton entry, 1789 Tax List, Allen County Public Library, Fort Wayne, Indiana. Microfilm, #0100, 1781-1797, 1799 – 1804.

[49] Kentucky. Fayette County. John Elliott entry. 1789 Tax List. Allen County Public Library, Fort Wayne, Indiana. Microfilm, #0100, 1781-1797, 1799 – 1804.

on the horses. Large sacks with a pocket in each end were thrown across the horses with hoops to hold the pockets open. Two or more children were stowed in each pocket with their heads sticking out on either side. A large child rode astride to guide the horse, and a small one rode behind."[50] If the timeline is accurate, the Bratton family arrived in Lexington around the fall of 1788. At this time, Jean was pregnant with their last child. In just a little under a decade since the Stevenson family had arrived and stayed at the Lexington blockhouse, the community had flourished. A stone courthouse stood on the public square and a public spring was available for everyone.[51] Additionally, education was available. The Transylvania Seminary had moved to Lexington recently and operated out of a two-story brick building. Tuition for students was five pounds with half of it paid in cash and the other half in property. The price for boarding a student was nine pounds a year and could be paid in property or tobacco, pork, corn, etc.[52] Also, men in the community desired an organization of freemasonry and they established one in Lexington as Lodge No. 25 on November 17, 1788. The ground that the lodge was built upon was donated by William Murray who became its first Grand Master.[53]

    The citizens of Lexington were various characters – settlers, merchants, adventurers, land speculators, preachers, and soldiers. Some had no money while others were quite wealthy. They represented all walks of life and sometimes they did not play nice. One violent practice that the poorer class of Kentucky citizens engaged in at this time was gouging. It was described as barbarous by Army officer Erkuries Beatty who served as paymaster for the Western Army in nearby Louisville. "When two men quarrel, they never have an idea of striking, but immediately seize each other, thumbs or fingers into the eye and push it out

---

[50] Little, James Alexander. n. d. *History of the Little Family.* Plainfield, Indiana: Publishing Association of Friends: 5.
[51] Ranck, George Washington. 1872. *History of Lexington, Kentucky: Its Early Annals and Recent Progress.* Cincinnati, Ohio: Robert Clarke & Company: 72.
[52] Ibid: 41-42.
[53] Ibid: 42.

from the socket till it falls on the cheeks," he said.[54] In the particular fight that Beatty witnessed, whilst the one man gouged out the other's eye, the other bit his adversary quite thoroughly, and both had each other by the testicles quite frequently. "It chills my blood with horror to see the unmanly, cruel condition these two men were left in today from this manner of fighting, and no person, although a number stood by, ever attempted to prevent them from thus butchering each other, but all was acknowledged fair play," he said. It did not surprise Beatty when soldiers insisted on carrying their dirks, swords or pocket pistols when they traveled.[55] Such a barbarous practice should have been shockingly new to William Bratton as Virginia had ruled maiming and defacing as a felony in 1752, specifically forbidding the offenses of biting, slitting or cutting off a nose or lip, or putting out an eye.[56] In 1772, Virginia amended the act to add that the felony specifically included gouging. Hopefully the Bratton family settled amidst the gentler citizens of Lexington upon their arrival.

George Bratton might have known Reverend Adam Rankin from Augusta County, Virginia. Rankin preached at the Mt. Zion Presbyterian Church in Lexington as well as the nearby Mt. Pisgah Church. The Mt. Zion Presbyterian Church was a log house on the southeast corner of Walnut and Short Streets. The Bratton family would not have seen Reverend Rankin for long though. Because of dissension between the congregation and Reverend Rankin over the usage of the literal version of Psalms in the Bible versus another version by a Dr. Watts, Rankin left Lexington and spent several years in London before he returned to Lexington in 1792.[57] Another option to attend church for George and Jean and their family was the nearby Walnut Hill Presbyterian Church that was in its fourth year of establishment. Members who attended this church meeting met in a log cabin under the spiritual

---

[54] Erkuries Beatty Diary (25 April 1787) New York Historical Society Library. New York, NY.

[55] Ibid.

[56] Hening, William Walter. 1821. *Hening's Statutes At Large*. Vol. 8. Richmond, Virginia: J. & G. Cochran: 520.

[57] Ranck, George Washington. 1872. *History of Lexington, Kentucky: Its Early Annals and Recent Progress*. Cincinnati, Ohio: Robert Clarke & Company: 108-109.

guidance of another Virginian native, Rev. James Crawford.

It is probable that a portion of that same congregation at Mt. Zion who were in dissension with Reverend Rankin, also disapproved of gambling or racing, but such events occurred in Lexington at this time. Communication about such events was not limited to the local grapevine of gossip. In 1789, the first newspaper was printed in Lexington as the Kentucky Gazette. In an advertisement that ran in the Gazette in August, citizens were informed that a purse-race would take place on the second Thursday in October 1789 in Lexington. One could enter their horse be it mare or gelding but to determine a winner, there would be three-mile heats with a best two in three. Each person that entered a horse to win the purse had to pay two guineas to John Fowler the day before the race at the tavern run by a Mr. Collins.[58]

While the horse race might have held some excitement for George Bratton and sons Robert, William, and even Adam and George, the ladies of the household might have found the arrival of a new baby more riveting. Jean Elliott Bratton delivered a new addition to the Bratton family. Their daughter, Nancy A. G. Bratton, was born on July 5, 1789. Because the middle initials for Nancy were A.G, the baby was probably named after George Bratton's sister Agnes Bratton Givens, establishing Nancy's middle names as most likely Agnes Givens. In addition to the large Bratton family, according to the tax list in Lexington dated August 3, 1789, George Bratton was taxed for one enslaved person above the age of twelve and eight horses.[59] Also, it is possible that the John Elliott family was living with them, or at least nearby, for he and George submitted their vouchers the same day to Bartlett Collins, Commissioner of the Tax. Collins in turn included the vouchers with those collected from the rest of his district and gave them to Fayette County clerk Levi Todd. (Todd was the grandfather of the future Mrs. Mary Lincoln Todd

---

[58] Ranck, George Washington. 1872. *History of Lexington, Kentucky: Its Early Annals and Recent Progress*. Cincinnati, Ohio: Robert Clarke & Company: 128-129.

[59] Kentucky. Fayette County. George Bratton entry, 1789 Tax List, Allen County Public Library, Fort Wayne, Indiana. Microfilm, #0100, 1781-1797, 1799 – 1804.

and Bartlett Collins could have been the tavern owner aforementioned.)

A strange phenomenon on October 31, 1789 no doubt befuddled the Bratton family as it did everyone else in Lexington. It became so dark in the afternoon that people had to eat by candlelight. The darkness lasted for three hours and then resumed to a normal dusk until the darkness of night naturally fell.[60] It was probably an eclipse that the townsfolk did not expect, and their reaction was reported in the Gazette.

As 1790 approached, George and Jean Bratton decided to move their family into neighboring Woodford County. It is possible that George moved his family in the spring of 1790, but this is unverifiable, and he was not listed on the 1790 tax list for either Woodford or Fayette counties, however, they were living there by 1791. On the Woodford County tax list for 1791, dated July 25, George Bratton listed himself as the male over age twenty-one. He was taxed for one enslaved boy under sixteen and nine horses.[61] At this time, George and Jean's children were the following ages – Robert, seventeen; Anne, fifteen; William, twelve (but he would be age thirteen in two days); Jenny, eleven; Adam, six; George Jr., five; Archibald, four; and Nancy, two. Because the tax list does not show that George owned any land yet, he and his family might have lived with his brother Alexander Dunlap on land in the Pisgah community or renting land there or in another community.

The first Kentucky home that George Bratton provided for his family might have been similar to the cabin that Isaac Drake built for his family just two years earlier. It was located further north, closer to the Ohio River in the village of Washington. In its most raw form, this first cabin might have been one large room without windows, with a wooden chimney with a clay lining, and a roof on one side only. The floor of the cabin would have been dirt until the puncheons, or planks of wood, were cut from nearby trees,

---

[60] Ranck, George Washington. 1872. *History of Lexington, Kentucky: Its Early Annals and Recent Progress*. Cincinnati, Ohio: Robert Clarke & Company: 128-129.

[61] Kentucky. Fayette County. George Bratton entry, 1791 Tax List, Allen County Public Library, Fort Wayne, Indiana. Microfilm, #0100, 1781-1797, 1799 – 1804.

hewed with a broad-ax, and set into place.[62] Gradually the roof would have been expanded, a window added, and a stone chimney constructed. In his own house, George might have added two pegs driven into one of the log walls as a convenient place to hang his hunting rifle, though he might have also kept his axe and scythe handy at night for protection. In addition to the rifle, axe, and scythe, George probably owned several husbandry implements, cooking utensils, and a mechanical tool such as an auger.[63] If he was lucky or wealthy enough, which is probably the case due to his ownership of so many horses, he would have also owned a cross-cut saw, a drawing-knife and a frow which was an L-shaped tool for cleaving wood. These tools would have been used for the construction of his cabin by making it possible to manipulate wood into planks, boards, pins, hinges, a door, and a latch.[64]

While the homes of George and Isaac might have shared characteristics, is it unlikely that George Bratton's cabin was ever as primitive for he had one thing that Isaac Drake did not – manpower. With the help of Robert, William, and the enslaved boy, a more than adequate cabin would have been erected in no time. It is likely that in addition to his cabin, he and the boys also constructed an attached lean-to for the horses. George's axe was essential is his success of settling out. It was used in not only the construction of buildings, but also in the tasks of providing fuel, clearing land, creating fences, tilling fields, marking boundary lines, and even hunting.[65] Furthermore, if he were wealthy enough, he had more than one axe for use by the boys. They would have helped him clear enough land for a corn and a vegetable garden. The garden would have included a "truck-patch" planted with watermelons, muskmelons, pumpkins, turnips, etc. Additionally, to add to the pantry, George, Robert, William, and the enslaved boy would have hunted for deer,

---

[62] Drake, Dr. Daniel. 1870. *Pioneer Life in Kentucky: A Series of Reminiscential Letters from Daniel Drake, M.D. of Cincinnati to His Children*. Cincinnati, Ohio: Robert Clarke & Company: 15-20.
[63] Hall, James. 1835. *Sketches of History, Life and Manners in the West*. Vol. 2. Philadelphia, Pennsylvania: Harrison Hall: 67.
[64] Ibid.
[65] Ibid: 68.

turkey, and other abundant wild animals. Robert and William might have had their own rifles.

Robert and William carried a man's load and their sisters Anne and Jenny helped their mother Jean in the new cabin. Their younger siblings Adam, George and maybe even Archibald, would have had their own chores. The younger children would have foraged in the woods for hickory nuts, walnuts, winter grapes, wild mushrooms, and berries.[66] They would have been given the task of scaring away animals from the vegetable patch once the crops were growing.

As George Bratton established his new domain, like so many others, history left little personal trace of the man he was. Instead, a general sort of conjecture can be made about his personality. He was a military man, still a Virginian at this time who like others around him "transferred to the soil of Kentucky all the pride, the local attachment, the love of country....an athletic, vigorous race, with hardy frames, active minds, and bold spirits...obliged to think and act for themselves, they acquired independence of thought, and habitual promptitude of demeanor...daring, impetuous and tenacious of their honor; chivalrous, fond of adventure, courteous to females and hospitable to the stranger."[67] Unfortunately, like many Virginians, he was also an enslaver. As such, he would have been interested in the tragic scandal that exploded at this time in Woodford County which involved a criminal case against a twelve-year-old enslaved boy named Bill who was enslaved by a person with the last name of James. This might have been Ann James, a widow who moved to Woodford County from Maryland with numerous children. She had been living in Woodford County since May 27, 1790 when she appeared at court and took an oath in relation to her importation of enslaved people.[68] Whom the youth killed or

---

[66] Drake, Dr. Daniel. 1870. *Pioneer Life in Kentucky: A Series of Reminiscential Letters from Daniel Drake, M.D. of Cincinnati to His Children*. Cincinnati, Ohio: Robert Clarke & Company: 47.

[67] Hall, James. 1835. *Sketches of History, Life and Manners in the West*. Vol. 2. Philadelphia, Pennsylvania: Harrison Hall: 94-96.

[68] Ardery, Mrs. William Breckenridge. 1999. *Kentucky Court and Other Records: Wills, Deeds, Orders, Suits*. Staunton, Virginia: Genealogical Publishing Company: 162.

why was not reported but tragically, he was tried for murder and became the youngest teen executed in Kentucky history when he was hanged on July 30, 1791.[69]

George Bratton was in court himself in 1791. He was sued by Paul Faught over an unsatisfactory business deal. The men who heard and determined the suit were John Finney, William Nall, Martin Nall, William Steele and Richard Young. The committee ultimately favored Faught, however, neither man escaped hefty court costs, and both were ordered to pay with tobacco. Upon the court's demand, Paul Faught paid the following men for their time on his behalf as witnesses in court - Richard Bohannon, fifty pounds for two days as witness; Julius Blackburn, fifty pounds for two days as witness; William Davis, James Wilson, Samuel Gregory and James Dickey, twenty-five pounds each for one day as witness; and Ephraim Bates, one-hundred pounds for four days as witness. George Bratton was ordered to pay the following men in tobacco for their services as well – Abraham Lauderback, seventy-five pounds for three days as witness; James Hall, 195 pounds for three days as witness and sixty miles of travel; and William Ramsey, 104 pounds for two days as witness and twenty-seven miles of travel.[70] George either bartered for the tobacco with other goods he had or he grew the tobacco himself but if he was not a landowner at that time, he soon would be. Regardless, George was not satisfied with the decision and appealed the verdict. One year later, in August 1792, he appeared with his attorney in court to state that errors had occurred in the processing of the suit. He stated, "the declaration does not state that the Plaintiff is the only man who was applied to by Andrew Hambleton to mail rails and refused to do it."[71] No doubt it was to George's dismay that the appeal was found ungrounded and the verdict against him was upheld.

Although George could not dodge civil embroilment in his community, he and his family were successful in avoiding tragedy from Native American raids. Others were not so lucky. In a nearby

---

[69] Aguirre, Adalbert. "Slave Executions in the United States." *The Social Science Journal*, 36, no. 1 (1999): 1-31.
[70] Kentucky. Woodford County. Order Book B. Paul Faught vs. George Bratton civil case: 23-26.
[71] Ibid: 26.

settlement in Woodford County, several people were massacred just months before George's appeal was denied. The settlement, Cook's Station, lay several miles below the North and South forks of the Elkhorn River called Innis Bottom and was settled by several extended families by the name of Cook. They built their cabins in the woods amidst the thick cane and undergrowth and though they were only three to four hundred yards apart, the brush created a living screen of privacy.[72] The Native Americans, about 100 Wyandots, struck on April 28, 1792 according to inhabitant Reverend Abraham Cook who was a teenager at the time of the attack.[73] His brothers Jesse and Hosea Cook were killed outside their cabins while shearing sheep. Hosea managed to crawl to the door of one cabin before dying on the doorstep. Their two wives, Betsy Bohannon Cook who was Jesse's wife, and Betsy Edrington Cook who was Hosea's wife, opened the cabin door and dragged Hosea into the cabin with them and bolted the door. Besides Hosea lying dead on the floor, they had two infants with them, one belonging to each wife. The ladies became the target of many Wyandot warriors whooping outside their door. Several times, the Wyandots tried to set the cabin on fire but each time the women were successful in extinguishing the flames. They used water, broken eggs and finally in desperation, Hosea's bloody clothing. When the Wyandots tried to break down the door, the women tried to use the one gun in the cabin. When no bullets could be found that were the right size for the gun, Betsy Bohannon Cook bit a large bullet into two pieces and loaded the gun. She then shot a Wyandot brave through the chinking in the logs.[74] Fearing that soon a larger force of white men would appear, the Wyandot warriors left the settlement. Others were killed besides Jesse and Hosea Cook - two sons of their sister Bathsheba Cook and her husband William Dunn, and Lewis

---

[72] R. T. Dillard, "A Fragment of Kentucky History." *The Observer & Reporter*, Frankfort, Kentucky, November 14, 1843.

[73] Jillson, Willard Rouse. 1936. *Early Frankfort and Franklin County: A Chronology of Historical Sketches Covering the Century 1750-1850.* Louisville, Kentucky: The Standard Printing Company: 70.

[74] R. T. Dillard, "A Fragment of Kentucky History." *The Observer & Reporter*, Frankfort, Kentucky, November 14, 1843.

Mastin, the husband of another sister, Margaret Cook.[75] Many accounts of this massacre abound because such depredations went beyond just causing vigilance or wariness in the settlers, especially the women - it terrified them. "The alarm of my mother and aunts, communicated of course to all the children, was deep," recalled Daniel Drake, son of Isaac Drake, who was seven at this time. "I well remember that Indian wars, midnight butcheries, captivities, and horse-stealings, were the daily topics of conversation."[76] Thus, it is likely that conversations like this also took place in the Bratton household and that the topic was one that the Bratton children heard often.

Later, in 1792, according to the tax list for Woodford County, George Bratton owned 112 acres of land. It is unclear where it was exactly located as a deed for the land is not registered in Woodford County, Fayette County, Mercer County nor Franklin County. (It is possible that a deed for the land was filed in Fayette County but that it no longer exists due to a fire at the land office on January 31, 1803. Kentucky pioneer Asa Farrar speculated the fire was set on purpose by the perpetrators so certain land claims would be destroyed.)[77] On the tax list, George designated himself as a white male over twenty-one, and also listed a white male between the ages of sixteen to twenty-one who would have been his son Robert, age eighteen. George had two enslaved people in his household with one being a male under age sixteen. George also owned thirteen cattle and seven horses. The Commissioner of Tax for George Bratton's district of Woodford County was William Steele. This was most likely the same William Steele who served on the committee in his suit with Faught. In the process of taxation, Steele distributed the lists to all males over twenty-one in his district who were considered tithable, or responsible to pay tax. He then later collected and checked these tax vouchers for accuracy before turning them into clerk Cave Johnson. Johnson

---

[75] R. T. Dillard, "A Fragment of Kentucky History." *The Observer & Reporter*, Frankfort, Kentucky, November 14, 1843.

[76] Drake, Dr. Daniel. 1870. *Pioneer Life in Kentucky: A Series of Reminiscential Letters from Daniel Drake, M.D. of Cincinnati to His Children*. Cincinnati, Ohio: Robert Clarke & Company: 23.

[77] Staples, Charles R. 1996. *The History of Pioneer Lexington*. Lexington, Kentucky: The University Press of Kentucky: 39, 60.

had served as clerk to the Quarter Sessions of the Woodford County Court for several years already.

By February 1793, George was back in court, this time as a plaintiff. George sued William Scruggs for trespass relative to an incident involving force and injury. Scruggs with his attorney James Hughes declared, "He is in no wise guilty of the premises in manner and form as the plaintiff against him hath declared."[78] While they worked out their differences in court, their community was involved in a much larger, more serious situation. Native American depredations had continued to occur there and in other Kentucky counties. As a result, President George Washington called for troops to secure Fort Washington. (This fort was built in June 1789 where Cincinnati is now located.) He asked Kentucky Governor Isaac Shelby to supply many of those troops. On July 6, 1793, the Kentucky Gazette ran an official notice which called for a return of the militia.[79] According to the Kentucky Constitution, all able-bodied white males, aged eighteen to fifty-five were eligible for militia duty.[80] William was age fourteen at this time; however, his brother Robert was of eligible age.

Dutifully answering the call for volunteers, Robert Bratton served as a private in Horatio Hall's Regiment, a mounted cavalry unit in the Kentucky Volunteer militia.[81] Hall's Regiment was under Captain Ezekiel Hayden's Company B of mounted cavalry that was commanded by Major General Charles Scott. He enlisted on October 10, 1793. He was marked as present on a muster roll on November 11th at Fort Washington. In a payroll dated November 15, 1793, he was paid $36 for thirty-six days of service

---

[78] Kentucky. Woodford County. Quarter Sessions Court Cases, Vol. 1. George Bratton vs. William Scruggs civil case: 26. Kentucky Department of Library and Archives.
[79] Works Progress Administration. 1939. *Military History of Kentucky*. State Journal, Frankfort, Kentucky: 35.
[80] Ibid: 33.
[81] National Archives of Records Administration (NARA); Washington D.C.; *Compiled Service Records of Volunteer Soldiers Who Served 1784 -1811* Service database entry for Robert Bratton. (accessed 23 April 2014). Ancestry.com.

from October 10 - November 14, 1793.[82] Besides being paid $1 per day, Robert, as a private, might have received a ration which consisted of "a pound of fresh beef or pork, one pound of wheat bread or flour, one pound and a quarter of cornmeal, a gill of spirituous liquor when to be had, a quart of salt, a quart of vinegar, two pounds of soap, and one pound of candles to every 100 rations."[83] Soldiers received these rations the year before, but due to the call for so many soldiers who were needed to repel Native American attacks, it is unclear if soldiers were still offered the same rations.

Robert Bratton again enlisted as a private on July 10, 1794 and served until Oct. 26, 1794 for a total of 109 days in Captain John Franciscoe's Company under Major William Price's Battalion of Mounted Volunteers commanded by General Charles Scott. The payroll indicated that these soldiers were "called into service by the President of the United States" who was still George Washington at that time. Ezekiel Hayden served as a lieutenant in this company under John Franciscoe.[84] During this stint of duty, Robert participated in the Battle of Fallen Timbers led by General Anthony Wayne. Wayne's successful efforts against Native Americans in the Ohio area of the Northwest Territory followed the previous dismal results of General Arthur St. Clair and his defeat by Little Turtle. This whole struggle existed between the two parties because the American government believed these lands were ceded to them by the British in the Treaty of Paris in 1783 whereas the Native Americans stated that the British had no right to give the land to anyone. They remained angry because even when treaties delineated a boundary between settlers and Native Americans, the settlers consistently ignored the boundaries and crossed into Native American lands to live. This happened repeatedly with new boundaries and treaties which

---

[82] National Archives of Records Administration (NARA); Washington D.C.; *Compiled Service Records of Volunteer Soldiers Who Served 1784 -1811* Service database entry for Robert Bratton. (accessed 23 April 2014). Ancestry.com.

[83] Works Progress Administration. 1939. *Military History of Kentucky*. State Journal, Frankfort, Kentucky: 35.

[84] Clark, Murtie June. 2009. *America Militia in the Frontier Wars, 1790-1796*. Baltimore, Maryland: Genealogical Publishing Company: 55.

kept their rage simmering. However, after their defeat at the Battle of Fallen Timbers, they had no choice but to retreat. When his service was at an end, Robert returned to his father's farm.

In the tax list for Woodford County in September 1794, George Bratton still owned 112 acres of land. He listed himself as a tithable white male over twenty-one. He again listed only one white male between 16 and 21. This tally mark was most likely for his son Robert, now age twenty, even though he was away fighting in the militia from July to October, or it could have been for William who was now age sixteen. There was still one enslaved boy in the household who was tallied as a black male under age sixteen. George owned five horses and nine cattle. William Steele again served as Commissioner of Tax for George's district and Steele gave the tax vouchers to Cave Johnson again. Additionally, there was another Bratton listed in a different district of Woodford County, a John Bratton who listed himself as a white male over age twenty-one with one cow. It is unclear if this was George's brother or cousin.[85]

In addition, George returned to court again in Woodford County for the final deliberation in his case against William Scruggs. Again, George was unlucky in court. The jury of John Jamison, Lewis Perry, John Williams, Isaac Ware, Michael Kirkham, David Sutton, Thomas Bates, William O'Bannon, David Durst, William Hubble, Charles Smith, and Jacob Alexander delivered their verdict in favor of Scruggs. They also ordered that George reimburse Scruggs for the costs of his defense.[86] Determining which court to attend became increasingly difficult for George because county boundaries around him were shifting for the creation of new Kentucky counties. The new county of Franklin, which contained the town of Frankfort, was acquired from the counties of Woodford, Mercer and Shelby. After the final establishment of Franklin County, George's 112 acres of land was now located in Franklin County instead of Woodford. In examining a 1794 Kentucky map of established county

---

[85] Kentucky. Woodford County. George Bratton entry, 1794 Tax List, Allen County Public Library, Fort Wayne, Indiana. Microfilm, #0394, 1790-1797, 1799 – 1815.

[86] Kentucky. Woodford County. Quarter Sessions Court Cases, Vol. 1. George Bratton vs. William Scruggs civil case: 105.

boundaries and particularly the Woodford County boundaries and the pending Franklin County boundaries, George's 112 acres of land was located south of Frankfort.[87] Instead of traveling to Versailles in Woodford County for business, George Bratton began traveling to nearby Frankfort.

Also in 1794, in the Pisgah community where George's brother Alexander Dunlap continued to live, there was a buzz jumping from household to household about a new academy. For days, the Presbyterian Church members had been constructing a little stone building next to the church. It was replacing the two-room, log schoolhouse with a dogtrot that had been there previously. The schoolteacher Andrew Steele lived in one of the rooms and taught in the other and charged four pounds a year for his services.[88] No doubt he had to find another home for himself and his students during construction of the new building. By December, it was completed and ready to be used. It was renamed the Kentucky Academy. The whole process for this education upgrade was begun by Reverend David Rice, whose home first housed classes for Transylvania Seminary in nearby Lexington. Rice was disappointed with how small an influence Presbyterian principles impacted educational curriculum at the university so he influenced the establishment of the academy and petitioned national individuals to invest in it.[89] It was quite a coup for him to elicit funds of $100 from both Presidents George Washington and John Adams.[90] He also received $50 from Aaron Burr. The academy became the first public school incorporated by

---

[87] The Newberry Library; Chicago, Illinois; *Atlas of Historical County Boundaries*. (accessed 23 April 2014). https://digital.newberry.org/ahcb/map/map.html#KY.

[88] Pisgah Presbyterian Church and Academy, Louisville, Kentucky. Historic American Buildings Survey (photographs, measured drawings, written historical and descriptive data), National Park Service, U.S. Department of the Interior. Prints and Photographs Division, Library of Congress (HABS KY 120-PISG V, 1 and 2-).

[89] "Transylvania University Early Documents." TUA1, Special Collections, Transylvania University, Lexington, Kentucky.

[90] Works Progress Administration. 1942. *Kentucky: A Guide to the Bluegrass State*. New York, New York: Harcourt, Brace and Company: 84.

the Kentucky Legislature.[91] It is possible that William Bratton attended the Pisgah school and then attended the Kentucky Academy when it opened. At some point in Kentucky, he did receive instruction in reading and writing either at home or at school. At this same exact age, Alexander Little, a son in the Thomas Little family mentioned previously in relation to their journey to Kentucky, created a mathematics booklet of twenty-six pages during his school on the Kentucky frontier (possibly in Mercer County) that he referred to as his Cypheren Book.[92] The cover was blue and made of homespun cloth. Inside, he filled the pages with mathematical principles, financial calculations and tables of weights and measures. It also included mathematics for land surveying.[93] If William attended the Kentucky Academy, he might have also had a mathematical booklet he worked in.

It is also possible that William received his schooling as part of his apprenticeship as a gunsmith. The age and to whom he was bound into an apprenticeship to learn the gunsmith trade is unknown.[94] If William was not the over sixteen-year-old male listed in his father's household in 1794, it is probable that he was already bound out as an apprentice at that time. There were about two handfuls of known gunsmiths working in Kentucky before 1794 – Samuel Boone, John Fitch, William Graham, John Harvey, Michael Humble, Matthew Jones, James McQuidey, William Price, Daniel Bryan, William Settle, Thomas Simpson, and Edward West. To determine whom William might have been bound to, we can perhaps rule out several of these since they were associated with military forts. James Harvey was an armorer and blacksmith at Fort Jefferson in 1780; John Harvey was an armorer at Fort Clark in 1780; Matthew Jones was an armorer at Fort Nelson in 1782; James McQuidey was an artificer

---

[91] Works Progress Administration. 1942. *Kentucky: A Guide to the Bluegrass State*. New York, New York: Harcourt, Brace and Company: 84.
[92] Little, Alexander. Cypheren Book. 1795-1796. Blog post and images. Special Collections, Honnold-Mudd Library, Claremont College. (Accessed 25 April 2014).
https://scl-blog.library.claremont.edu/2009/09/24/alexander_little_his_book_1795/
[93] Ibid.
[94] James T. Fields to Eva Dye Letter. 18 November 1901. Eva Emery Dye Collection. Oregon Historical Society. Portland, Oregon.

and armorer at Fort Nelson from 1779-1781; and William Price was an armorer at Fort Nelson in 1784.[95] Of the gunsmiths left, the one that lived the closest to the Bratton family was William Graham. He was also a Virginian native who relocated to Franklin County. He lived there in August 1801.[96] It is unknown whether he entered into contracts to support boys in apprenticeships but he did have a son James who learned the gunsmith trade from him. Graham was only ten years older than William, so he might have been deemed too young or not established enough to be a significant gunsmith master for William. Next, geographically, the closest gunsmiths to William Bratton were Samuel Boone, Edward West, and Daniel Bryan. Samuel Boone, a cousin of Daniel and Squire Boone, lived in Shelby County, north of Frankfort on Brashear Creek. His Kentucky flintlock rifles were considered to be very beautiful pieces. They were on average about fifty-five to sixty-one inches long with finely wrought brass and silver mountings, highly finished stocks, and beautifully browned barrels.[97] Edward West ran a gunsmith and silversmith shop in Lexington that was conducting business when the Brattons first arrived in Lexington in 1789. He was also a talented inventor who invented a hemp-breaking machine, a wire-bound cannon, a nail-cutting machine, a pistol, an arms lock, and a machine used cut or press molding on tin gutter pipe.[98] Unfortunately, even though West filed patents in Washington D. C. for many of his inventions, a fire in 1814 (as part of the War of 1812) destroyed the paperwork. He did employ apprentices but whether or not they learned both trades of gunsmithing and silversmithing is unknown.[99] If they were so engaged, then William Bratton did not apprentice under West. Daniel Bryan, a nephew of Daniel Boone,

---

[95] Kelly, Walter H. "Arms, Arms Makers and Arms History in Kentucky," manuscript. University of Louisville, Kentucky, 1957.
[96] Kentucky. Franklin County. William Graham entry. 1801 Tax List, Allen County Public Library, Fort Wayne, Indiana. Microfilm, #0118, 1797, 1801-1815.
[97] Kelly, Walter H. "Arms, Arms Makers and Arms History in Kentucky," manuscript. University of Louisville, Kentucky: 1957.
[98] Ibid.
[99] West, Edward. Business advertisement. Kentucky Gazette. December 18, 1790: 3.

was a gunsmith who, like West, lived in Fayette County. He produced guns that were indicative of the area. His rifles were maple with the metalwork on each was finely designed and executed.[100] Many times, Bryan's guns were unsigned because he and his family ran a large shop with up to 25 gunsmiths in which each one would work on a different part of the rifle.[101] Besides the gunsmith shop, Bryan also operated a paper mill, a gunpowder mill, a grist mill and a distillery. Perhaps in knowing of William Bratton's future endeavors of also running a mill and distillery besides doing gunsmith work, Daniel Bryan is the strongest potential candidate for whom William fulfilled an apprenticeship under.

As an apprentice, by law, William could expect to be provided with lodging, clothing, schooling, and if he was lucky, a wage. His education was to include reading, writing, mathematics, and mechanics of gunsmithing.[102] Such an education made for long days. He would have worked in a gunsmith shop that was poorly lit and crowded with equipment – a forge, a boring machine, a rifling bench, etc. Crafting one barrel took about a week. A gunsmith also often carved detailed engraving on the stock of a gun, and so would have imparted that skill to his apprentice. Additionally, apprentices learned how to make springs and screws to repair used guns and also often learned how to make tomahawks and knives, bullet molds and possibly powder horns. While in Europe, individual tasks of making a gun were allotted to different guilds – barrel makers, stocker, lock maker and mountings maker – but because of a lack of skilled labor, an American gunsmith did it all.[103] Moreover, if a blacksmith was not available in the area in which they lived, a gunsmith might have

---

[100] Montfort, Guy. "A Fine Lexington Style Rifle by Marvin Kemper." Contemporary Longrifle Foundation. 2013. http://www.contemporarylongriflefoundation.org.
[101] Eblen, Tom. "A Historic Icon, Kentucky Long Rifle Increasingly Seen as a Work of Art, too." Herald-Leader, 11 March 2014.
[102] Gorin, Sandra. *Indentures to Apprenticeships.* List-serv post. 8 December 2005. https://archiver.rootsweb.ancestry.com.
[103] Kindig, Joe. 1960. *Thoughts on the Kentucky Rifle in the Golden Age.* York, Pennsylvania: Trimmer Printing, Incorporated: 11.

repaired other things as well.[104] Usually, boys were apprentices until the age of twenty-one. They received a new suit of clothes and were now able to make their own way in the world. If indeed William Bratton was able to apprentice within close range of his family, he was able to keep abreast of their comings and goings, and of their latest news.

    Near the end of 1794 the most exciting event for the year in the Bratton family occurred. On the day after Christmas, Anne married Corporal Joseph Bimson.[105] Because of continually shifting county borders, Joseph and Anne's marriage bond was filed in Mercer County. Joseph Hutton served as Bimson's security when Bimson posted a marriage bond for fifty pounds to Governor Isaac Shelby to secure his intention to marry Anne. George Bratton gave his consent for their marriage since Anne was not yet twenty-one.[106] The witnesses to this consent were John Ward and Samuel Hutton, a brother or father to Joseph Hutton. This was the first time the Hutton name arose in legal documents that involved members of the Bratton family but it was not the last. The Hutton family also hailed from Augusta County, Virginia and migrated to Kentucky in 1780.[107] They lived at McMurtry's Station until they settled along land between the south fork of the Benson River's Big Creek and Hammond Creek in their own station.[108] Their station was on the west side of the Kentucky River south of Frankfort near the Bratton land. Because several Huttons show up in future legal documents for various events and for more than one Bratton member, it is clear that the Hammond Creek neighborhood is where they all lived. Samuel Hutton and his family lived in a larger three-story log home with open porches on two levels and an outside staircase on the front

---

[104] "The Gunsmith and his Shop." Pricketts Fort Memorial Foundation. (Accessed 20 June 2014). http://www.prickettsfort.org

[105] Kentucky. Mercer County. *Kentucky, County Marriages Records, 1797-1954.* (Accessed 15 May 2014). Ancestry.com.

[106] Ibid.

[107] U.S. Revolutionary War Pension and Bounty-Land Warrant Application Files, 1800-1900. James Hutton Revolutionary War pension record. (database online.) Provo, Utah: Ancestry.com Operations Inc.: 2010.

[108] Kentucky. Franklin County. Samuel Hutton land record. 13 January 1798.

of the house.[109] The joints of the logs were saddle-notched and the roof had gable ends. On one side of the house, the fireplace was centered so that it ran upward past the peak of the roof and was used in the front room on the first two stories. The stone basement stood over a spring to serve as a springhouse.[110] (The Hutton house was still standing in 1968.)

It is unclear when Joseph Bimson first arrived in the Hammond Creek neighborhood. He first surfaced in Kentucky in 1789 in Louisville but what he was doing there is undetermined. His native origin is also undetermined.[111] It is possible that he was an American soldier at Fort Nelson though no military records have identified him as a soldier then. He might have ended up there after a journey by boat down the Ohio River. Even if he was not a soldier before, he became one to defend Kentucky from Native American attacks. Like Robert Bratton, he answered the call to arms in 1793, and served as a Corporal in Captain David Kennedy's company B of mounted volunteers in David Caldwell's Battalion. He served for fifty-three days for the wage of $66.25 at $1.25 per day. On September 23, 1793 during his service, he was present at Fort Washington.[112] He served another term in the Kentucky militia the next summer again as a Corporal while he courted Anne. He mustered in on July 7, 1794 and served in Lieutenant Stephen Arnold's company B of mounted volunteers in Whittaker's Battalion. Originally, Bimson's company was led by Captain John Arnold, however Arnold was soon given new orders to form a company of spies, which he did, and the command was transferred to his brother Stephen Arnold. Bimson served this term until October 26, 1794. It equaled 112 days of which he was

---

[109] Lancaster, Clay. 2014. *Antebellum Architecture of Kentucky*. Lexington, Kentucky: University Press of Kentucky: 16-17.

[110] Lancaster, Clay. 2014. *Antebellum Architecture of Kentucky*. Lexington, Kentucky: University Press of Kentucky: 16-17.

[111] Kentucky. Jefferson County. Joseph Bimson entry. 1789 Tax List, Allen County Public Library, Fort Wayne, Indiana. Microfilm, #0100, 1781-1797, 1799 – 1804.

[112] National Archives of Records Administration (NARA); Washington D.C.; *Compiled Service Records of Volunteer Soldiers Who Served 1784-1811*. Service database entry for Joseph Bimson. (accessed 15 May 2014). Ancestry.com.

paid $140.00 at $1.25 per day.[113]

As a resident in the Hammond Creek area, there was one civil incident that embroiled Joseph Bimson. This incident involved a bond that was given to him by Jones Varswell in July 1794 with the expectation that Bimson would pay for it in the near future. However, over a year later, he had not made any payment to Varswell and understandably, Varswell was not happy about it. On September 14, 1795, Varswell posted a notice in the Kentucky Gazette and warned people that he did not receive any value for the bond from Bimson and that if Bimson tried to assign it to anyone, Varswell would not pay them for it.[114] Besides this one small hiccup in 1794, Bimson and Anne's life as well as those of the Bratton family, contained the everyday normal activities of frontier life. The only significant change they experienced was that the surrounding population in Franklin County grew so rapidly that nearby Frankfort was designated as the new state capital.

---

[113] National Archives of Records Administration (NARA); Washington D.C.; *Compiled Service Records of Volunteer Soldiers Who Served 1784-1811*. Service database entry for Joseph Bimson. (accessed 15 May 2014). Ancestry.com.

[114] Varswell, Jones. Business advertisement. Kentucky Gazette. 18 Dec. 1795: 3.

CHAPTER THREE
Franklin County, Kentucky, 1795-1803

Now firmly established as a citizen of the newly formed Franklin County, Kentucky, George Bratton was included in the 1795 tax list for Franklin County. His eldest son Robert Bratton, now age twenty-one, warranted his own name and entry in the tax logs. It is impossible to know if Robert still lived in his father's household, or whether he had his own home, or if he worked for another man and lived at that man's residence. Regardless, tax information for both men was turned into Commissioner Thomas Lillard on the same day. Lillard did not finalize and turn in his accumulated Franklin County information until late 1796.[115] Property west of the Kentucky River, including land that had before been considered Mercer County but was now within Franklin County, was under Lillard's jurisdiction.[116] Robert paid the tax for himself but was not taxed for anything else.[117] His father George was listed several entries above him and he was taxed for one horse, but he was not taxed for any other males between sixteen to twenty-one. If William lived with him, then George was charged a tithe for William who was age seventeen

---

[115] Early Kentucky Tax Records: From the Register of the Kentucky Historical Society. Frankfort, Kentucky: Clearfield Publishing Company, 2001: 47.
[116] Jillson, Willard Rouse. 1936. *Early Frankfort and Franklin County: A Chronology of Historical Sketches Covering the Century 1750-1850*. Louisville, Kentucky: The Standard Printing Company: 104.
[117] Kentucky. Franklin County. Robert Bratton entry. 1795 Tax List, Allen County Public Library, Fort Wayne, Indiana. Microfilm, #0100, 1781-1797, 1799 – 1804.

in 1795.[118] As discussed previously, the most plausible explanation for the absence of William from tax records of his father's household is that he was living in another household as a gunsmith apprentice. Likewise, William was not found on any militia records. He did not participate in the local militia in 1796 when he became age eighteen as deemed by the law since he was indentured out at this time to a gunsmith. Gunsmiths were exempt from militia duty because their gunsmithing activities were considered their service to the militia. According to the tax list, it is possible that George Bratton was not doing too well financially. He was not taxed for land or livestock. In addition, he signed an IOU on April 7, 1796 to James Dunn for nine pounds, seventeen shillings and nine pence. George signed his own name but the rest of the IOU was filled out by the witness John January. The IOU was written on the back of a piece of paper that contained business interactions with an Isaac Sellers for various sundries but for mostly whiskey. The looping handwriting for the business interaction matches January's so even the paper the IOU was written on was borrowed by George.[119]

If George was in the nearby town of Frankfort for business, it was bustling with enormous activity. There was a lot of building underway for necessary infrastructure. Already, a stone statehouse had been built in 1793 on the public square with a designated Market Street. During 1796, before the Governor's Mansion was built on the corner of High and Clinton Streets, Governor James Garrard, his wife, and his numerous children were housed in the Major James Love home. It was rented for the Governor by the commonwealth

---

[118] Kentucky. Franklin County. George Bratton entry. 1795 Tax List, Allen County Public Library, Fort Wayne, Indiana. Microfilm, #0100, 1781-1797, 1799 – 1804.

[119] Kentucky. Franklin County. Civil Court Cases, Vol. 1, Kentucky Department of Library and Archives: James Dunn vs. George Bratton civil case.

for 100 pounds.[120] More was paid for the mansion. Twelve hundred pounds was allotted by the commissioners of public buildings, Bennet Pemberton, William Trigg, and Daniel Weisinger, to build and furnish it sufficiently with cupboards, beds, a desk, tables, chairs, a chest of drawers, and a bookcase. In addition, legislators wanted a fence erected around a two-acre plot for a vegetable garden.[121] Even though the dwelling was called the Governor's Mansion, the design and construction of it was modest, which was in alignment with the concept of a simple gubernatorial democracy. The dwelling was indicative of a modest Kentucky farmhouse instead of a more imposing, formal and affluent mansion. It stood four stories high with a small attic and a basement. It had four chimneys at the ends of the dwelling and numerous windows on the two main stories. A dogtrot connected the dwelling to an outside kitchen. Besides the vegetable garden, a pasture was created for livestock and bordered the house on one side.[122]

The only other stone structure in Frankfort at this time was Daniel Weisinger's tavern which stood out among all the other buildings constructed of wood. Some of the wood buildings were built of hewed logs and others were built of unhewn logs. Because of its state capital status, Frankfort was bustling. It had an ideal geographic position on the Kentucky River and became a point of shipment for flatboats making their way to the Ohio River via the Kentucky River. The town became an economic hub for manufacturing, mining and agricultural products. The atmosphere of the budding capital was a curious mix of rough infrastructure and backwoods frontiersman with affluent businessmen trying to make a deal and a living. In one description of Frankfort at this time, "there

---

[120] Clark, Thomas D. and Margaret Lane. 2002. *The People's House: Governor Mansions of Kentucky*. Lexington, Kentucky: University Press of Kentucky: 5-11.

[121] Clark, Thomas D. and Margaret Lane. 2002. *The People's House: Governor Mansions of Kentucky*. Lexington, Kentucky: University Press of Kentucky: 5-11.

[122] Ibid.

were no sidewalks in this rough and, in many respects, straggling village. The streets were without substantial covering of any kind, and were difficult of passage at all times of the year, dusty and rough in the summer months, wet and loblollied throughout the late fall, winter and early spring. Travelers, of whom there were many, explorers, soldiers, adventurers, land speculators, and settlers moved through this strategically located town, on the old road from Lexington to Louisville at the Falls of the Ohio, in ever-increasing numbers. Here, in an elemental society, where hunters in deerskin breeches and coonskin caps met, mingled and bartered, for hard money was scarce, with aristocrats from the eastern tidewater dressed in broadcloth and silk tops, tavern jollity afforded the principal amusement and entertainment of life."[123] With Weisinger's tavern being an exception, other taverns in Frankfort were "stoutly-built, well-chinked log structures with great open fireplaces of stone, where logs blazed brightly" and homemade corn whiskey was served.[124] Thomas Love operated a tavern conveniently near the ferry on the southwest corner of Wilkinson and Wapping Streets. Philip Bush operated another tavern.

One Frankfort citizen gave a descriptive account of a specific occasion in which extreme measures were needed to offset the muddy streets. While legislators and their wives ate a formal dinner at Weisinger's Tavern, a very heavy rain fell which turned the streets into a quagmire. After dinner, they were supposed to attend a ball at the statehouse. Seeing the river of mud, legislators linked their hands to another legislator, formed human rickshaws, and began ferrying the women across the treacherous, wet streets to the statehouse door. Apparently, the ball was to go on.[125] According to farmer

---

[123] Jillson, Willard Rouse. 1936. *Early Frankfort and Franklin County: A Chronology of Historical Sketches Covering the Century 1750-1850.* Louisville, Kentucky: The Standard Printing Company: 66.
[124] Clark, Thomas D. and Margaret Lane. 2002. *The People's House: Governor Mansions of Kentucky.* Lexington, Kentucky: University Press of Kentucky: 5-11.
[125] Ibid.

and agricultural lobbyist Robert Wilmot Scott, affairs of these in Frankfort were not to be missed. A Christmas party held by Governor Garrard and his wife included a dinner of "two large turkeys, two pieces of beef of about twenty-five pounds each, and bacon and ducks," dessert, and a peach wine that Mrs. Garrard made herself.[126] Scott himself attended a Frankfort ball and was very content with its quality. "I left the ball and reached home about one o'clock, well tired and better satisfied that fashionable society was nowhere superior to that of Frankfort, Ky., though it is true that the belles had more accomplishments, that is immodest airs and fancy millinery about them in Washington than in Kentucky. And what is more, my suspicions were confirmed that the ladies of Washington were not the most pure in soul and chaste in deed of all the Fair in which I had seen. P.S. several of the most fashionable young ladies wore short dresses and pantalets."[127] The ladies must not have worn pantalets at this time in Frankfort. The progress of such society, along with the new statehouse, the hospitable taverns, and increasing river traffic and trade was a huge improvement over the previous landscape of wild grapevines and sinkholes on the south side of Frankfort, and a mud flat surrounded by three beaver dams on the north side.[128]

Such parties no doubt excluded George Bratton who remained somewhat poor. As of March 1, 1796, George had not paid his debt to James Dunn when he was asked for it, and as a result he was sued. The suit was filed in Woodford County and the sheriff there looked for him.[129] According to the 1796 Franklin County tax list, George remained in the same financial

---

[126] Clark, Thomas D. and Margaret Lane. 2002. *The People's House: Governor Mansions of Kentucky*. Lexington, Kentucky: University Press of Kentucky: 5-11.
[127] Ibid.
[128] Darnell, Ermina Jett. 1966. *Filling in the Chinks*. Frankfort, Kentucky: Roberts Printing Company: 15.
[129] Kentucky. Woodford County. Civil Court Cases, Vol. 1, Kentucky Department of Library and Archives: James Dunn vs. George Bratton civil case.

situation. He was taxed for one horse and no land. Again, George is listed as a white male above twenty-one with no other males in his household sixteen or above.[130] Robert was listed three rows down from George and was not taxed for any property or livestock.[131] George's son-in-law, Joseph Bimson, was listed thirteen rows up from George. He was taxed as a tithable male over twenty-one, and was taxed for two horses and five cattle but no land.[132] Whereas George and Robert's information was collected on May 17, 1796 by Daniel Weisinger, serving as a Franklin County tax commissioner, Weisinger received Bimson's information on March 20, 1796.

Just a year later, on June 20, 1797, George Bratton no longer even owned a horse. Perhaps he had to sell it to pay off his debt to Dunn. Again, he was listed as the only tithable male in his household. Besides himself, his household included his wife Jean, age forty-seven; daughter Jenny, age sixteen; son Adam, age twelve; son George Jr., age ten; Archibald, age nine, and daughter Nancy, age seven. William still worked as a gunsmith apprentice. George's eldest son Robert Bratton is again on the tax list for Franklin County. He listed himself as a white male above age twenty-one. He was not taxed in any other column, not even for a horse.[133] Joseph Bimson no longer owned his two horses or five cattle and he listed himself as the only tithable male in his household of him and wife Anne. George, Robert and Joseph were three of ninety tithable white males in a total population of 441 people.[134] Having to pay taxes did not help George's finances. He again looked to

---

[130] Kentucky. Franklin County. George Bratton entry. 1796 Tax List, Allen County Public Library, Fort Wayne, Indiana. Microfilm, #0100, 1781-1797, 1799 – 1804.

[131] Ibid: Robert Bratton entry.

[132] Ibid: Joseph Bimson entry.

[133] Kentucky. Franklin County. Robert Bratton entry. 1797 Tax List, Allen County Public Library, Fort Wayne, Indiana. Microfilm, #0100, 1781-1797, 1799 – 1804.

[134] Jillson, Willard Rouse. 1936. *Early Frankfort and Franklin County: A Chronoogy of Historical Sketches Covering the Century 1750-1850.* Louisville, Kentucky: The Standard Printing Company: 66.

borrow money to keep his finances afloat. He and Thomas Wilson borrowed thirty pounds from Thomas Bereman on September 26, 1797 as witnessed by Francis Major.[135] Bereman was a neighbor who owned one horse, thirty cattle and 200 acres of land.[136]

The children were occupied with far happier pursuits. On a Monday evening at 6 p.m. in September 1797, George's young children might have spied something they had never seen before in the sky. South of Frankfort, in Lexington, a Frenchman named M. Lassellard, raised an air balloon that was ten feet in diameter. This activity took place at the home of M. Sangrain on High Street. The balloon managed to travel a mile before it caught on fire and burned up entirely.[137]

As the new year of 1798 rolled in, the Kentucky legislature tackled the controversial issue of inoculation against smallpox. There was interest throughout the state about the process but for fear of an epidemic, Kentucky legislators felt strongly against it. To discourage physicians or quacks, they voted on January 30, 1798, to pass an act that regulated the inoculation process. "Be it enacted by the General Assembly, that if any person or persons whatsoever shall willingly or designedly presume to import or bring into this commonwealth, from any country or place whatever, the small-pox, or any variolous or infectious matter of the said distemper, with a purpose to inoculate any person or persons whatsoever; or by any means to propagate the said distemper within this commonwealth, he or she so offending, shall forfeit and pay the sum of one thousand pounds for every offense committed...."[138]

---

[135] Kentucky. Franklin County. Civil Court Cases, Vol. 1, Kentucky Department of Library and Archives: Thomas Bereman vs. George Bratton and Thomas Wilson civil case, 1798.

[136] Kentucky. Franklin County. Thomas Bereman (Berryman) entry. 1795 Tax List, Allen County Public Library, Fort Wayne, Indiana. Microfilm, #0100, 1781-1797, 1799 – 1804.

[137] Lassellard, M. Article. Kentucky Gazette. 27 September 1797.

[138] Kentucky. General Assembly. 1798. "Journal of the 2nd Session of the 6th General Assembly of the Commonwealth of Kentucky." Lexington, Kentucky: John Bradford, printer.

Furthermore, "every physician, doctor, or other person undertaking inoculation at any house, shall cause a written advertisement to be put up at the nearest public road or other most notorious adjacent place, giving information that the small pox is at such house, and shall continue to keep the same set up for as long as the distemper or infection remains there, under the penalty of forty shillings for every day the same is omitted, or neglected to be paid by the physician or doctor."[139] A Dr. Samuel Brown, who lived in Lexington for several years, was one of the primary medical figures that introduced the area to the inoculation of smallpox.[140]

There was exciting news at the end of the summer in 1798 for citizens of Frankfort and Franklin County. A new, weekly newspaper called The Palladium began printing on August 9, 1798. Several months later, the newspaper reported record freezing temperatures on Halloween. On that Monday morning, the temperature was eighteen degrees Fahrenheit but by sunrise, the temperature had only climbed four degrees to twenty-two degrees Fahrenheit. It was determined by pioneer citizens that it was the coldest temperature ever recorded for the end of October for the greater Lexington area since it had been settled.[141]

As of November 1798, George nor his associate Thomas Wilson had repaid Thomas Bereman the thirty pounds they owed him. Bereman hired Thomas Todd as his attorney who filed a formal complaint against the two men. In turn, Nathaniel Richardson, the Sheriff of Franklin County, was asked to bring the two men to jail until their court date on

---

[139] Kentucky. General Assembly. 1798. "Journal of the 2nd Session of the 6th General Assembly of the Commonwealth of Kentucky." Lexington, Kentucky: John Bradford, printer.
[140] "Samuel Brown (1769-1830)." Dickinson College: Dickinson College Archives & Special Collections, 2005. (accessed 16 May 2014.) http://archives.dickinson.edu/people/samuel-brown-1769-1830.
[141] The Palladium, weather article. Frankfort, Kentucky. 13 November 1798.

November 24, 1798.[142] It is unclear if Thomas Wilson ever paid back his portion, but somehow George's son Robert Bratton was roped into the legal mess. Possibly as George's heir, he was liable for the debt if his father did not pay. Furthermore, George and Robert signed their own obligation to Nathaniel Richardson for the thirty pounds on Dec. 15, 1798. This transfer of debt indicated that Richardson paid the thirty pounds to Bereman and transferred the IOU so that now George Bratton owed the debt to Richardson instead. Wilson was not represented in the new document.[143] The conclusion of this matter and to what satisfaction it was resolved is unknown, and though George was usually the one being sued in most of the cases in his life, he remained satisfied enough with the justice system to pursue another case. He became involved in a legal case in Augusta County, Virginia even though he and his family had been living in Kentucky for a decade. The court case was active in April 1799 and was listed as Bratton vs. Montgomery, so this time it was George who was suing. It was noted by the court that George lived in Kentucky but the conclusion of the case is unknown.[144]

Though George was embroiled in this conflict in Virginia and possibly still involved in local legal entanglements, the safety of him and his family and their situation at home in Kentucky rose in concern as the summer passed. Whole neighborhoods and communities were alarmed and on guard as murderers known as the Harpe brothers rampaged through the Kentucky countryside. The Harpes were either brothers or cousins from North Carolina and unbeknownst to most

---

[142] Kentucky. Franklin County. Civil Court Cases, Vol. 1, Kentucky Department of Library and Archives: Thomas Bereman vs. George Bratton and Thomas Wilson civil case, 1798.

[143] Kentucky. Franklin County. Civil Court Cases, Vol. 1, Kentucky Department of Library and Archives: Thomas Bereman vs. George Bratton and Thomas Wilson civil case, 1798.

[144] Chalkley, Lyman. 1912. *Chronicles of the Scotch-Irish Settlement in Virginia: extracted from the Original Court Records of Augusta County, 1745-1800*. Vol. 2. Rosslyn, Virginia: Commonwealth Printing Company: 22.

Kentucky residents, had already been killing people way before they even entered Kentucky. By August 15, 1799, thirty to thirty-five murders were already attributed to them since July and the list continued to grow – William Ballard of Knox County, Tennessee, a Mr. Langford, Isaac Coffey, James Brazell, John Trabue, and John Tully. The pair had been captured at one time and were locked up in jail in Danville, Kentucky but they escaped. They were on the move from the Wolf River in the Cumberland Mountain area to Stockton Valley to Marrowbone along the north branch of the Cumberland River which frustrated the men that were tracking them.[145] It was not until the end of August that a posse successfully placed themselves close enough to the duo to do them some damage. Whether their goal was to apprehend them to bring them to justice or outright kill them, the posse shot Micajah Harpe which resulted in his death. The tale that many residents heard was that John Leiper rode up close to Micajah Harpe, jumped off his horse as he aimed his gun and shot him. At that time, Micajah Harpe dropped his own gun, began bleeding profusely but continued riding very slowly before expiring. Wiley Harpe unfortunately escaped. The final death count committed by these two men was over forty people but it could be more. On December 16, 1799, the Kentucky government paid the men in the posse for their successful apprehension of Micajah Harpe… "that the governor did offer a reward of three hundred dollars, for the apprehension of the said Harp; and whereas sundry good citizens of the commonwealth, who went in pursuit of said Harp, were, while in the attempt to apprehend him, reduced to the necessity of slaying him; whereby doubts have been entertained whether they are entitled to the aforesaid reward: To remove all doubts, therefore, Be it enacted, that John Leiper, James Tompkins, Silas McBee, Matthew Christian, Moses Stegall, Neville Lindsey, and William Gresham, who slew the said Harp in attempting to apprehend him, shall be entitled to receive three hundred dollars…One hundred dollars of

---

[145] The Palladium. Harpe brothers report. Frankfort, Kentucky. August 15, 1799.

which shall be appropriated to the said John Leiper, and the residue to be equally divided among the others. And be it further enacted, that Alexander McFarling, John McFarling, and Robert White, who from motives of public good, incurred very considerable expense and toil in the pursuit of the said Harp, and other his associates, fugitives from justice be allowed one hundred and fifty dollars, for their trouble and expenses incurred in such pursuit." [146] John Leiper, a large man who weighed about 210 pounds and was at least six feet tall, was a woodsman who lived in the Highland Lick area in western Kentucky. Michael Christian was from Henderson County, Kentucky.[147]

Other news in December that was not quite as titillating for Franklin County residents as the capture of Micajah Harpe and escape of Wiley Harpe but just as relevant - a bridge would soon be built over Kentucky River at the end of Ann Street on the south side of Frankfort. The erection of the bridge was to be completed by an association of Frankfort citizens known as the Frankfort Bridge Company. Christopher Greenup, Daniel Weisinger, and William Trigg were appointed commissioners for the purpose of keeping a subscription book to sell stock in the company at $400 per share. Once forty shares were sold, seven of the shareholders would then be elected directors of the company. One of the decisions they would make was what rules and regulations would be established pertaining to the collection and accounting of the tolls, the preservation of the bridge, and other matters in conducting and regulating the business of the Frankfort Bridge Company. The General Assembly also passed a slate of acceptable amounts that could be charged for tolls: "For every man or woman, 5 cents; for every child over five years old, 5 cents; for every horse, mare,

---

[146] Kentucky. General Assembly. 1798. "Journal of the 2nd Session of the 6th General Assembly for the Commonwealth of Kentucky." Lexington, Kentucky: John Bradford, printer.

[147] Young, Chester Raymond, Ed. 1981. *Westward into Kentucky: The Narrative of Daniel Trabue.* Lexington, Kentucky: The University Press of Kentucky: 151, 197.

or colt, 5 cents; for every wagon, 50 cents; for every cart, 37.5 cents; for every riding carriage with four wheels, 50 cents; for every riding carriage with two wheels, 37.5 cents; for every head of cattle, 2 cents; for every head of sheep, goats, or hogs, 1 cent; and for every hogshead of tobacco rolled or carried across that is not in a wagon or cart, 25 cents." The collected tolls would then be split amongst the shareholders in proportion to their shares. However, a deduction for the expenses of collection would first be subtracted before the remaining amount would be dispersed.[148]

It is also by this time that the dynamics of the George Bratton family began to experience huge changes. First, they experienced the death of Jean, their beloved wife and mother. Her death occurred at some point between 1790 and 1799; however, no record of her death exists by document or headstone. Even the whereabouts of her burial is unknown. Usually burials at this time occurred in ground where a family lived, either in a little family graveyard or in a church cemetery. If Jean was buried in the ground where the Bratton family lived in the Hammond Creek neighborhood, there is no record or information passed down orally to validate a location. If George Bratton rented ground, she could have been buried there with permission granted by the owner. Graves for other pioneers in the area at that time are scarce as well, though one exception is for Jane Montgomery McBrayer, a Bratton neighbor, who died in 1796. Her grave is in her family graveyard, the McBrayer Cemetery.[149] It is difficult to best calculate in that decade when Jean likely died. If Jean died in the early 1790s, her eldest daughters Anne and Jenny would have helped with the younger children and the household duties of cooking, cleaning and laundry, thus preventing any

---

[148] Kentucky. General Assembly. 1800. "Journal of the 1st Session of the 8th General Assembly for the Commonwealth of Kentucky." Frankfort, Kentucky: William Hunter, printer.

[149] Ancestry. *Find A Grave*. Database with images. (http://findagrave.com: accessed 17 July 2014), memorial 65886417, Jane Montgomery McBrayer (unk.-1796), McBrayer Cemetery, Alton Station, Anderson County, Kentucky; gravestone photograph by Kate Jacques.

huge transparent shift of household dynamics that would have signified her death. If she died in the latter part of the 1790s, the younger children would have been old enough to care for themselves and could even contribute to household chores themselves. Many men who found themselves widowed with young children usually remarried quickly but George was not in such dire straits as far as caring for children, and could wait until he was ready to enter another marriage. By the latter half of 1799 or in the first half of 1800, he began courting a woman by the name of Rutha Ashley. It is unknown if this was a pet name or full name because other records indicated that her name could also have been Susanna. In 1797, the only Ashley listed on the Franklin County tax list in the same district as George Bratton is a Susanna Ashley who did not own any land but owned one horse.[150] Because she was listed as a woman on the tax list, it is most likely she was a widow. It is certainly possible that Susanna could have had a daughter Rutha in her household but later relevant records refer to her as Susanna Bratton. During his courtship, George was listed on a tax list for more than one county. He was listed on February 18, 1800, for Warren County, Kentucky. At this time, he owned no land there. On the tax list for Warren County, George listed himself as a white male above twenty-one. Also, he listed a male, age sixteen to twenty-one, who was most likely Adam, now age sixteen. Although William was now twenty-one, he did not pop up on either the 1800 Franklin County tax list or the Warren County tax list but he probably still lived in another man's household finishing up his apprenticeship. Usually apprenticeships were completed when the apprentice reached age twenty-one meaning William's apprenticeship was winding down. According to the Warren County tax list, George also owned two horses.[151] Additionally, George successfully

---

[150] Kentucky. Franklin County. Susanna Ashley entry. 1797 Tax List, Allen County Public Library, Fort Wayne, Indiana. Microfilm, #0100, 1781-1797, 1799 – 1804.
[151] Ibid: George Bratton entry.

made arrangements with local authorities in regards to the taxation for his situation there - "ordered that George Bratton have credit with the sheriff of this County for one dollar and eight cents tax paid for the year Eighteen hundred, satisfactory proof being made to the Court of same."[152] At this time, George and his family had not yet officially moved from Franklin County, but George was improving a 400-acre claim near Little Trammel Creek in Warren County. His parcel of land was described as beginning at a white oak and dogwood and running northeast to a corner and then southwest to another corner.[153] In fact, it was not until a few months later on July 22, 1800 that George entered into a bond with Governor James Garrard for fifty pounds as assurance that he was committed to his upcoming marriage. On the same day, Susanna appeared before the Franklin County Clerk to consent that she was of age to marry without permission. A woman had to be at least twenty-one to represent herself. She signed her own name as Ruth Ashley.[154] Shortly after the bond was approved, George Bratton married Susanna Rutha Ashley in Franklin County.[155] It is unknown whether Susanna brought any of her own children to the marriage, but she gained a household full of teenagers and young adults - Jenny, age nineteen; Adam, age; fifteen; George Jr., age thirteen; Archibald, age twelve, and Nancy, age ten.

    It was very soon after the marriage that George Bratton, his new wife, and his children moved to their new home in Warren County, Kentucky located further west and farther south than where Franklin County sat. Though the rest of the

---

[152] Ford, Barbara Oliver. 1986. *Early Tax Lists of Warren County, Kentucky, 1797-1807*. B.O. Ford, publisher.

[153] Gorin, Sandra. 1993. *Warren County, Kentucky Order Book*. Book A. Glasgow, Kentucky: Gorin Genealogical Publishing: 344.

[154] Kentucky. Franklin County. Marriage Bonds. Ruth Ashley entry. 22 July 1800.

[155] Kentucky. Franklin County. Franklin County Marriage Records. George Bratton to Rutha Ashley. Archives, University of Louisville, Lexington, Kentucky.

family moved, once his apprenticeship concluded, William stayed in Franklin County with his brother Robert and his sister Anne and most likely moved in with Anne and her husband Joseph Bimson. The toil and trade in which William was employed at this time could have been gunsmithing but it did not make him a great profit. The next year, on May 30, 1801 both William and his brother Robert were listed on the tax list in Franklin County, Kentucky. Robert, age twenty-seven, was listed as above age twenty-one, and he owned one horse but he did not own any land. William, age twenty-two, was also listed above twenty-one, but he did not own a horse or any land.[156]

William Bratton might have been mildly amused when he heard about a young man named Mr. Brown from a nearby neighborhood who made a $100 wager that he could walk from Frankfort to Lexington in one day between sunrise and sunset. Brown succeeded with apparent ease since he concluded the task with two hours to spare.[157] Like the story about Mr. Brown, William also probably heard of the shocking tale about a man, his two sons, and his thirteen enslaved people who were traveling down the Ohio River on a flatboat. The two sons killed their father only to be killed by their enslaved people. Then, the enslaved people tried to flee to live with local Native Americans, the Creeks, but they were caught by the federal army.[158]

Warren County, Kentucky inhabitants probably heard this scandalous story as well. By this time, George Bratton and his young family lived in a house, probably a dog-trot cabin. The improvement of his 400-acre claim was sufficient enough that the government issued George a warrant or title to his land

---

[156] Kentucky. Franklin County. Robert Bratton and William Bratton entries. 1801 Tax List, Allen County Public Library, Fort Wayne, Indiana. Microfilm, #0100, 1781-1797, 1799 – 1804.
[157] The Palladium. Brown article. Frankfort, Kentucky: 7 August 1800.
[158] Friend, Craig Thompson. 2010. *Kentucke's Frontiers*. Bloomington, Indiana: Indiana University Press: 218.

issued on June 15, 1801.[159] The nearest towns of significance were the growing town of Bowling Green and the oldest town of Martinsville, which was founded in 1785 by Hut Martin, a crony of Daniel Boone's who came from Virginia in 1777 to Boonesborough.[160] Like many other frontiersmen before him, Martin discovered the beautiful ground above the Big Barren River in Warren County while hunting. After Native American hostilities quieted enough for Martin's satisfaction, he and many other families traveled back to this area to settle. A grant was issued to the settlers of the Big Barren River by Patrick Henry who served as Governor of Virginia, as the land was still considered a part of Virginia in the county of Kentucky at that time. Martin staked his claim where he discovered a large spring on the north bluff of the river. Four other families adjoined his property and a village was born. Due to its prime location on the river and plentiful game, the village flourished and was home to about 300 people in just five years. It then doubled to 600 people in the next decade and teemed with flatboat business.[161] It was an ideal, convenient place of commerce for George Bratton and his family when they arrived in the county.

In 1802, George still owned 400 acres but owned only one horse.[162] A rustic picture of his place might be gained through the perspective of Frenchman Andre Michaux, who traveled through Warren County during the summer that year. Michaux was following the most traveled southwest route from Lexington to Nashville, Tennessee through the following locations - Harrodsburg to Hays Inn to Skeggs Inn to Bears

---

[159] Gorin, Sandra. 1993. *Warren County, Kentucky Order Book*. Book A. Glasgow, Kentucky: Gorin Genealogical Publishing: 344.

[160] Lee, Patsy Ground. 2012. "Martinsville, Warren County's Lost City." *Smith's Grove Gazette*: 1-4. (submitted by Lee to The Kentucky Explorer as written by her great-great-uncle Victor Moulder, circa 1905.) The website address for the online article posted 16 October 2012 is defunct.

[161] Ibid.

[162] Kentucky. Warren County. George Bratton entry. 1803 Tax List, Allen County Public Library, Fort Wayne, Indiana. Microfilm, #0100, 1781-1797, 1799 – 1804.

Wallow to Dripping Spring, across the Big Barren River, to a night possibly spent outdoors, and then over the border to Tennessee. Michaux encountered a Mr. McFadden who ran a ferry boat on the Big Barren River which Michaux thought was one-third broader than the Green River.[163] Three miles past the ferries were two of the oldest settlements which Michaux believed to have been at least fourteen-years-old which would have made their establishment around 1788 (One of these settlements was most likely Martinsville).[164] In one of the settlements, he noted that a boat loaded with salt had arrived from the French town of St. Genevieve located on the Mississippi River about 100 miles south of the mouth of the Ohio.[165] Somewhere just south of Warren County, Michaux stayed the night with a Mr. Jacob Kesly whom Michaux recognized as a member of the Dunker/Dunkard sect due to his long beard. (Dunker refers to German people of the Baptist faith known as the German Baptist Brethren.)[166] Though he seemed grateful for a place to stay at all, Michaux found Kesly's home to be pretty primitive. "My landlord's house was as miserably furnished as those I had lodged at for several days proceeding, and I was again obliged to sleep on the floor. The major part of the inhabitants of Kentucky have been here too short a time to make any great improvements; they have a very indifferent supply of anything except Indian corn and forage."[167]

In 1802, in Franklin County, William, Robert Bratton and Joseph Bimson all showed up on the tax list. William did not have any land or cattle, and he was only taxed as a white male over age twenty-one. Robert Bratton was also taxed as a white male over twenty-one but he is additionally taxed for one

---

[163] Michaux, Andre. 1802. *Travels to the West of the Alleghany Mountains.* London, England: D.N. Shury Publishers: 146.
[164] Ibid.
[165] Ibid.
[166] Falkenstein, George. 1900. *The German Baptist Brethren or Dunkers.* Lancaster, Pennsylvania: The Pennsylvania – German Society: 7.
[167] Michaux, Andre. 1802. *Travels to the West of the Alleghany Mountains.* London, England: D.N. Shury Publishers: 146.

horse. Joseph Bimson owned a little more. He was taxed for owning thirty acres near the Benson River, land that was part of the parcel originally entered and patented by Thomas Paxton. He was also taxed for one horse.

In 1803, neither William nor Robert were listed on the Franklin County or the Warren County tax list. Their brother-in-law, Joseph Bimson was on the list but probably sold his land near the Benson River since the previous year because he was only taxed as a white male over twenty-one who owned two horses.[168] It is a bit of a puzzle why William and Robert Bratton were not listed on the tax list because they lived in Franklin County. Robert served as a bondsman on April 21, 1803 for the wedding of Jonathan Hutton and Susannah Watkins.[169] Jonathan was another brother in the Hutton family in the Hammond Creek neighborhood. Both Bratton brothers probably attended a party to celebrate the wedding. William most likely continued working and living in Franklin County for a couple more months until he like many other young men heard startling news that traveled swiftly along the river routes…preparations for a military expedition to go west of the Mississippi River were underway and they were looking for hardy, unmarried men. When he heard about the opportunity, William Bratton's interest was piqued.

---

[168] Kentucky. Franklin County. Joseph Bimson entry. 1803 Tax List, Allen County Public Library, Fort Wayne, Indiana. Microfilm, #0100, 1781-1797, 1799 – 1804.

[169] Downing, George C. "Early Marriage Bonds of Franklin County, Kentucky, 1803, 1804, 1805." The Register of the Kentucky Historical Society. Vol. 12, No. 36: 79.

CHAPTER FOUR
Adventuring with Lewis and Clark

Unbeknownst to William Bratton in January 1803, huge plans by President Thomas Jefferson were beginning to fall into place. He wanted a body of men to travel westward to map new lands, document new life forms, and solidify friendly relationships with Native Americans. In January, Jefferson formally submitted a confidential proposal to Congress to approve his plan of western exploration. He proposed that the exploration be a military endeavor with all of the might of the U.S. Army behind it and that he would need $2500 from the U.S. government to execute it (approximately $50,000 in today's economy).[170] Also at this time, Congress and Jefferson used savvy diplomatic finesse, maneuvers, and negotiations with Napoleon to buy neighboring lands owned by France. When Spain had recently ceded the Louisiana territory back to France, suddenly U.S. citizens could not use the Mississippi River and the port of New Orleans. This caused an economic uproar in western states, especially Ohio, Kentucky, and Tennessee, where people used the river as their main highway to transport goods to market. Napoleon wanted to grow France's empire on the North American continent but he was also distracted with his activities closer to home of continuous warfare, especially with Great Britain, and the need for more money to maintain his army there. Congress and

---

[170] President Thomas Jefferson to Congress, 18 January 1803; Series 1, General Correspondence, 1651-1827; Thomas Jefferson Papers; Manuscript Division, Library of Congress, Washington D.C. (accessed 23 Sept 2014). http://hdl.loc.gov/loc.mss/mtj.mtjbib012083

Jefferson secured France's neighboring lands as the Louisiana Purchase for eighty million francs though twenty million francs of it was the release of a debt owed by France to us for lost costs from past seizures of ships, and the other sixty million francs was to be paid over twenty years. The remaining sixty million francs was equal to $11, 250,000 American dollars at the time but was measured as a low price for 875,000 acres.[171] Thus, in the early months of 1803, President Jefferson and Congress were very busy indeed. After Jefferson's proposal for the expedition was approved in February, he appointed his personal secretary Captain Meriwether Lewis to command it.

By spring 1803, Lewis selected rifles and other weapons from the federal arsenal at Harper's Ferry. Because the expedition was a military operation with sizable goals, Lewis asked former Lieutenant William Clark to co-captain the operation with him. Clark had previously served over Lewis in 1795 when Lewis joined his company of sharpshooters and riflemen in their Chosen Rifle Company. It was a company within the Second Sub-Legion under Anthony Wayne in the U.S. Army. Captain Clark was the perfect man to co-command with Lewis due to both life and military experiences on the Kentucky frontier. He had experience with guns, with Native Americans, with commanding men, with mapping, with letter writing, etc. It was a very successful partnership.

Captain William Clark's Kentucky frontier extended from Louisville northward to Clarksville, a town across the Ohio River in Indiana Territory. The 1000 acres of land that first became Clarksville was part of 150,000 acres of land awarded to General George Rogers Clark and the soldiers in his regiment by the Virginia General Assembly for their successful Illinois campaign fought in the 1770s.[172] The population of Clarksville in 1803 was only about forty residents and it did

---

[171] Cerami, Charles A. 2003. *Jefferson's Great Gamble: the Remarkable Story of Jefferson, Napoleon and the Men Behind the Louisiana Purchase.* Chicago, Illinois: Sourcebooks, Incorporated: 204-205.

[172] Kramer, Carl E. 2003. *The Corps of Discovery and the Falls of the Ohio.* Jeffersonville, Indiana: Sunnyside Press: 7-8.

not grow very fast due to several reasons. First, it was located too close to an annual flood plain from the nearby Mill Creek. Second, it was located on the Indiana Territory side of the rapids of the Ohio River and the rapids were hard to cross. Third, settlers there were not very safe from Native American attacks despite the location of Fort Clark nearby on Silver Creek. Finally, many members of the governing body lived across the river in Louisville. [173] General Clark permanently moved to Clarksville in early 1803 when he built a log cabin high above the Ohio River on a beautiful spot called Point of Rocks, also referred to as Clark's Point.[174] Due to its isolated but majestic location overlooking the lower rapids of the Ohio River near the upper end of the Falls, General Clark's cabin was described as "a lonely cottage" by visitor Josiah Espy just two years later. Though Espy appreciated the "full and delightful view of the falls, particularly the zig-zag channel which is only navigated at high water," he observed, "the General has not taken much pains to improve this commanding and beautiful spot, but it is capable of being made one of the handsomest seats in the world."[175] As the younger brother of General Clark, Captain Clark was a frequent visitor to the cabin and lived there at times.

While the still secret potential adventure offered by Lewis and Clark was brewing, something else undoubtedly snagged Bratton's attention along with the rest of his community. Not too many miles west of Frankfort, on July 7, 1803, a girl was murdered. The gory details were reported by The Palladium newspaper in Frankfort - "A shocking murder was committed on Monday last, a few miles from Shelbyville, on the body of a young woman of the name of Bean, by a Negro fellow belonging to Mrs. Stephen Smith, of Shelby County. The unfortunate girl was returning early in the morning to her

---

[173] Kramer, Carl E. 2003. *The Corps of Discovery and the Falls of the Ohio.* Jeffersonville, Indiana: Sunnyside Press: 10-11.
[174] Ibid: 13.
[175] Espy, Josiah. 1805. *A Tour in Ohio, Kentucky and Indiana Territory in 1805.* Robert Clarke & Company, published in 1871.

father's, from a neighbor's house where she had stayed all night, when she was met by the unfeeling monster, who speedily put an end to her existence. Her cries were heard by some persons at work in a cornfield near the spot, who, we are sorry to learn, were not sufficiently alarmed, instantly to desist from their labor and fly to her assistance, until roused by the noise of a number of hogs contending for the carcass. The feelings of her unhappy parents must be excruciating indeed, and will doubtless draw a tear from the eye of Humanity. But if it were possible in such a state to receive consolation, it must afford them some to hear that the unprincipled villain is in custody, and likely to meet the punishment due to his atrocious crime. We understand he was immediately apprehended, confessed the fact, and is lodged in Shelby jail. Revenge for some offense given him by her father is the cause he assigns for committing the murder."[176] Another account provided additional but conflicting details. It contended that the perpetrator was named Ned and that he was in fact a free man. Allegedly, he had been ordered to leave the premises of the Bean property a few days before he committed the crime. Because being ordered to leave someone's property does not logically seem to warrant such a strong action of revenge as murder, one can speculate that there was definitely more going on in this situation. Perhaps Ned worked for Mr. Bean for several days prior and was not paid for his work when he was kicked off the property. Perhaps in the act of kicking Ned off his property, Mr. Bean used very insulting language. Clearly, Ned did not feel that involving the justice system would result in his favor. Instead, he allegedly and violently took matters into his own hands and exacted his retribution on Mr. Bean's daughter Elizabeth "Betty" Bean. While in jail for the murder, Ned sold his body upon his death to local medical students and used the money to eat delicacies until the day arrived that he was hanged which was just over a month from when he was

---

[176] The Palladium. Elizabeth Bean article. Frankfort, Kentucky. 7 July 1803: 3.

arrested.[177] The local newspaper, The Palladium, reported "The negro who perpetrated the shocking murder mentioned in our paper of the 7th ult., was executed at Shelbyville, on the 10th instant. His behavior we are told showed him to be devoid of sensibility or fear. He died as he lived, a hardened criminal."[178]

On July 18, 1803, within a week and a half of the murder (which Captain Clark might have heard about as well), Clark wrote Lewis to accept Lewis' proposal of co-commanding the military expedition westward. Then one of his first tasks was to begin securing able men for the endeavor. Lewis had a specific idea of what kind of men they would need. He wanted Clark to "engage some good hunters, stout, healthy, unmarried men, accustomed to the woods, and capable of bearing bodily fatigue in a pretty considerable degree"[179] and that Clark was authorized to "engage any other man not soldiers that I may think useful in promoting the objects of success of this expedition."[180] When Clark made his intentions public, word most likely spread like wildfire by mouth from Louisville along the roads and rivers spreading throughout the Kentucky countryside.

Within a week, men began to arrive in Louisville or Clarksville to present themselves to Clark, however, no primary sources exist that make it perfectly clear as to which location was used the most in initially interviewing candidates for the expedition. Clark's letters were written from both Clarksville and Louisville at the time. Logically, Louisville would have been the better location because it was a larger town than Clarksville and more hospitable for lodging the large number of men who traveled there. Using William Bratton's

---

[177] Willis, George L. 1929. *The History of Shelby County, Kentucky*. Louisville, Kentucky: C.T. Dearing Printing Company.
[178] The Palladium. Ned article. Frankfort, Kentucky. 13 August 1803: 3.
[179] Thwaites, Reuben Gold, Ed. 1905. "Meriwether Lewis letter to William Clark, 19 June 1803." *Original Journals of the Lewis and Clark Expedition, 1804-1806*. Vol. 7. New York, New York: Dodd, Mead & Company: 226-230.
[180] Ibid.

traveling distance as an example, men were coming from at least two counties away. Also, Louisville would have been more convenient because it eliminated the need for all of the potential prospects to hire a river pilot to take them across the Ohio River and navigate the tricky falls in order to land in Clarksville. And although Clark sometimes lived with his brother General Clark at Point of Rocks at certain times, he also rented a townhouse near his family in Louisville so he could have easily set up a temporary operation there.[181] Regardless of the location, men began to express their interest pretty quickly. Among the men who applied, there were men who met the physical requirements but who lacked in other areas and Clark turned them away.[182] Several others were pampered sons of gentlemen who were unsuited for the adventure.[183] These men were the epitome of the kind of men Meriwether Lewis was not looking for and unlike those Clark might have already had in mind for the job. By August 1, 1803, Clark had already enlisted three men. Two of the men, Joseph and Reubin Field, were brothers who traveled from their father's farm in the Fish Pools area of Jefferson County, a little over eight miles southeast of Louisville to meet with Clark.[184] Because of their proximity to Louisville and the expediency by which they were enlisted, it is probable that the Field brothers already knew Clark and could have even worked for him or someone Clark knew before. The Field brothers were hunters and woodsmen who grew up on the Kentucky frontier since they and their

---

[181] Kramer, Carl E. 2003. *The Corps of Discovery and the Falls of the Ohio.* Jeffersonville, Indiana: Sunnyside Press: 35.

[182] Thwaites, Reuben Gold, Ed. 1905. "William Clark to Meriwether Lewis letter, 21 August 1803." *Original Journals of The Lewis and Clark Expedition, 1804-1806.* Vol. 7. New York, New York: Dodd, Mead & Company.

[183] Letter, William Clark to Meriwether Lewis, 24 July 1803.

[184] Appleman, Roy E. "Joseph and Reubin Field, Kentucky Frontiersman of the Lewis and Clark Expedition and their Father, Abraham." *Genealogies of Kentucky Families.* 1981. Filson Club History Quarterly, Baltimore, Maryland: Genealogical Publishing Company: 489.

father first arrived in the area in 1785.[185] The third man Clark enlisted was Charles Floyd. Clearly, they were all eager for adventure.

Although Clark continued to receive interest in the trip, he refrained from giving anyone else an official acceptance per instructions given by Lewis in a letter written August 3, 1803, but not received by Clark until August 20, 1803. Lewis told him "I am pleased to hear that you have engaged some men for this service, your contract with them had better be with the condition of my approval, as by the time I shall arrive more will have offered themselves and a better selection may of course be made; from the nature of this enterprise, much must depend on a judicious selection of our men; their qualifications should be such as perfectly fit them for the service, otherwise they will rather clog than further the objects in view."[186] In reference to the interest by pampered gentlemen's sons, Lewis also had an opinion for Clark. He said, "I am well pleased that you have not admitted or encouraged the young gentlemen you mention, we must set our faces against all such applications and get rid of them on the best terms we can."[187] Also, Lewis wanted to make sure that Clark relayed to the interested men up front that they would not serve just one purpose on the expedition but would contribute to whatever needed accomplished. He told Clark "if a good hunter or two could be conditionally engaged I would think them an acquisition, they must however understand that they will not be employed for the purposes of hunting exclusively but must bear a portion of labor in common with the party."[188]

It is unknown when in the summer of 1803 William Bratton arrived in Louisville or Clarksville to join the many other men who approached Clark about going on the

---

[185] Appleman, Roy E. "Joseph and Reubin Field, Kentucky Frontiersman of the Lewis and Clark Expedition and their Father, Abraham." *Genealogies of Kentucky Families.* 1981. Filson Club History Quarterly, Baltimore, Maryland: Genealogical Publishing Company: 489.
[186] Letter, Meriwether Lewis to William Clark, 3 August 1803.
[187] Ibid.
[188] Ibid.

expedition. If he went by road, he traveled from his neighborhood near Hammond Creek in Franklin County to Louisville on what they called the "Big Road." It was created in the 1780s, and was fifteen-feet wide. It was used every day by 1792.[189] William would have either ridden a horse, walked, caught a ride riding double with someone else, or on a wagon. It is doubtful but not impossible that William owned a horse by now. Because he was not listed on the 1803 tax list, it is unknown if indeed he owned one, but if he did not, he could have borrowed one. Because his brother Robert was not listed on the 1803 tax list either, it is also unknown if he owned a horse. His brother-in-law Joseph Bimson owned two horses, so William could have borrowed one from him.[190] Also, William might not have traveled alone but with other young men in his community who were also interested in securing a spot. The other way of getting to Louisville was by boat. He could have caught a ride with a small craft that would have flowed along the Kentucky River into the Ohio River and down to Louisville.

If William arrived in the first two weeks of August, it is possible that he could have even been one of the young men whom Clark put off until Lewis arrived. Clark told Lewis in one letter that he had "many applications from stout likely fellows but have refused to retain some and put others off with a promise of giving an answer" until after he heard or saw from Lewis.[191] Although Clark referred to having many applications, no actual applications from the expedition are known to exist. Clark's term of "applications" might have meant that the men reported to his base of operations and were lined up to interview with him and undergo tests to show their skills of shooting and strength. Men might have even brought references with them known then as letters of introduction. If

---

[189] Jillison, Willard Rouse. "Old Bridgeport and its Environs." *The Register of the Kentucky Historical Society*. Vol. 54, No. 186. Jan. 1956.

[190] Kentucky. Franklin County. Joseph Bimson entry. 1803 Tax List, Allen County Public Library, Fort Wayne, Indiana. Microfilm, #0100, 1781-1797, 1799 – 1804.

[191] Letter, William Clark to Meriwether Lewis, Louisville, 21 August 1803.

William brought letters of introduction, he could have laid a sound foundation of very high recommendations for himself. He might have secured one from his father or a Dunlap cousin validating his connection with Clark as a distant cousin. Maybe he reminisced with Clark about visits to the home of his uncle John Dunlap and Dunlap's wife Anne Clark back in Virginia. Additionally, as mentioned before, William's own maternal grandmother was a Clark that could have been a common ground they might have referenced if indeed they had never met before. On the other hand, William could have secured a letter of recommendation from Captain John Arnold who lived close to his neighborhood of Hammond Creek in Franklin County. William's brother-in-law John Bimson served under Arnold briefly in 1794 before Arnold headed a spy division in the border war against hostile Native Americans. Arnold was so fierce that the Native Americans called him "Black Wolf."[192] Even if Arnold had never had direct contact with William Clark or his brother General Clark, it is probable that they all knew of one another. Besides Arnold being well respected as a military man, he was also a wealthy landowner and had lived in the area for a long time. His family had moved to the area by 1783 and established Arnold's Station as an outpost at the mouth of the Kentucky River and Little Benson Creek in the 1780s when the settlers lived in forts for safety. Additionally, Captain Arnold was wealthy and probably employed many of the young men in the neighborhood at one time or another. Because he was a man that William Bratton well respected as future transactions between him and William imply, it is possible that William could have carried a letter of introduction from him. If William did not bring any letters of introduction with him, he had only the presentation of himself and his skills to set him favorably apart from other men.

 Another man selected for the expedition, Alexander Willard, was not able to show up at this leg of the expedition preparations because he already served in the U.S. government with soldiers under Major Amos Stoddard at Kaskaskia.

---

[192] Jackson Gazette. John Arnold obituary. 4 September 1830.

Illinois. He said that when the expedition reached Illinois and more men were needed, there were many men at this point of the expedition who still vied for spots. He told his children and grandchildren that there were over 100 hundred men trying to outdo each other as they were inspected and tested for "their hardihood and all around qualities."[193] In his old age, Willard would "lay on his couch out in the shade on the porch and reviewed over and over and with great pride how he was one of the few selected, that "there was none stronger, no one who could endure more out of the great number" of "young men who came for inspection."[194]

So, if William Bratton was one of the men in August 1803 told by Clark to wait until Lewis arrived to find out if he was selected, he might have gone back home to wait another month, or he might have found lodging in Louisville, or he might have camped outside. If William wasn't in Louisville or Clarksville by August 1803 after having heard about the expedition on the Kentucky River or by people coming up the Big Road, then he definitely would have heard the news after it was published in local newspapers. On August 25, 1803, a Louisville newspaper published a small article that read "an expedition is expected to leave here shortly, under the direction of Capt. William Clark and Mr. Lewis (private secretary to the President) to proceed through the immense wilderness of Louisiana to Western or Pacific Ocean."[195] The Louisville newspaper could have traveled to Frankfort by boat within days of its printing. If not, the news was definitely in Frankfort by September 1, 1803 when The Palladium newspaper in Frankfort reported that exact news and more - "The Louisville paper of the 25th ult. contains the following information: - An expedition is expected to leave this place shortly, under the direction of Capt. William Clark and Mr.

---

[193] Calista Scott Letter. Eva Emery Dye Collection. Oregon Historical Society. 9 March 1903.
[194] Ibid.
[195] Eastern Argus. Lewis and Clark Expedition article. 29 September 1803: 2.

Lewis (private secretary to the President) to proceed through the immense wilderness of Louisiana to the Western or Pacific Ocean. The particular objects of this undertaking are at present matters of conjecture only, but we have good reason to believe that our government intend to encourage settlements and establish seaports on the course of the Pacific Ocean, which would not only facilitate our Whaling and Sealing voyages, but enable our enterprising merchants to carry on a more direct and rapid trade with China and the East Indies."[196] Regardless of how William Bratton heard about the expedition, he planned to be there when Lewis arrived. Unbeknownst to him, two more men had already been quasi-selected for the expedition since Lewis also did some hiring of his own. Though their employment was not official at first, Lewis picked up George Shannon and John Colter along his trip on the Ohio River from Pittsburg towards Louisville of which he informed Clark in another letter, "I have two young men with me whom I have taken on trial and have not yet engaged them but conditionally only, tho' I think they will answer tolerably well."[197]

Meriwether Lewis, George Shannon and John Colter arrived in Louisville on October 14, 1803 and their activities in preparation for the expedition were definitely of interest to the surrounding communities. The Palladium newspaper in Frankfort reported, "Captain Lewis arrived at this port on Friday last. We are informed that he has brought barges & c. on a new construction that can be taken in pieces for the purpose of passing carrying-places, and that he and Captain Clark will start in a few days on their expedition to the Westward."[198]

It is unknown whether Clark was there to meet Lewis in Louisville or whether they did not see him until the next day in Clarksville when Lewis hired river pilots to help him transport the keelboat through the falls. Once Lewis and Clark were

---

[196] The Palladium. Lewis and Clark Expedition article. Frankfort, Kentucky: 1 September 1803: 2.
[197] Letter, Meriwether Lewis to William Clark, 28 September 1803.
[198] The Palladium. Lewis and Clark Expedition article. Frankfort, Kentucky: 29 October 1803: 3.

united, the administration of the expedition began to move forward. The men who Clark had talked with before, the ones he "put off with a promise of giving an answer" after he saw or heard from Lewis were now invited back to show off their skills.[199] William Bratton's time to shine had finally arrived as the two men began to earnestly select men. Again, it is not conclusive that the evaluations of men were conducted in Louisville or Clarksville, but it was most likely done at Clarksville and more specifically near Clark's Point since the location of operations was now established there since Lewis' arrival. Lewis and Clark were comparing several things about the men – their physicality, their outdoor skills, their attitude, their character, and their suitability. William definitely stood out among other hopefuls as he was formally enlisted into the Lewis & Clark Expedition at the Falls of the Ohio by Clark on October 15, 1803. The other successful applicants who were also enlisted at that time were Nathaniel Pryor, George Gibson, and John Shields.

    Once the selection and enlistments were decided upon, the activities of the enlisted men were numerous. Besides packing, they probably had to begin training. Again, because this was a military expedition and these men were not soldiers, they had to learn to execute what was expected from them as military men. Additionally, they might have traveled back across the river to say goodbyes depending on how far away from home they were, and they might have bought things that the government was not providing like their rifle and their shot pouch. Another possession that William Bratton took with him was a compass housed in a block of wood that he either purchased or was given for the trip. "The block was about 1¾ inches wide and 2½ inches long. The compass rested on a needle set in a depression in the block and was covered with round glass, which was held in place by a spring around the inside of the depression. A hinged cover was over the top. The block was so arranged that it could also be used as a

---

[199] Letter, William Clark to Meriwether Lewis, 21 August 1803.

sundial."[200] It would have looked almost identical to the one that Lewis carried that is now in the Smithsonian Museum. Another possible pre-departure event which the men did according to one source was to travel to nearby Pisgah Church in Woodford County to hear a sermon by Reverend Adam Rankin before they set out on the expedition. Because no other primary documents have been found to support this, nor any other sources have cited it, it is unknown if this actually occurred. It seems unlikely that the men would have traveled from Louisville or even further from Clarksville to Pisgah in Woodford County to do this, especially if they traveled upstream on the Kentucky River. Nevertheless, maybe they traveled by a small craft and took an opportunity to practice moving a boat upriver even if they were yet only partially staffed. If a sermon did take place by Reverend Rankin, it seems more believable that Reverend Rankin would have instead traveled to Clark's Point to give it.

On October 26, 1803, Lewis & Clark and the men they had selected so far boarded a boat and headed west. Another Clark brother, Jonathan Clark, jumped aboard and rode with them as far as the farm of his son-in-law Benjamin Temple.[201] The Palladium in Frankfort also reported on their departure. "Louisville (Ken.) – Capt. Clark and Mr. Lewis left this place on Wednesday last, on their Expedition to the Westward. We have not been enabled to ascertain to what length this route will extend, as when it was first set on foot by the President, the Louisiana country was not ceded to the United States, and it is likely it will be greatly extended – they are to receive further instructions at Kohokia."[202]

*Author's note - *Because whole books are written on the expedition alone, the rest of the chapter is going to be organized*

---

[200] Mariner, Myrtle Fields. "Wm. Bratton" *Heroes of 1812*. Nebraska Society of United States Daughters of 1812; 1930: 96.
[201] Jonathan Clark diary. 26 October 1803 (JCDB, 6:400-402)
[202] The Palladium. Lewis and Clark Expedition article. Frankfort, Kentucky: 5 November 1803: 2.

as chronological entries that mostly center on information directly written about William Bratton in the journals by expedition members. Below the entries, there is also information that denotes what we learn about William from the entries, and also information that has passed down through William's descendants from stories William shared with his children about the expedition. There is also information about the expedition that was discovered with current technology and included where it fit chronologically. The information from the journals is quoted and attributed from whoever's journal it was gleaned. The spelling and abbreviations were kept the way they were originally written. A journal entry from several people on the same date might be given to establish the most comprehensive description of certain events and activities. Additionally, information is included about the expedition that is from the Native American perspective of one or two of the tribes with whom the expedition members interacted.

9 July 1804
Capt. Clark's journal – "sent one man back to the mouth of the River to mark a tree, to let the party on shore see that the boat had passed the river."

John Ordway's journal – "sent Bratton back to the Creek to blaze some trees, so the hunters might see we had passed."

12 July 1804 – Camp New Island
Capt. Clark's journal – "The commanding officers, Capt. M. Lewis & W. Clark constituted themselves a court martial for the trial of such prisoners are guilty of capital crimes, and under the rules and articles of war punishable by DEATH. Alexander Willard was brought forward charged with lying down and sleeping on his post whilst a sentinel, on the night of 11th instant by John Ordway, Sergeant of the guard. To this charge the prisoner pleads guilty of lying down, and not guilty of going to sleep. The court after duly considering the evidence adduced, are of the opinion that the prisoner Alex. Willard is

guilty of every part of the charge exhibited against him. It being a breach of the rules and articles of war (as well as tending to the probable destruction of the party) do sentence him to receive one hundred lashes, on his bare back, at four different times in equal proportion, and order that the punishment commence this evening at sunset, and continue to be inflicted by the guard every evening until completed."[203]

William told his children that instead of switches, the men used their ramrods when they were expected to help mete out this punishment.[204]

19 July 1804
Capt. Clark's journal – "W. Bratton hunting on the L.S., swam to the island."

John Ordway's journal – "G. Drewer joined us with two deer this evening. Bratton also. He found Callimous opposite where we camped & a large quantity. (Sweet flag we call it)."

From Clark's journal, we know William Bratton could swim. As expected from William's life in Kentucky, he was a proficient hunter and forager. Sweet flag was used to soothe an upset stomach.[205]

7 August 1804
Capt. Clark's journal – "At 1 o'clock, dispatched George Drewer, R. Fields, Wm. Bratton, and Wm. Labieche back after the deserter Reid with order if he did not give up peaceably to put him to death."

---

[203] Jones, Landon Y. 2000. *The Essential Lewis and Clark*. New York, New York: HarperCollins Publishers: 4, 5.
[204] Chesterson, Maud J. Bratton. "William Bratton: His Service in the Lewis and Clark Expedition, 1804-1806 and in the War of 1812." Indiana Pamphlet-00000106839277, Indiana State Library.
[205] Scott, B.V. 1863. *The Voice of Nature to the Invalid; or the Oxford Pioneer Medical Truth Versus Medical Mystery*. London, England: Job Caudwell, printer: 60.

John Ordway's journal – "we then sent G. Dreyer, W. Bratton, R. Fields, and W. Labuche back to the ottaus village after M.B. Reed who had deserted from us with orders to fetch him dead or alive."

Charles Floyd's journal – "on the 4th of this month one of our men by the name of Moses B. Reed went Back to our Camp where we had Left in the morning, to get his Knife which he Had Left at the Camp ⟨bout⟩ the Boat went on and He Did not Return, ⟨pore⟩ that night nor the Next day nor Night, upon examining his nap-Sack we found that he had taken his ⟨Cal⟩ Clothes and all His powder and Balls, and had hid them out that night and had made that an excuse to Desert from us with out any Just Case we never minded the Said man until the 7th we Sent 4 men after him we expect he will make for the ottoe town as it is not more than 2 days Journey from where he Run away from us."

Patrick Gass's journal – "We set out early this morning and continued our voyage till 12, when four of our people were dispatched to the Oto nation of Indians after the man who had not returned on the 4th, with orders to take him, dead or alive, if they could see him."

Whitehouse's journal – "the party consisted of 4 their names first G. Druier, R. fields, Bratton, and William that was Sent after Ms. Read that Deserted in Latd 41 17 00 N."

As a woodsman and hunter, William had very good tracking skills.

September 1804

In September of 1804, Captain Lewis wrote his associate James Findley a letter in which he expressed his opinion to Findley that all of the men were good boatmen and that most of them were good hunters.[206]

If William did not have many boating skills at this time, he was quickly learning and was adept enough to be lumped in with everyone else as being considered a good boatman.

6 January 1805
John Ordway's journal – "Bratton caught a fox in a steel trap where it had a hole in the pickets. It had frequently come through it in to the Garrison after bones where we divided meat."

11 May 1805
Capt. Lewis' journal – "About 5 P. M. my attention was struck by one of the Party running at a distance towards us and making signs and hollowing as if in distress, I ordered the perogues to put too, and waited until he arrived; I now found that it was Bratton the man with the soar hand whom I had permitted to walk on shore, he arrived so much out of breath that it was several minutes before he could tell what had happened; at length he informed me that in the woody bottom on the Lard. side about 1½ below us he had shot a brown bear which immediately turned on him and pursued him a considerable distance but he had wounded it so badly that it could not overtake him; I immediately turned out with seven of the party in quest of this monster, we at length found his trail and pursued him about a mile by the blood through very thick brush of rosebushes and the large leafed willow; we finally found him concealed in some very thick brush and shot him through the skull with two balls; we proceeded dress him as soon as possible, we found him in good order; it was a monstrous beast, not quite so large as that we killed a few days past but in all other respects much the same. The hair is remarkably long fine and rich tho' he appears partially to have

---

[206] Lexington Herald Leader. Meriwether Lewis to James Findley letter article. September 1804.

discharged his winter coat; we now found that Bratton had shot him through the center of the lungs, notwithstanding which he had pursued him near half a mile and had returned more than double that distance and with his talons had prepared himself a bed in the earth of about 2 feet deep and five long and was perfectly alive when we found him which could not have been less than 2 hours after he received the wound; these bear being so hard to die rather intimidates us all; I must confess that I do not like the gentlemen and had rather fight two Indians than one bear; there is no other chance to conquer them by a single shot but by shooting them through the brains, and this becomes difficult in consequence of two large muscles which cover the sides of the forehead and the sharp projection of the center of the frontal bone, which is also of a pretty good thickness. The fleece and skin were as much as two men could possibly carry. By the time we returned the sun had set and I determined to remain here all night, and directed the cooks to render the bear's oil and put it in the kegs which was done. There was about eight gallons of it."

John Ordway's journal – "one of the party which had a lame hand was walking on shore. Towards evening, he came running and hollering to the perogues chased by a brown bear which he had wounded bad. Some of the hunters went out with him and killed it. It was nearly of the same description as the one killed some days past, but much fatter. We camped before night to dress the bear after coming 17 miles today."

1 July 1805
Capt. Lewis' journal – "I directed Bratton to assist in making the tar tomorrow, and selected several others to assist in putting the boat together."

11 July 1805
Capt. Lewis' journal – "This morning Capt. Clark dispatched Bratton to meet the canoes which were detained by the wind

to get a couple of axes. He obtained the axes and returned in about two hours. This man has been unable to work for several days in consequence of a whitlow on one of his fingers, a complaint which has been very common among the men."

Capt. Clark's journal – "I dispatch W. Bratten (who cannot work he haveing a tumer rising on his finger) to meat the Canoes & bring from them two axes, which is necessary for the work at the perogues or Canoes, and is indespenceable   he returned in about two hours & informed that one Canoe was within three miles, about 1 o Clock the Canoe which Bratten left arrived haveing killed a Buffalow on the river above our Camp, at which place the bend of the river below & that above is about 1 mile apart."

A whitlow is an infection that can be extremely painful, that is under and around the fingernail or toenail and is sometimes deep into the bone.[207]

12 July 1805
Capt. Lewis' journal – "The canoes not having arrived and the wind still high I dispatched Sergt. Gass with three men to join Capt. Clark and assist in completing the canoes retaining only a few who in addition to those in the canoes that I expect every moment, will be sufficient to man the six canoes and take up all the baggage we have here at one load. I feel excessively anxious to be moving on. The canoes were detained by the wind until 2 P. M. when they set out and arrived at this place so late that I thought it best to detain them until morning. Bratton came down today for a couple of axes which I sent by him; he returned immediately."

4 September 1805
The expedition stopped to rest on the Lolo Trail, and Clark named their camp Travelers' Rest in his journal. At Travelers'

---

[207] Chuinar, Eldon G. 2002. *Only One Man Died: the Medical Aspects of the Lewis and Clark Expedition.* Fairfield, Washington: Ye Gallon Press: 297–98.

Rest, expedition members met with members of the Salish tribe, known today as the Confederated Salish Kootenai tribe. The Salish encountered the expedition at nearby Ross's Hole that is on the East Fork of the Bitterroot River, and recorded this encounter in their history. The Bitterroot River was named for the bitterroot plant that grew all over the region and also at Travelers' Rest. The Salish and other Native Americans ate the bitterroot and also used it for trade.[208] The Salish met with the men of the expedition several times while they were at Traveler's Rest. Unbeknownst to the Expedition, their dancing on the night before they left was part of a prayer dance the Salish were performing marking the fulfillment of a prophecy. The prophecy foretold that strange people would come, that the Salish life would be changed, and that if the Salish survived, they would be stronger.[209] And the Salish did not try to kill members of the Lewis & Clark Expedition because of York. They thought he was a powerful medicine man. Instead they fed them and helped the Corps of Discovery determine how best to proceed in getting to the Pacific Ocean.[210]

5 September 1805

They stayed there several days. The exact campsite was located by principal investigator and historical archaeologist Daniel S. Hall with Western Cultural, Inc. in Missoula, Montana. He and his team used a variety of sources. The foremost sources were information such as topographical features, astronomical observations, campsite descriptions, and detailed maps included in the expedition journals.[211] Second, they used modern technology

---

[208] Knudsen, Susan L., "Cultural landscape report for the Lewis and Clark Expedition's Travelers Rest campsite near present-day Lolo, Montana" (2003). *Graduate Student Theses, Dissertations, & Professional Papers.* 1955. University of Montana. https://scholarworks.umt.edu/etd1955.

[209] Ronda, James P. 1984. *Lewis & Clark Among the Indians.* Lincoln, Nebraska: University of Nebraska Press: 188.

[210] Steven Small Salmon, speaker. "Lewis & Clark: An American Epic." Gilder Lehrman Institute of History teacher seminar. Missoula, Montana. 16 July 2014.

[211] Knudsen, Susan L., "Cultural landscape report for the Lewis and Clark Expedition's Travelers Rest campsite near present-day Lolo, Montana"

and mapping techniques to discover new information in the modern landscape. "The interdisciplinary investigation consisted of historical and ethnographic research, remote sensing techniques (magnetometer, electromagnetic conductivity, metal detectors, and mercury vaporizer analysis), historic archaeological excavations and laboratory analysis (carbon 14, lead isotope, magnetic susceptibility, and artifact analysis) conducted to verify the site's location," according to Hall's report titled Travelers Rest National Historic Landmark: Validation and Verification of a Lewis and Clark Campsite.[212] One of the major finds to clinch the exact location of Travelers' Rest was the discovery of mercury in one area and small lead pools in another. By the location between these two elements, scientists were able to determine that the camp was indeed set up along military parameters, specifically diagrammed according to the leading military guide, a Revolutionary War drill manual, by Baron Frederick William Von Steuben. Steuben who accrued most of his military experience in the Prussian army crossed paths with Benjamin Franklin in Paris in 1777. Franklin by letter presented Steuben to General George Washington and the Continental Congress who in turn secured Steuben's services towards winning the Revolution. Steuben joined Washington at Valley Forge in 1778 where he tasked with training the American forces.[213] Through drills and field regulation procedures, he was able to mold forces with order and discipline into a more highly trained fighting machine. As he proceeded with his task, he wrote down the drills and instructions in French that after being translated became the primary military guide for training American military until 1812.[214]

In his manual, Steuben included specific instructions titled Order of Encampment, on how a military camp should be laid out

---

(2003). *Graduate Student Theses, Dissertations, & Professional Papers.* 1955. University of Montana. https://scholarworks.umt.edu/etd1955.

[212] Hall, Daniel S. "Travelers Rest National Historic Landmark: Validation and Verification of a Lewis and Clark Campsite." Western Cultural, Inc.: June 2003.

[213] Von Steuben, Baron Frederick William. 1794. *Revolutionary War Drill Manual.* New York, New York: Dover Publications, Inc.: reprint, 1985.

[214] Ibid: 77-85.

as well as instructions entitled Necessary Regulations for Preserving Order and Cleanliness in Camp. The following instructions of Steuben's were used by Lewis & Clark to set up their expedition camps but of course the terrain and their small amount of men might not have allowed for every regulation to be followed precisely but Von Steuben's guide was used to maintain a semblance of order in and adventure of the unknown: (the following steps below are verbatim from his manual) [215]

- The tents of the non-commissioned officers and privates are to be pitched in two ranks, with an interval of six paces between the ranks, and two feet between each tent.
- Captain tents are to be in one line, twenty feet from the rear of the men's tents; the captains in the right wing opposite the right of their respective companies.
- When a regiment enters a camp, the field officers must take care that the encampment is pitched regularly; that the sinks and kitchens are immediately dug in their proper places; and that no tents are pitched in any part of the camp contrary to the order prescribed.
- The kitchens are to be dug behind their respective companies, forty feet from the field officers' tents. The horses and wagons are to be placed in a line, twenty feet behind the kitchen. The sinks (latrines) of the first line are to be three hundred feet in front, and those of the second line the same distance in the rear of the camp.
- The place where the cattle (or meat of any kind in the case of the expedition) are killed must be at least fifty paces in the rear of the wagons or horses, and the entrails and other filth immediately buried.
- Whenever a regiment is to remain more than one night on the same ground, the soldiers must be obliged to cut a small trench round their tents, to carry off the rain; but great care must be taken they do not throw the dirt up against the tents.

---

[215] Von Steuben, Baron Frederick William. 1794. *Revolutionary War Drill Manual*. New York, New York: Dover Publications, Inc.: reprint, 1985.

- The soldiers should not be permitted to eat in their tents, except in bad weather, and an officer of a company must often visit the messes, see that the provision is good and well-cooked, that the men of one tent mess together, and that the provision is not sold or disposed of for liquor.
- The quartermaster must be answerable that the parade and environs of the encampment of a regiment are kept clean; that the sinks (latrines) are filled up, and new ones dug every four days, and oftener in warm weather; and if any horse or other animal dies near the regiment, he must cause it to be carried at least half a mile from camp, and buried.
- When a private arrives at camp or quarters, he must clean his arms, prepare his bed, and go for necessaries, taking nothing without leave, nor committing any kind of excess.

As the men made their way through Lolo pass, they were unprepared for the amount of snow that obscured their way. They eventually made it through but they experienced much hardship due to severe cold and little food. This might have been the point in their journey where they killed an old female wolf which William told his children that "the worst morsel of which he partook on the journey was an old she wolf that was suckling her young."[216]

19 October 1805

Expedition members encountered the Umatilla people after meeting the Nez Perce after crossing the Bitterroot Mountains. The Umatilla people thought expedition members were really strange for several reasons. First, they had never seen a black man before and York was also a tall, muscular man. The children were taught to behave from birth through Coyote stories in which monsters would attack children who did not behave and many of them thought he might have been one of those monsters. Second, many of the expedition members kept reaching into their pockets and putting something in their mouths. It looked to the

---

[216] Chesterson, Maud J. Bratton. "William Bratton: His Service in the Lewis and Clark Expedition, 1804-1806 and in the War of 1812." Indiana Pamphlet-00000106839277, Indiana State Library.

Umatilla like they were eating their own flesh. It was most likely jerky that they had in their pockets. The expedition members also had individual kernels of Mandan corn and when they pulled it out, it looked like teeth to the Umatilla. Lastly, the Corps bargained with the Umatilla for numerous dogs for food, however they thought it strange that they were not eating one specific dog, Seamen. They did not understand why the one dog was sacred and the rest of the dogs were not.[217]

18 November 1805
Capt. Clark's journal – "I Set out with 10 men and my man York to the ocean by land, i.e. Sergt. Ordway & Pryor, Jos. & Ru. Fields, Go. Shannon, W. Brattin, J. Colter, P. Wiser, W. Labieche & P. Shabono one of our interpreters & York. I Set out at Day light and proceeded on a Sandy beach."

28 December 1805
Capt. Clark's journal – directed "Jos. Fields, Bratton, Gibson to proceed to the Ocean at some convenient place, form a camp, and commence making salt with 5 of the largest kettles."

5 January 1806
Capt. Lewis' journal – "These lads also informed us that J. Fields, Bratton and Gibson (the Salt makers) had with their assistance erected a comfortable camp, killed an Elk and several deer and secured a good stock of meat; they commenced the making of salt and found that they could obtain from 3 quarts to a gallon a day; they brought with them a specimen of the salt of about a gallon, we found it excellent, fine, strong, & white; ⟨salt;⟩ this was a great treat to myself and most of the party, having not had any since the 20th ultm.; I say most of the party, for my friend Capt. Clark declares it to be a mere matter of indifference with him whether he uses it or not for myself I must confess I felt a considerable inconvenience from the want of it."

---

[217] Roberta Conner, speaker. *Lewis & Clark: An American Epic.* Gilder Lehrman Institute of History teacher seminar. Missoula, Montana. 15 July 2014.

The men on the expedition who might have visited Clatsop Indian homes was the men at the salt-boiling camp – Joseph Field, William Bratton, and George Gibson, because there were seven Indian homes in the vicinity where the salt camp was established.[218]

10 February 1806
Capt. Lewis' journal – "Willard arrived late in the evening from the Saltworks, had cut his knee very badly with his tomahawk. He had killed four Elk not far from the Salt works the day before yesterday, which he had butchered and took a part of the meat to camp, but having cut his knee was unable to be longer useful at the works and had returned. he informed us that Bratton was very unwell, and that Gibson was so sick that he could not set up or walk alone and had desired him to ask us to have him brought to the Fort."

11 February 1806
Capt. Lewis' journal – "also sent Colter and Wiser to the Salt works to carry on the business with Joseph Fields; as Bratton has been sick we desired him to return to the Fort also if he thought proper; however in the event of his not coming Wiser was directed to return."

15 February 1806
Capt. Lewis' journal – "about 3 P. M. Bratton arrived from the salt works and informed us that Sergt. Pryor and party were on their way with Gibson who is so much reduced that he cannot stand alone and that they are obliged to carry him in a litter. Bratton himself appears much reduced with his late indisposition but is now recovering fast. Bratton informed that the cause of Sergt. Pryor's delay was attributable to the winds which had been so violent for several days as to render it impossible to get a canoe up the creek [1] to the point where it was necessary to pass with Gibson."

---

[218] Ronda, James P. 1984. *Lewis & Clark among the Indians*. Lincoln, Nebraska: University of Nebraska Press: 188.

17 February 1806
Capt. Lewis' journal – "continue the barks with Bratton, and commenced them with Gibson his fever being sufficiently low this morning to permit the use of them."

21 February 1806
Capt. Lewis' journal – "gave Willard and Bratton each a dose of Scotts pills; on the former they operated and on the latter they did not."

7 March 1806
Capt. Lewis' journal – "Bratton is much worse today, he complains of a violent pain in the small of his back and is unable in consequence to set up. We gave him one of our flannel shirts, applied a bandage of flannel to the part and bathed and rubbed it well with some volatile liniment which I prepared with spirits of wine, camphor, castile soap and a little laudinum. He felt himself better in the evening."

21 March 1806
Capt. Clark's journal – "our sick men Willard and bratton do not seem to recover; the former was taken with a violent pain in his leg and thye last night. Bratton is now so much reduced that I am somewhat uneasy with rispect to his recovery; the pain of which he complains most seems to be seated in the small of his back and remains obstinate. I believe that it is the rheumatism with which they are both afflicted."

23 May 1806
John Ordway's journal – "Wm bratton having been so long better than 3 months nearly helpless with a Severe pain in his back we now undertake Sweeting him nearly in the manner as the Indians do only cover the hole with blankits having bows bent over above the hole. We expect this operation will help him."

24 May 1806
Capt. Lewis' journal – "William Bratton still continues very unwell. He eats heartily, digests his food well, and has recovered

his flesh almost perfectly yet is so weak in the loins that he is scarcely able to walk, nor can he sit upright but with the greatest pain. We have tried every remedy which our ingenuity could devise, or with which our stock of medicines furnished us, without effect. John Shields observed that he had seen men in a similar situation restored by violent sweats. Bratton requested that he might be sweated in the manner proposed by Shields to which we consented, (i.e., sunk a circular hole of 3 feet diameter and four feet deep in the earth.) He kindled a large fire in the hole and heated well, after which the fire was taken out a seat placed in the center of the hole for the patient with a board at bottom for his feet to rest on; some hoops of willow poles were bent in an arch crossing each other over the hole, on these several blankets were thrown forming a secure and thick awning of about three-feet high. The patient being stripped naked was seated under this awning in the hole and the blankets well secured on every side. The patient was furnished with a vessel of water which he sprinkles on the bottom and sides of the hole and by that means creates as much steam or vapor as he could possibly bear, in this situation he was kept about twenty minutes after which he was taken out and suddenly plunged in cold water twice and was then immediately returned to the sweat hole where he was continued three quarters of an hour longer then taken our covered up in several blankets and suffered to cool gradually. During the time of his being in the sweat hole, he drank copious draughts of a strong tea of horse mint. Shields says that he had previously seen the tea of Sinnecca snake root used instead of the mint which was now employed for the want of the other which is not be found in this country — this experiment was made yesterday; Bratton feels himself much better and is walking about today and says he is nearly free from pain."

4 July 1806

Capt. Clark's Journal – "This being the day of the decleration of Independence of the United States and a Day commonly Scelebrated by my Country I had every disposition to Selebrate this day and therefore halted early and partook of a Sumptious Dinner of a fat Saddle of Venison and Mush of Cows (roots)."

8 June 1806
Capt. Lewis' journal – "Bratton has so far recovered that we cannot well consider him an invalid any longer, he has had a tedious illness which he boar with much fortitude and firmness."

On June 30, 1806, the men arrived back at their old camp of Travelers' Rest. Just that day before arriving, the hunters in their group traveled ahead of the main party and successfully kept everyone supplied with venison. It is unclear if William Bratton had resumed his duties as a hunter due his past illness but as Captain Lewis wrote that they could not consider him sick anymore near the beginning of the month, it is likely that since several more weeks had past, Bratton was probably able to hunt. He could even have been pretty eager by then to revel in the added freedom and privacy that hunting afforded him.

The men stayed at Travelers' Rest until July 3, 1806 then they divided forces. Captain Lewis took George Drewyer, the Field brothers, Werner, Frazier, Sargent Gass, Thompson, McNeal, and Goodrich with him. They were headed to the Falls of the Missouri where he would leave Thompson, McNeal, and Goodrich who would get their baggage and canoes ready to portage. Meanwhile, Lewis and the rest of the men would ascend and explore the Maria's River. Captain Clark took the remaining men with him. They left at 8 a.m. with supplies and fifty horses. Their first part of their mission was to return to Jefferson's River to pick up the cache and canoes they had left there. The men included York, Labiche, Potts, Sergeant Ordway, Sargent Pryor, Bratton, Collins, Colter, Cruzatte, Shields, Shannon, Lepage, Hall, Gibson, Howard, Willard, Whitehouse, Windsor, and Weiser. Also included was Charbonneau, his wife Sacagawea, and their son Pomp. Once they all reached Jefferson River, Sargent Pryor and two men would travel on land by horse to the Mandans in order to take a letter from Lewis to Hugh Haney in hopes he could begin talking to the Sioux Chiefs about visiting the United States government. The second part of the mission for the rest of their group was to descend the Yellowstone River to its nearest point to the three forks of the Missouri River where they would meet up with Lewis and his men at the Falls.[219]

Clark's men had to continually look for scattered horses but they reached their cache on the Jefferson River by July 8, 1806. As they neared the spot where their cache was buried, Clark described many of them as more than eager for one of the items. "Some articles, as before mentioned the most of the Party with me being Chewers of Tobacco become So impatient to be chewing it that they Scercely gave themselves time to take their Saddles off their horses before they were off to the deposit. I found every article Safe, except a little damp," he wrote. "I gave to each man who used tobacco about two feet off a part of a role took one third of the ballance myself and put up ⅔ in a box to Send down with the most of the articles which had been left at this place." The men worked to dig out their canoes, dry them, and then pack them with most of their supplies. Clark did pack the supplies he wanted for his trip down the Yellowstone River on the horses. Ordway and nine of the men piloted the canoes down for the first leg of the trip with Captain Clark and the rest of the men taking the horses down. About fifteen miles down, both groups met up on the banks to encamp. The next day, Captain Clark rode with the canoes on the Jefferson River, and Sargent Pryor was accompanied by six men on horseback, these men being those who would accompany Captain Clark to the Yellowstone River. Captain Clark ordered Pryor to move moderately but to try to join the group by water at their encampment at night but sometimes this was not attainable.

By July 13, 1806, Captain Clark's water party and land party reached a location just north of the three forks of the Missouri within one hour of each other. It was after dinner, at this location, that Ordway took ten men in six canoes to further their descent to meet up with Captain Lewis and his party. Captain Clark now was accompanied by York, Sargent Pryor, Gibson, Hall, Windsor, Labiche, Bratton, Shannon, Shields,

---

[219] Lewis & Clark Journals. University of Nebraska. Lincoln, Nebraska. (accessed 25 June 2015). https://lewisandclarkjournals.unl.edu/.

Charbonneau, Sacagawea, and Pomp. They had only proceeded three days before the hooves of their horses were almost worn through due to the rocky terrain. Captain Clark became determined to create canoes but the task wasn't as easy as making frames and attaching animal skins because the Yellowstone River was so rough. They would have to make canoes out of wood. They traveled three more days until they found cottonwood trees large enough to make canoes. It was none too soon because George Gibson had suffered a serious and immensely painful injury falling off his horse, and traveling was somewhat agonizing for him. They made camp and settled in for their arduous task of making several canoes. They stayed at this "canoe camp" from July 19 through July 24, 1806. During this stretch of time, their party suffered another mishap. They woke up one morning to find half of their horses gone. Captain Clark sent William Bratton, Shannon, and Charbonneau to look for them. Despite numerous attempts to find them, the horses were never recovered. Besides making canoes and searching for horses, the men were also hunting and then dressing the animal skins to make clothes. "Keeping the men clothed remained a problem throughout the remainder of the journey. Leather clothing wore out quickly under the conditions of the rough use to which it was put."[220]

The likely location of the canoe camp was discovered through the research of Billings historian and cartographer Ralph Saunders. Armed with convincing information, he persuaded Tom Rust, assistant professor at Montana State University Billings, to help him prove it. Rust, Saunders, and MSUB students were able to conduct an archaeological study and geographical analysis from 2011-2014 to determine if Saunders' location of an island on Yellowstone River was the right site.[221] They also engaged the help of local boy scouts.

---

[220] Moore, Jr., Robert J. and Michael Haynes. 2003. *Lewis & Clark, Tailor Made, Travel Worn: Army Life, Clothing & Weapons of the Corp of Discovery.* Helena, Montana: Farcountry Press: 245.

[221] National Park Service, post. "Clark Canoe Camp on the Yellowstone." (accessed 25 April 2015). https://www.nps.gov/places/clark-s-canoe-camp-on-the-yellowstone.htm

They used a "magnetometer and soil resistance meter to assess soil disturbances and compaction," reported the Billings Gazette. They found a lead ball, .375 caliber size, and another piece of flattened lead near a likely fire pit site. The isotope analysis from the lead found at the canoe camp matches that from the artifacts found at the expedition campsite at Travelers Rest indicating that the metal used in both was taken from the same mine in Kentucky. They also found evidence of mercury using a mercury vapor analyzer which also matches the findings at Travelers' Rest.[222]

3 August 1806
Captain Clark's Journal – "landed and Sent **Labeech** to kill the ram, which he did kill and brought him on board. This ram is not near as large as maney I have Seen. However he is Sufficiently large for a Sample. I directed **Bratten** to Skin him with his head horns & feet to the Skin and Save all the bone. I have now the Skin & bone of a Ram and Ewe & a yearlin ram of those big Horn animals."

"The distance from the **Rocky Mountains** at which place I struck the **River Rochejhone** to its enterance into the **Missouri** 837 Miles 636 Miles of this distance I decended in 2 Small Canoes lashed together in which I had the following Persons. **John Shields, George Gibson, William Bratten, W. Labeech**, Toust. **Shabono** his wife & child & my man **York**."

8 August 1806
Captain Clark's Journal – "Sergt. Pryor bing anxious to overtake me Set out Some time before day this morning and forgot his Saddlebags which contains his papers &c., I Sent **Bratten** back with him in Serch of them."

---

[222] French, Brett. "Evidence Builds that Yellowstone Island was Clark's 1806 Canoe Camp." Billings, Montana: Billings Gazette: 27 April 2014.

12 August 1806
Captain Lewis' Journal – "at 1 P. M. I overtook Capt. Clark and party and had the pleasure of finding them all well."

28 August 1806
Captain Clark's Journal – "Sent out Bratten and Frazier to kill the barking Squirel. and Gave directions to all of them to kill the Magpye."

5 November 1806
Jonathan Clark diary - "Captains Lewis & Clark arrived at the Falls of the Ohio on their return from the Pacific Ocean after an absence of a little more than three years."[223]

Upon Bratton's discharge, Captain Meriwether Lewis said "in virtue of the authority vested in me by the President of the United States, hereby discharged from the military service of the said states, and as a tribute fully due the merits of the said William Bratton, I with cheerfulness declare that the ample support which he gave me under every difficulty, the manly fairness which he evinced on every necessary occasion and the fortitude with which he bore the fatigues and painful sufferings incident to that long voyage, entitles him to my highest confidence and sincere thanks, while it eminently recommends him to the consideration and respect of his fellow citizens.[224]

It took about six months for the federal government to compensate the men of the expedition. In "an Act making compensation to Messers. Lewis and Clarke and their companions," Captain Lewis and Captain Clark each received a land warrant of 1600 acres, and the rest of the expedition

---

[223] Jonathan Clark diary. 5 November 1806. The Filson Historical Society. Louisville, Kentucky.
[224] Indiana Historical Bureau, post. "William Bratton discharge papers." (accessed 23 April 2015) https://www.in.gov/history/state-historical-markers.

members received a land warrant for 320 acres. The government specified that each warrant could be "at the option of the holder or possessor, be located with any register or registers of the land offices, subsequent to the public sales in such office, on any of the public lands of the United States, lying on the west side of the Mississippi, then and there offered for sale, or may be received at the rate of two dollars per acre, in payment of any such public lands."[225] Additionally, the men received double pay for the time they served in the expedition. William eventually sold his to Samuel Barclay, a citizen of Warren County, Kentucky.

---

[225] U. S. Congress. U.S. Statutes at Large, Volume 6. Private Laws and Resolutions – 1845. United States, - 1845, 1789. Periodical. https://www.loc.gov/item/llsl-v6/.

CHAPTER FIVE
Return to Franklin County, Kentucky, 1807-1812

It was probably very surreal for William to re-enter society compared to where he had been and what he had seen in the last two years. He and his fellow expedition members probably discussed this together while traveling back. In fact, two Scottish gentlemen told the expedition members that the general public believed the Corps of Discovery was dead.[226] Besides alerting his family that he was alive and in good health, another task near the top of William's list was probably thinking about how he would support himself. He was still a gunsmith and a hunter, but he had also cultivated many new skills on the expedition and had greatly increased his network of contacts. First, he probably saw his family. William's family in Bowling Green were no doubt clamoring to see him in addition to his friends and family in Frankfort. From Louisville, he either traveled towards Bowling Green in Warren County, Kentucky to visit his father and siblings to let them know how he fared or traveled back to Franklin County to his brother-in-law and sister's house, the residence of Joseph and Anne Bimson.

During William's absence, Joseph and Anne were in close contact with the rest of her family in Warren County. Bimson had some sort of friendly business deal with his father-in-law George Bratton to grow corn on George's land in Warren County. Maybe they were partners. Sometime in the spring of 1806, Bimson made a deal concerning the corn with Thomas

---

[226] Lewis & Clark Journals. University of Nebraska Lincoln. 20 Sept. 1806. (accessed 26 April 2015)
https://lewisandclarkjournals.unl.edu/item/lc.jrn.1806-09-20.

Middleton that did not sit well with Bratton brothers-in-law Adam, George Jr. and Archibald. In a later court case, as administrator of George Bratton's estate, Archibald entered a plea of trespass against Middleton accusing Middleton of stealing $700 of corn and corn crop by-products in November 1806. Middleton denied the theft. As part of the common law court case, Middleton and Archibald Bratton met at Mary Stuart's house, a neighbor to the Brattons, to gather her testimony as evidence in the case. The parcel of land was ten acres in size and yielded forty-five to fifty bushels of Indian corn per acre. The problem with the court case for Archibald is that almost fifteen years had elapsed since the alleged crime, and both Bimson and George Bratton were no longer living. It is unclear why Archibald even as administrator of his father's estate felt entitled enough to press charges when they were not involved in the original business dealing, and neither his father nor Bimson had filed charges themselves. Clearly, Archibald felt a lot of enmity for Middleton that did not abate over time. Though he tried to gather witness testimony, many neighbors just could not remember specific details. The Warren County court found in favor of Middleton.[227]

In that same year, shortly after William Bratton's return from the expedition and right after the corn harvest, tragedy struck William and other members of the Bratton family. Their sister Anne Bratton Bimson died in the winter of 1806. In December 1806, William was granted administration of her estate. As part of the process, he entered a bond with the Franklin County clerk for $200. His neighbor Captain John Arnold served as his security.[228] By the middle of January, it is clear that Anne's husband Joseph Bimson was now also deceased when William filed a court order requesting that John Arnold, David Wilson, James Paxton, and William Robinson, Sr.

---

[227] Kentucky. Warren County. Civil Court Cases. Kentucky Department of Library and Archives: Archibald Bratton vs. Thomas Middleton civil case, 1820.

[228] Kentucky. Franklin County. Anne Bimson estate administration record, Order Book D.

appraise the personal estate of Joseph and then file their report at the next court session.[229] Joseph Bimson and Anne had no living children so the process of administrating their estates was pretty straightforward but no actual documentation beyond the approval of William's administration and the request for an appraisal, like a will or inventory exists.

On May 20 1807, on the tax list for Franklin County, Kentucky, William's brother Robert Bratton listed himself as over age twenty-one and he owned one horse. He did not own any land at that time.[230] William was not listed on the tax list. About this time though, William decided that as an occupation, he would use his experience as a boatman to earn a living. He helped operate a boat that shipped goods up the Kentucky River to the Ohio River and then down the Mississippi River to New Orleans.[231]

While it is not possible to know exactly what William experienced as a boatman, a good idea can be gleaned from the voyage journals of two people, seventeen-year-old John G. Stuart, who made a trading trip by boat from Fayette County to New Orleans in 1806, and Fortescue Cuming who spent two years on and off the rivers from 1807-1809. Though Stuart began his journey at Cleveland's Landing that was forty land miles and 140 water miles south of Frankfort on the Kentucky River, and he had to bring his goods north to the Ohio River, we can pick his story up at Frankfort which was probably still William Bratton's home base. Stuart was hired by George W. Halley to transport tobacco, flour, and whiskey by flatboat.[232]

---

[229] Kentucky. Franklin County. Joseph Bimson estate administration record, Order Book D: 132, 141.

[230] Kentucky. Franklin County. Robert Bratton entry. 1807 Tax List, Allen County Public Library, Fort Wayne, Indiana. Microfilm, #0100, 1781-1797, 1799 – 1804.

[231] James T. Fields to Eva Dye Letter. 18 November 1901. Eva Emery Dye Collection. Oregon Historical Society. Portland, Oregon.

[232] Stuart, John G. "A Journal, Remarks or Observations in a Voyage Down the Kentucky, Ohio, Mississippi Rivers." Frankfort, Kentucky: Kentucky Historical Society: 1806.

Fortescue Cuming was an Englishman who wrote about his journey by boat from Maysville, Ohio to New Orleans so his experience does not mirror William and Stuart's until he reached the point where the Kentucky River emptied into the Ohio River.

Near Frankfort - April 1806

Stuart wrote in his journal that when the spring rains arrived, the river began to rise rapidly. At thirty feet high, the water became too high. "Through the whole course of the day, large trees and timber of all kinds has been in a manner flying past. Also a cow, three or four canoes, and this evening the wreck of a large new produce boat, we cannot tell who has lost her," Stuart wrote. He also saw hogsheads of tobacco lodged in some places. When they were able to resume floating, the traffic on the river was so busy, Stuart noted that they passed twenty-two flatboats and two keelboats. As they are neared Frankfort, he saw many warehouses. They passed Frankfort that afternoon. It is here that his journey and William's journeys sync in that what Stuart began to see at this point is comparative to what William probably experienced as a boatman just a year or two later when he worked on the rivers.

Just past Frankfort there was a rocky shallow part of the Kentucky River where the water was rough. Spots such as these were called riffles and this specific riffle was referred to as the Frankfort riffle, and the men had to pull the boat hard to the right to avoid going aground. Later in the same day, they approached the Elkhorn riffle that Stuart designated as the worst one of the Kentucky River, and they had to pull the boat hard to the left and then to the right to avoid it. There was an island at the mouth of the Elkhorn River. They also passed the mouth of Benson Creek and Captain John Arnold's place which Stuart thought was possibly one of the "handsome seats" he saw on the Kentucky River.

When Stuart reached the Ohio River, there was a little town there by the name of Newport, but this was not the same town across from Cincinnati, but another little town of the same name that a year later changed its name to Port William and then later to Carrollton. It was not a very big town and Stuart called it "a trifling place." It made a better impression on Cuming two years later who described it as "delightfully situated" just above the mouth of the Kentucky River. In 1808, the town was eighty –one hundred feet wide in Cuming's estimation and contained about twenty-one houses, many of them brick, but all of them rundown. Cuming attributed the shabby shape of the town to the lack of improvement or infrastructure needed to support the growth of a town.[233]

Louisville, Kentucky

When Stuart and his fellow boatmen landed temporarily about a mile above the Falls, Stuart walked just a little ways and saw Louisville on the left which he noted was "a handsome little town, it contains some elegant buildings." He saw Jeffersonville on the right side of the river in Indiana Territory. This was probably the same place where Cuming and his companions stopped in 1808 when he wrote about his view of Louisville from a harbor just inside Bear Grass creek just off the Ohio River. He too enjoyed the view of Louisville and Jeffersonville from there. He noted that Jeffersonville was a "neat village of thirty houses" about a mile away. When Cuming was able to walk around Louisville, he found that "Louisville consists of one principal and very handsome street, about a half-mile long, tolerably compactly built and the houses generally superior to any I have seen in the western country with the exception of Lexington. Most are of handsome brick, and some are three stories, with a parapet wall on the top in the modern European taste, which in front gives them the appearance of having flat roofs. I had thought Cincinnati one of the most beautiful towns I had seen in America, but Louisville, which is almost as large, equals it in beauty, and in the opinion of many excels it. It was considered as unhealthy which impeded its progress, until three or four years ago, when probably in consequence of the

---

[233] Thwaites, Reuben Gold, ed. 1907. *Early Western Travels, 1748-1846*. Vol. 4. Cleveland, Ohio: The Arthur H. Clark Company: 260.

surrounding country being more open, bilious complaints ceased to be so frequent, and it is now considered by the inhabitants as healthy as any town on the river. There is a market house where there is a very good market every Wednesday and Saturday. The courthouse is a plain two-story stone building with a square roof and small belfry. There are bells here on the roofs of the taverns as in Lexington, to summon the guests to their meals. Great retail business is done here, and much produce is shipped to New Orleans."[234]

When Cuming visited Louisville, one of its residents was famed naturalist and artist John James Audubon. Audubon lived there with his wife Lucy Bakewell Audubon, and was in business as a storekeeper. Unfortunately, he was not very successful at it because he spent more of his time drawing birds in the nearby woods than doing business in his store. They lived in the Indian Queen tavern owned by John Gwathmey.[235]

Another important visitor arrived in Louisville in 1809, Nicholas Roosevelt, of the Roosevelts of New York. He stayed in Louisville for three weeks where he talked with boatmen and merchants about the industry of powering boats by steam. He described his experiments upon many eastern rivers and upon the Hudson, but Louisville were unconvinced that boats by steam could navigate the swirling, sometimes muddy waters of the Ohio and Mississippi in which dangerous lurked unseen below the water line.[236]

---

[234] Thwaites, Reuben Gold, ed. 1907. *Early Western Travels, 1748-1846*. Vol. 4. Cleveland, Ohio: The Arthur H. Clark Company: 260.

[235] Yater, George H. 1979. *Two Hundred Years at the Falls of the Ohio: a history of Louisville and Jefferson County*. Louisville, Kentucky: The Heritage Corporation: 30.

[236] Petersen, William J. 1995. *Steamboating on the Upper Mississippi*. New York, New York: Dover Publications, Incorporated: 53.

Falls of the Ohio

Stuart and his fellow boatmen arranged help crossing the Falls with a river pilot by the name of Nelson who might have been Captain John Nelson, the son-in-law of one of the main Falls pilots, Captain James Patton. Stuart saw thousands of swallows and some hawks that were hovering over the Falls. He also wrote that they used the Indiana chute as all the other chutes were impassable that day.[237] Cuming wrote a more detailed description of the Falls. "The rapids or falls of the Ohio are the next objects which strike the observer. They are formed by a range of rocks and low islands, which extend across the river, the deepest channel through which is near the Indiana shore, and has only six feet water, and that even very narrow when the river is low. Cuming and his boat crew were also ushered over the falls by ship pilot Captain Nelson "by the Kentucky shute, and in forty-five minutes we moored at Shippingport where we found Commodore Peters's boat and officers, and captain Nevitt's gun boat, all bound to New Orleans in a few days."

The Falls were severely daunting, and people had three "chutes" to choose from - the Kentucky chute, the middle chute, and the Indiana chute - in moving their cargo and boats down the river. It was always dangerous to traverse for people and their cargo. Water levels and weather had to be a certain standard for the Falls to be even passable. Because of this, sometimes people had to wait a week or more in Louisville or Jeffersonville to move their cargo. The business of not just piloting people and their cargo over the Falls, but also storing their cargo and providing the travelers with room and board, caused Louisville and Jeffersonville to develop into two of the largest towns on the Ohio River.[238] In the fall of 1810, in an accounting by the pilots kept over a seven-month period, cargo

---

[237] Stuart, John G. "A Journal, Remarks or Observations in a Voyage Down the Kentucky, Ohio, Mississippi Rivers." Frankfort, Kentucky: Kentucky Historical Society: 1806.

[238] Kramer, Carl E. 2003. *The Corps of Discovery and the Falls of the Ohio*. Jeffersonville, Indiana: Sunnyside Press: 4-5.

included butter, corn, oats, lard, bacon, pork, flour, thousands of barrels of whiskey and cider, onions, apples, beans, dried fruit, shoe thread, linen, yarn, cordage, hemp, hogs, horses, and tobacco, etc. They piloted about 740 boats over the Falls with only one-third of them crossing in high water.[239] Because of the risk involved in navigating the Falls, many boat owners insured their cargo.

When the Tarascon brothers, and a Mr. Berthoud wrecked their boat at the Falls of the Ohio in 1805, they were inspired a year later to found the town of Shippingport, the town Cuming mentioned stopping in after he was navigated safely through the Falls. So it was not there when William Bratton and the Corps of Discovery had passed westward in 1804, but it was existed when they returned, and when Stuart went through as well. He and his fellow boatmen landed their boat on the opposite shore across from the Berthoud & Co. warehouse to unload hemp. They stayed for a few days in Louisville and Stuart visited a boat owned by Berthoud & Company called the Western Trader that was large enough that some men were calling it a ship and others were calling it a square-rigged brig. Stuart also noted that he found a fresh human jawbone on the beach. Because of only referring to this occurrence as one sentence in his journal, such an occurrence in the early 1800s did not receive any further investigation indicating that perhaps finding fresh human bones was not terribly unusual and the task might be impossible to discover to whom it belonged.[240] Shippingport provided another place on the river where businessmen built warehouses and teamsters employed in Louisville portaged cargos for owners working to get their boats down the Falls. As Stuart witnessed, sometimes, new

---

[239] Petersen, William J. 1995. *Steamboating on the Upper Mississippi*. New York, New York: Dover Publications, Incorporated: 54.

[240] Stuart, John G. "A Journal, Remarks or Observations in a Voyage Down the Kentucky, Ohio, Mississippi Rivers." Frankfort, Kentucky: Kentucky Historical Society: 1806.

boats were built in Shippingport, and then cargo loaded and sent down to New Orleans.[241]

The shipping business was so vibrant, thousands of boats arrived in New Orleans each year by river from the North. The smallest boat that might be on the river would be a log canoe which could cost as little as three dollars. A larger canoe, six to eight-feet-wide and forty to fifty feet long, was called a pirogue. Both types of boats were heavy and unsuitable for long portages. A boat called a skiff with a flat bottom could hold two to three men, and an even larger one, called a bateau, could hold a family. A bateau could be used downstream and upstream using long oars. Flatboats could vary in size and were more hospitable in transporting families. They were twenty to sixty feet in length depending on the distance they were destined to travel.[242] Two other popular boats were keelboats and barges. Keelboats could haul twenty to forty pounds of cargo. Keelboats were sturdy and ideally suited in combating the unseen snags in the Mississippi River due to a thick four-inch timber on the bottom of the boat that ran from bow to stern. They were seven to nine feet wide and forty-five to seventy-five feet long. Some keelboatmen even used a mast and sails sometimes to catch the breeze and better propel them downstream. Both keelboats and barges utilized the boatmen as steersmen in which they used poles to muscle the boats upstream.[243]

Cuming wrote "Shippingport is a fine harbor, there being no current in it, but the banks are rather low, so as to be inundated at very high floods. Mr. Berthoud, who has a handsome house here, is connected with Mr. Tarascon of Louisville in one of the finest ropewalks in the United States. It is twelve hundred feet long, of which seven hundred and fifty

---

[241] Yater, George H. 1979. *Two Hundred Years at the Falls of the Ohio: a history of Louisville and Jefferson County.* Louisville, Kentucky: The Heritage Corporation: 32.

[242] Petersen, William J. 1995. *Steamboating on the Upper Mississippi.* New York, New York: Dover Publications, Inc.: 51.

[243] Ibid: 52.

are covered. A little above the port is a mill wrought by the Ohio, the race being formed by a small bank, which has been cut through purposely."[244] Stuart noted that when they left Shippingport, they lashed their boat to eight other flatboats and one keelboat and began their journey towards New Orleans. About thirty other boats lined the banks above and below the Falls. The men on the boats divided into three watch teams and were able to float westward down the Ohio River at three to four miles per hour.[245] Men were on duty around the clock to navigate the boats around islands, several very rocky.

Sullivan's Ferry – Seven miles below Shippingport

A gentleman with the last name of Sullivan probably ran a ferry business here. On the Indiana Territory on the northside, there was a road that ran 120 miles northward to Vincennes, that capital of Indiana. At this time, Indiana was not yet a state.

Salt River and Doe Run – 25 miles below Shippingport

Cuming described Salt River as eighty yards wide "with some neat settlements on each side of it, and also on the opposite bank of the Ohio, which latter bank housed six families. There was also a small creek nearby called Doe Run that ran into the Ohio. Cuming and his crew landed there to buy supplies. Cuming relayed the following prices for food, butter at twelve and a half cents per pound, a dozen eggs at six and a quarter cents, a quart of milk for six and a quarter cents, a chicken for twelve and a half cents each, and a turkey, depending on its size, was anywhere from twenty-five to fifty cents each.[246] Stuart noted on his trip that he and his party were greeted by two Native Americans in this general area who had food supplies for sale. The Native Americans were not fluent in

---

[244] Thwaites, Reuben Gold, ed. 1907. *Early Western Travels, 1748-1846.* Vol. 4. Cleveland, Ohio: The Arthur H. Clark Company: 260.

[245] Stuart, John G. "A Journal, Remarks or Observations in a Voyage Down the Kentucky, Ohio, Mississippi Rivers." Frankfort, Kentucky: Kentucky Historical Society: 1806.

[246] Thwaites, Reuben Gold, ed. 1907. *Early Western Travels, 1748-1846.* Vol. 4. Cleveland, Ohio: The Arthur H. Clark Company: 260.

English but the crew was able to trade them a half-gallon of whiskey for two venison hams. Between Stuart and Cuming's accounts, it is clear that commerce and trade along the Ohio River was prevalent.

Blue River, Indiana Territory

After passing the Blue River that ran into the Ohio River from Indiana Territory, Stuart's boat flotilla stopped for the evening. Stuart traded three pounds of tobacco for a forty to forty-five pound catfish. Cuming's crew also stopped at Blue River, and Cuming saw people living on both sides of it. The uppermost side was settled three years before and many were barely able to survive. Cuming spied "a large family of children and their mother almost naked," Cuming said. "Nothing apparently flourishing except a large garden of onions, for a few of which with a pound or two of Indian meal to make leaven, the woman would fix no price, but thinking herself badly paid with a quarter of a dollar, I gave her an eighth more to satisfy her," he said. There was also a settlement on the lower side that was settled by a Mr. Thomas Davidson who was from Carlisle, Pennsylvania. More people lived further up Blue River eight miles where Squire Boone, brother of frontier hero Daniel Boone, had settled six years earlier in 1802. Additionally, Indiana Governor William Henry Harrison who primarily lived in Vincennes, built and ran a grist and saw mill in the same area. It would later become known as Wilson's Springs and when county lines within Indiana were determined, it would fall within Harrison County, Indiana. Larger boats can navigate through Blue River for about 40 miles, but not to Vincennes which lies about 100 miles north of Harrison's mills.[247]

---

[247] Thwaites, Reuben Gold, ed. 1907. *Early Western Travels, 1748-1846*. Vol. 4. Cleveland, Ohio: The Arthur H. Clark Company: 262.

Owensboro, Kentucky

On May 1, 1806, Stuart's crew passed Owensboro, Kentucky. Along the river, Stuart observed "wretched little huts" scattered amidst the banks covered in thick cane. The crew estimated that they floated 80 miles in a twenty-four hour period. In this area on the Ohio River, Cuming also noted that there were little settlements here and there.

Flint Island – three miles south of it.

Three miles below an island in the river, called Flint Island, Cuming and his crew pulled over due to some rough waters from wind. There was a man by the last name of Wheatly formerly from Redstone, Pennsylvania that lived there in a cabin. He was about six feet in height and athletic looking, maybe in his thirties for Cuming described him as being in the prime of his life. Cuming struck up a conversation with him while he was splitting wood. Besides his cabin, Wheatly originally owned 1000 acres but it was now pared down to 340 acres, of which six acres were cleared and where he grew 500 bushels of corn the previous year.[248] Next, Wheatly told Cuming that a small tribe of Native Americans, the Miamis, lived about two miles away on Oil Creek. When Cuming asked him if there were ever any problems between him and the Native Americans, Wheatly replied while he was still cutting wood, "We never permit them to be troublesome, for if any of them displease us, we take them out of doors and kick them a little, for they are like dogs, and so will love you the better for it." Cuming felt that while Wheatly might be able to get away with treating the Native Americans like that due to his size, he doubted that the Native Americans would allow themselves to be treated that way by other white men not so impressively well-built. "He informed us that they frequently get the Indians together, take their guns, knives and tomahawks from them, then treat them with whiskey until they are drunk, when they set them by the ears, to have the pleasure of seeing them fight,

---

[248] Thwaites, Reuben Gold, ed. 1907. *Early Western Travels, 1748-1846.* Vol. 4. Cleveland, Ohio: The Arthur H. Clark Company: 263.

at which they are so awkward like young bears according to his phrase that they scuffle for hours without drawing blood, and when their breath is exhausted they will sit down quietly to recruit, and then up and at it again," Cuming wrote.[249]

Author's note – While I find Mr. Wheatly's attitude very offensive, I recognize that at that time, people believed in manifest destiny – the strong take what they want no matter the harm to whomever or from however they get it – and that he was of the generation that experienced warfare their whole lives with Native Americans following their life's path as pioneers.

Sinking Creek

Sinking Creek was located eight miles south of Wheatly's place. There was a ferry and a trace or path, not quite a road that headed northward seventy-five miles to Vincennes. Sinking Creek emptied into the Ohio and a settlement with a large double log cabin existed.

Squire Tobin's – 10 miles south of Sinking Creek

Squire Tobin, like Wheatly, was from Redstone, Pennsylvania and had lived on the Ohio River for three years as a farmer. While Cuming was at Tobin's landing, a large forty-ton keelboat arrived. "She was worked by a horizontal wheel kept in motion by six horses going round in a circle on a gallery above the boat, by which are turned two cog wheels fixed each to an axle which projects over both gunwales of the boat, one before and the other behind the horizontal wheel. Eight paddles are fixed on the projecting end of each axle which impel the boat about five or six miles an hour so that she can be forced against the current about twenty miles a day," Cuming wrote. The boat was owned by a Mr. Brookfield who also captained the boat. He had the boat built the previous year in Kentucky, about two miles above Louisville. He took the

---

[249] Thwaites, Reuben Gold, ed. 1907. *Early Western Travels, 1748-1846*. Vol. 4. Cleveland, Ohio: The Arthur H. Clark Company: 262.

boat to New Orleans and was now on way back, selling a cargo of sugar place to place on his way up the rivers. Brookfield expected to be back to his home soon and then to leave on another voyage shortly after his return. The largest problem Brookfield encountered in his voyage was that many of the horses died on the trip. Seven of the original nine horses used to power the boat had died so he had had to replace them along the way.

Blair's Ferry, Kentucky
Twelve miles below Green River, a road travels through Kentucky to the Ohio River where Blair's Ferry took travelers across to the road that continued on the Indiana side to Vincennes which was north fifty-four miles. It was just a mile below Blair's Ferry where Cuming encountered the Patterson family. He and several crew members took a skiff to land where they lived. Patterson was from Aberdeen, Scotland who immigrated to Grenada in the West Indies in the 1770s to manage a rum plantation called Harvey's Plains. Due to problems with his liver, Patterson moved to New York where he lived for several years and met his Mrs. Patterson. He moved his family to their farm on the Ohio River the previous year. "Mrs. Patterson thought they were to find a country abundant in everything, with little or no trouble, but now being undeceived by experience, she jocularly remarked, that if the current of the river would change, she would gladly seize the occasion to return immediately where she came from, Cuming wrote. He observed that the family had a comfortable situation. The Pattersons were entertaining neighbors and their table was loaded with food and though the Pattersons very enthusiastically invited them to eat with them, Cuming and men had to catch up to their boat.

Henderson, Kentucky

Henderson was a town that Cuming said had about twenty wooden cabins and houses, two stores and two large warehouses for tobacco. There lives a Mr. McBride who had a gin machine that carded and spun cotton when the wheel was turned. The machine worked by spinning eight threads at once winding them upon eight spools. The machine was so ingeniously simple, a child could operate it, and it took up no more room than a table would, Cuming wrote. The town of Henderson at that time experienced a business of 500 hogshead of tobacco being shipped there each year which continually attracted new settlers and even several wealthy ones. In four years, artist John James Audubon would move there. Across the river from Henderson was another road to Vincennes that was fifty-two miles northeast of Henderson.

Diamond Island

Diamond Island was beautifully situated, over four miles long, and contained about 800 acres of timbered land, described Cuming. The river was about a quarter of a mile wide on each side of the island as it flowed around it. In 1808, the island was owned by a Scotsman, Mr. Alvis who also owned property in South Carolina. Alvis had bought the island two years previously from a Mr. Wells. In addition to the island, Alvis also had almost 150 acres cleared on the Kentucky side of the river. Before Alvis worked it, that particular spot had been the former camp of twenty to thirty river pirates who attacked passing boats. Because the river was so narrow as it flowed around the island, it afforded no protection. Among those river pirates were the Mason gang, a Harper, and a Corkendale. Because of their murderous activities, the Kentucky government sent a militia to apprehend them. Cuming relayed this story as he heard it from Mr. Alvis, the river pirates "were surprised, and Harper, one of the Masons, and three or four more were shot, one in the arms of his wife who escaped unhurt though her husband received eleven balls. The rest dispersed, and again recruiting, became under Mason the father, the terror of the road through the wilderness through Nashville in Tennessee and the Mississippi Territory. About four years ago (1804) two of the gang, tempted by the reward of five hundred dollars for Mason dead or alive, offered by the governor of the Mississippi Territory, shot him, carried his head to Natchez, received the promised reward which they expected, and also what they did not expect, being both found guilty of belonging to the gang, and being executed accordingly."[250] At this spot as well, when the river pirates were not preying on river travelers, warriors from different Native American tribes in the nation would also attack river travelers as they considered the hunting grounds and water highways theirs. It also served as an outlet for revenge as whites encroached from the east, and it also provided goods as a prize for their efforts.

Uniontown, Kentucky
On the Kentucky (left) side of the river, past several islands, lived three families all related by the name of Robinson. Here, the Highland Creek flowed into the Ohio River and just past the Creek was a landing. A Mr. Austin and a Mr. Cooper both had land and houses situated there. There was also a framed house that was rented by a temporary settler by the name of Mr. Gilchrist. The landing was busy with boat traffic used by other families in the area. In the future, this settlement would become Uniontown, Kentucky.

Wabash River, Indiana Territory
The mouth of the Wabash River was on the right side, two and a half miles below what would become Uniontown, Kentucky. It is the largest river in Indiana and travels northward. Vincennes was 50 miles up its north of the mouth. Also, near the mouth of the river which spanned about 300 hundred-yards-wide at the time, there was a large island, five miles long and 3000 acres in size. The banks were low and the two cabins

---

[250] Thwaites, Reuben Gold, ed. 1907. *Early Western Travels, 1748-1846*. Vol. 4. Cleveland, Ohio: The Arthur H. Clark Company: 268.

that sat on the banks were flooded to the top of their eaves every spring. Cuming must have talked to the settlers there for he discovered that their cattle had drowned the year before when the river rose, and they saved themselves by retreating several miles away from the river. Another cabin with a tavern sign was nestled in the juncture where the two rivers met.[251]

Shawneetown, Illinois Territory
Shawneetown was on the right side of the river in Illinois Territory. It first began as a Native American town but the only evidence of the Native Americans that remained was their burial ground. Upon the burial ground, Cuming saw human bones and small copper bells. In 1808, the location was populated with settlers in twenty-four cabins and was quite busy due to a salt-works business within twelve miles of there that supplied salt to people within 100 miles. Cuming believed that their business extended to supplying salt to those within the whole Upper Louisiana territory. The U.S. Government had secured the area that the settlement sat on as well as the salt licks and the land that formed a tract from there to the Saline River. Because the settlers did not own where they lived, they were not motivated to improve the land more than what they needed to just get by. The Saline River was nine river miles below Shawneetown and had a mouth of about fifty yards wide that was deep enough that keelboats and batteaux boats could sail up it a little way. Up the Saline River is where the salt works was located.

Cave-in-Rock, Illinois Territory
Cuming and his crew began to see unique limestone rock formations on the Illinois Territory (right) side of the river. When they saw a cavern about forty-five feet deep, three feet wide and nine feet high, they thought it was Cave-In-Rock, a cave they had heard about. They launched a skiff from their boat and went in for a better look and Cuming noted that it had

---

[251] Thwaites, Reuben Gold, ed. 1907. *Early Western Travels, 1748-1846*. Vol. 4. Cleveland, Ohio: The Arthur H. Clark Company: 268.

a vault at its end where there were formations resembling the "hanging pipes of a large organ," and the side formed a gothic arch. But when they continued along the shore in their skiff, they realized that that couldn't have been Cave-In-Rock because just a third of a mile down, Cuming said, "one of the finest grottos or caverns I have ever seen, opened suddenly to view, resembling the choir of a large church as we looked directly into it." The mouth of the cave was fifty-five feet wide and framed by cedar trees, and both black and white oak trees. Inside, the cave was close to 160 feet deep and forty feet wide but at seventy-five feet into the cave, the floor inclined to where there were just a few feet between the floor and ceiling at the end. However, at that point there is a hole in the ceiling large enough for a man to crawl through. This hole is a sinkhole and acts as a drain for rainwater and other small material that works washes down in heavy rains.[252] Two crevices ran along the top of the cave and another opening was situated in the middle of it. It was also big enough for a man to crawl through and it led to an upper chamber that was ten feet high and four feet wide and was known as the upper cave. When the river is at its normal height, the cave sits halfway between the distance between the river and the top of the limestone bluff above it, but when it flooded the water would come up close to the lip of the cave and sometimes even passed the lip when the water was extremely high to where the water would run into the cave. Men and been able to paddle their canoes into it.[253] Names carved by previous river travelers were etched along the walls of the cave, some of them created as early as 1766. Another flatboat traveler, Christian Schultz, had visited the cave in 1807 and noted that there were smoke marks and wooden hooks in the walls. Besides river travelers, Native Americans first used the cave, but in 1797, it was used

---

[252] Rothert, Otto. 1924. *The Outlaws of Cave-in-Rock: historical accounts of the famous highwaymen and river pirates who operated in pioneer days upon the Ohio and Mississippi Rivers and over the Old Natchez Trace.* Cleveland, Ohio: Arthur H. Clark, Publisher: 19.
[253] Ibid: 20.

as another river hideout for the Mason gang.[254] When John G. Stuart passed the cave on his river journey on May 3, 1806, he merely described the cave as "picturesque rocks" "worth looking at." He and another member of their party, Joshua Baker, paddled their canoe over to explore it.[255]

It was just under a half mile after Cave-in-Rock where Cuming encountered his own "river pirate" by the name of Mrs. Perkins. She lived on a nice farm where he bought some buttermilk. He wanted to buy eggs as well but was shocked at the price she wanted for them. During the transaction, he "on demanding the price, and being asked by Mrs. Perkins, with an unblushing face, four times as much as we hitherto paid for the first article, and twice as much as had ever been demanded for the second, we left the eggs with her." So affronted by Mrs. Perkins' prices, Cuming did not hesitate to tell her "how much she ought to be ashamed to take such advantage of the necessities of travelers."

Fort Massac, Illinois Territory
Fort Massac was built in the 1750s by the French. It was in a dilapidated state in 1794 before it was rebuilt by Americans for use in fighting Native Americans.

New Madrid, Missouri
Stuart described New Madrid in 1806 as "a handsome situation but said to be unhealthy." After leaving New Madrid, a fierce wind that Stuart described as a hurricane drove their boat flotilla onto a sandbar where they were stranded for a half an hour until the storm let up a little. When they first became stuck, fellow boatman James Baker and another in their party by the name of Ramsey unlashed the remaining unstuck boats

---

[254] Rothert, Otto. 1924. *The Outlaws of Cave-in-Rock: historical accounts of the famous highwaymen and river pirates who operated in pioneer days upon the Ohio and Mississippi Rivers and over the Old Natchez Trace.* Cleveland, Ohio: Arthur H. Clark, Publisher: 25.

[255] Stuart, John G. "A Journal, Remarks or Observations in a Voyage Down the Kentucky, Ohio, Mississippi Rivers." Frankfort, Kentucky: Kentucky Historical Society: 1806.

and floated further down. Their impatience proved fatal to Ramsey's boat which wrecked and sank in minutes. When Stuart's boat that was still lashed to John Baker's and a boat belonging to a Mr. Spilman, followed them down the river, they were able to help Ramsay salvage what he could from the wreck. The next day, the men spent the whole day loading Ramsay's property onto the four boats but was able to again push off into the river the following morning. They were cruising through Missouri which was so flat that Stuart wrote that he had only seen one hill in an entire week.[256]

Devil's Elbow

On May 11, 1806, Stuart described dangerous obstacles on the river such sawyers, which were trees bobbing up and down in the river, and banks that were falling into the river. Sometimes the crew could not find a place to land their boat for the evening until after dark making it difficult to maneuver the boat easily. Again, storms with heavy rain and wind would arise unpredictably affecting their course of action. They passed some treacherous parts that Stuart called the Devil's Race Path, or Devil's Race Ground which was also near the Devil's Elbow and also called the Devil's Hackle.[257]

Fort Pickering and Memphis, Tennessee

Near a fourth bluff on the Mississippi River there was an active Spanish garrison called Fort Pickering. There was also a small town nearby which was Memphis, Tennessee. Stuart accompanied a Mr. Moss up to the fort. There was a small guard kept there and five artillery cannons mounted and usable. After their visit, due to fog, the crew waited for it to dissipate before they shoved off.

---

[256] Stuart, John G. "A Journal, Remarks or Observations in a Voyage Down the Kentucky, Ohio, Mississippi Rivers." Frankfort, Kentucky: Kentucky Historical Society: 1806.
[257] Thwaites, Reuben Gold, ed. 1907. *Early Western Travels, 1748-1846*. Vol. 4. Cleveland, Ohio: The Arthur H. Clark Company: 257.

In one place on the river, Stuart spied a great many number of vultures and eagles excitedly perched on a heap of driftwood. The sight was so curious to the men that one of their crew took the canoe to investigate. He found a dead man lodged within the wood who looked to have died four to five days previously.

St. Francis River, Arkansas

Just north of where the St. Francis River emptied into the Mississippi River, in 1806, there was an excessive amount of sawyers in the water and consequently a large amount of boat wrecks. Stuart and his crew saw soldiers traveling on seven to eight barges and keelboats. They passed Stuart's boat flotilla on their way to Nachitochas or Red River.

It is at this point that the mosquitoes began highly bedeviling Stuart and it being spring, they were not yet as thick as they would become when the summer months arrived. "They, I believe, are almost twice as large as in Kentucky," he wrote. They used tobacco to smoke them away at night.

Yazoo River, Mississippi

Near the Yazoo River in Mississippi, the temperatures began to rise, and coupled with the mosquitoes, Stuart and his fellow boatmen were beginning to be affected so much that some of them had problems sleeping. Stuart also noted he was seeing a lot of Cypress, Willow, and Cottonwood trees. On May 20, 1806, he saw Spanish Moss for the first time and called it Spanish Beards because of the way they draped down eight to ten feet long. He thought it resembled hemp after it was broken. [258] The next day, they began to see alligators.

---

[258] Stuart, John G. "A Journal, Remarks or Observations in a Voyage Down the Kentucky, Ohio, Mississippi Rivers." Frankfort, Kentucky: Kentucky Historical Society: 1806.

Natchez, Mississippi

Between the Yazoo River and Natchez, Stuart and his crew began to see settlements along the river as they passed Palmyra, the Grand Gulf, Bayou Pierre, all of these above Natchez. For the first time in some time, the crew had consistent access to fresh produce, and Stuart noted that the Indian corn was seven to eight feet high. When they arrived at Natchez, there were almost seventy other boats there. Stuart was able to write several letters and put them in the mail. It is here that he parted employment with G. Halley and agreed to proceed on to New Orleans with one of the Baker men. They left that very night, May 27, 1806, and floated through the night until noon the next day where they reached a place called the Heights located twelve river miles above Red River, Louisiana. There was a little town there. Stuart saw more troops docked there and boats bringing additional troops that had come down from St. Louis.[259]

Baton Rouge, Louisiana

As they floated southward, they soon passed Baton Rouge and Stuart described it as a handsome place. Plantation homes began to line the banks. "We passed several houses where they were dancing in full glee," he said, "fine plantations & handsome houses surrounded with beautiful orange & fig trees." He concluded that they were "a constant succession of the most beautiful seats in America." [260]

New Orleans, Louisiana

On June 4, 1806, Stuart and his crew reached New Orleans. This was Stuart's first visit to the city and he was not disappointed. In the port, he saw over 150 ships and over 300 flat boats. He thought the buildings of New Orleans were very grand. "My greatest expectations are gratified," he said. The

---

[259] Stuart, John G. "A Journal, Remarks or Observations in a Voyage Down the Kentucky, Ohio, Mississippi Rivers." Frankfort, Kentucky: Kentucky Historical Society: 1806
[260] Ibid.

next morning, he walked to the Market House where he considered that almost anything one would want was sold. He saw Irish potatoes, sweet potatoes, watermelons, plums, and cucumbers. Beside the market, the city was in a bit of an uproar because a fire had erupted in a rope factory that spread to several buildings but was eventually extinguished. The people were a hodgepodge of nationalities and that day, Stuart heard that a Spaniard had stabbed an American. This entire hubbub occurred amidst intense heat and thick mosquitoes. Stuart visited a Roman Church and watched some of its ceremonies. He also visited an establishment called Madame Jack's which might have been an infamous brothel located at this time on the New Orleans riverfront.[261] After several days of rambling through the city to see its curiosities, Stuart was ready to return home.

Back in Frankfort, Kentucky
When William Bratton was not on a boat trip, he still lived in Franklin County, Kentucky. Although his sister and brother-in law, Joseph and Anne Bimson, were deceased, William's brother Robert Bratton still lived there. On July 30, 1808, on the tax list for Franklin County, Kentucky, William listed himself as over age twenty-one and he owned one horse. He was not taxed as a landowner at this time.[262]

It is possible that William met Fortescue Cuming when he visited Frankfort in Franklin County in 1808 in between his river journeys. After Cuming visited Lexington, he made his way to Frankfort along the Leesburgh road. Twelve miles northwest of Lexington, he stayed overnight at an inn run by an African-American man named Daly. The home, stables, icehouse, and land were rented to him by the widow of a

---

[261] Wilds, John, Charles L. Dufour and Walter G. Cowan. 1996. *Louisiana, Yesterday and Today: A Historical Guide to the State*. Baton Rouge, Louisiana: Louisiana State University Press: 144.
[262] Kentucky. Franklin County. William Bratton entry. 1808 Tax List, Allen County Public Library, Fort Wayne, Indiana. Microfilm, #0100, 1781-1797, 1799 – 1804.

Colonel Lee for forty pounds of Virginia currency per year which equaled about $137. According to Cuming. Daly grew corn, oats and hay to supply the stables, and cultivated a kitchen garden which contained "culinary sweet herbs besides useful vegetables."[263] Soon after Cuming arrived, a commotion occurred between Daly and an enslaved woman from a nearby plantation. He used a cow skin to physically drive her away from the inn of which she did not like of course, so all the while she insulted him quite vigorously. Daly took the most offense at being called "Indian-looking" and "a black son of a bitch," Cuming said. Later, while Cuming and his male companion enjoyed dinner, Daly exhibited a softer side by playing the violin for them. Cuming found Daly's coffee to be especially delightful but found that the strength of it combined with a bit of indigestion kept him from sleeping that night.[264]

Cuming resumed his journey towards Frankfort the next morning and arrived there after riding eleven more miles. It took him two hours to travel on horseback. He first stopped at the Golden Eagle tavern owned by Daniel Weisiger where they "sat down to a sumptuous breakfast with two green silk air fans kept in motion over our heads by a little negro girl with a string from the ceiling in a room seventy-two feet long."[265] While walking around Frankfort, Cuming went into the statehouse and climbed the cupola to count every existing house there; his count totaled 90 homes. Most of the houses were brick or a dusky cream marble with blue and red veins. These fancier houses were replacing the older wooden homes that were first built. Other buildings in Frankfort included the statehouse, the courthouse, a state penitentiary, a market-house, a jail, and the Old Governor's Mansion which was occupied by Kentucky governor Christopher Greenup. He was outside the mansion when Cuming, his landlord, and William Hunter, a bookseller and printer, passed by on their way to see

---

[263] Cuming, F. 1810. *Sketches of a Tour*. Pittsburg, Pennsylvania: Cramer, Spear & Kichbaum: 168-173.
[264] Ibid.
[265] Ibid.

the penitentiary. The governor courteously saluted the three gentlemen. He was a widower at this time since his wife, Mary Catherine Pope Greenup, died the previous year. (Future inhabitants of the Mansion have claimed to see her ghost in a mirror or a face of a clock.[266]) He lived there one more year until the next Kentucky governor took office, General Charles Scott.

At the penitentiary, Cuming, Hunter, toured the main building and various outbuildings which housed workshops and storehouses. The buildings covered an acre. Several cedar-log pipes directed water by gravity from Cove Spring to the penitentiary. The pipes were provided by the Frankfort City Waterworks and the penitentiary was their first project. The main building was enclosed by a sixteen-foot high stone wall topped with an additional three-foot brick entablature that was rounded on top, and also projected out a foot, to prevent any scaling attempts by its inmates.[267] Upon his visit, Cuming counted twenty-four "miserable wretches" who were confined for various crimes with correlating sentences, though none of the sentences exceeded ten years. Because it was Sunday, the inmates were allowed to rest instead of working at various tasks that they completed the other six days of the week. These tasks utilized their skills as coopers, nailers, stonecutters, carpenters, etc. Many of the men during Cuming's visit were playing fives, a version of hand tennis. A Captain Taylor supervised the penitentiary as the Superintendent. He was from Mercer County and had rescued the mismanagement of the penitentiary two years before. Cuming described him as a large and strong man, about fifty years of age, who was a "great mechanical genius." Taylor had two pistols strapped to his waist and kept a distinctive two-inch, dark-brown beard that reached from ear to ear. Cuming could not decide if Taylor was

---

[266] Clark, Thomas D. and Margaret Lane. *The People's House: Governor's Mansions of Kentucky*. Lexington, Kentucky: University Press of Kentucky, 2002: 5-11.

[267] Cuming, F. 1810. *Sketches of a Tour*. Pittsburg, Pennsylvania: Cramer, Spear & Kichbaum: 168-173.

merely eccentric or whether Taylor wanted his beard to lend him a fierce appearance. Cuming also found it peculiar that Taylor preferred to separate himself from his family in Mercer County to supervise felons in Frankfort.[268]

Again, at this time, William and Robert Bratton were making visits to Warren County from Frankfort. During the winter in 1808, the Barren River in Warren County rose very high, impacting William Bratton's family there. William's brother Adam was familiar with the Barren River and he boarded a flatboat loaded with a hogshead of tobacco from a place above a footbridge. The water was so high that the bank he boarded from was about forty feet above the normal level of water. Adam Bratton was about age twenty-three when this occurred.[269] Years later, he showed a nephew where this bridge was located.

On May 31, 1809, William Bratton was listed on the tax list for Franklin County. He listed himself as over age twenty-one and he did not own land or a horse at this time.[270] However, he did think about owning land just not in Franklin County. He applied for a survey and was the grantee for 200 acres along the Barren River in Warren County.[271] Though Robert still lived in Franklin County, he was not listed on the tax list.

In 1810, William was involved in a curious court case in Warren County with his father George Bratton and George's friend Henry Grider. William sued them because they borrowed $150 from him on December 8, 1808 and they still had not paid him back by 1810. He submitted an IOU from them to the Warren County court. Philip Stucker was the

---

[268] Cuming, F. 1810. *Sketches of a Tour*. Pittsburg, Pennsylvania: Cramer, Spear & Kichbaum: 168-173.
[269] Younglove, John E. "A Diary of Warren County, 1808-1889." http://kentuckyexplorer.com/nonmembers/01-04013.html (now defunct).
[270] Kentucky. Franklin County. William Bratton entry. 1809 Tax List, Allen County Public Library, Fort Wayne, Indiana. Microfilm, #0100, 1781-1797, 1799 – 1804.
[271] Kentucky. Warren County. Book 11: 95. William Bratton land grant. *Kentucky Land Grants*, Vol. 1: 297.

witness to the borrowing of money in 1808.[272] At this time, William's brother Robert also sued them. On the same day that they borrowed from William, they also borrowed $50 from Robert. Philip Stucker was also the witness to this transaction, and he signed his name to the IOU that George Bratton and Henry Grider gave Robert Bratton.[273] Additionally, William's brother Adam sued Henry Grider for an unpaid debt of $24.50 that Grider borrowed from Adam on January 10, 1810. Grider had not repaid him by July despite several attempts by Adam to recoup the debt. As proof that Henry Grider owed him the money, Adam submitted the IOU to the court that Grider had issued him. Fellow Warren County resident Simon M. Hubbard had witnessed the borrowing of the money that January day.[274] Each time that the suits were brought to court, a warrant was issued to the Warren County sheriff to bring the men into court to plead their case. The cases remained unresolved in 1810.

At tax time, on June 10, 1810, Robert Bratton was listed in Franklin County. He listed himself as over the age of twenty-one and he owned one horse. He did not own land at this time.[275] William is not found on the 1810 Federal Census nor on the tax list for Franklin County. He was probably boating abroad the rivers delivering cargo. William and Robert Bratton were two residents among a population in Franklin County in 1810 of 1099 people that included 407 enslaved people.[276]

William was in Franklin County on November 10, 1810

---

[272] Kentucky. Warren County. William Bratton vs. George Bratton and Henry Grider. Common Law/Ordinary Cases, 1810, Box 11, Case #1350; Warren County Circuit Court. Kentucky Department of Library and Archives.

[273] Ibid: Case #1351; Warren County Circuit

[274] Kentucky. Warren County. Adam Bratton vs. Henry Grider. Common Law/Ordinary Cases, 1810, Box 11. Warren County Circuit Court. Kentucky Dept. of Library and Archives.

[275] Kentucky. Franklin County. Robert Bratton entry. 1810 Tax List, Allen County Public Library, Fort Wayne, Indiana. Microfilm, #0100, 1781-1797, 1799 – 1804.

[276] Kramer, Carl. 1986. *Capital on the Kentucky: A Two-Hundred Year History of Frankfort and Franklin County.* Frankfort, Kentucky: Historic Frankfort.

when he wrote a letter to Martin Grider of Warren County regarding a land transaction in Warren County.[277] He wrote, "Sir, This is to inform you that I have paid the full amount of the 200 acres of land under the 20 dollar act and have returned the plat and certificate into the register's office. And the amount of what's paid on the other land is 12 dollars and 50 cents and I leave 7 dollars and 50 cents with Captain John Arnold for you which will be my part. I wish you to return the plat and certificate into the register's office and in six months after we can get a patent and when that is done, I can make you a deed for your part of the land."[278] He signed it at the bottom. This deed was eventually recorded in Warren County on January 25, 1819 in which William conveyed to Grider 200 acres of land.[279] William's letter to Martin Grider was delivered by Captain John Arnold, William's neighbor in the Hammond Creek area of Franklin County (as described in Chapter 3.) Arnold's brother Stephen had moved to Warren County so it is possible that Arnold was traveling to Warren County anyway to visit him and took the letter with him as a favor to William. (*Author's Note - This letter is the earliest document found in William Bratton's writing. The fact that he was literate was proved when he was a viable candidate to take Sargent's Floyd's position on the Lewis & Clark expedition. Only literate men were considered because whoever took the position was responsible for keeping a journal. Bratton lost the vote to Patrick Gass and no journal of William Bratton's kept during the expedition is known to exist but many documents from later in his life that contain his handwriting did survive.*)

As time rolled along into 1811, William continued to work in the keelboat business. In May 1811, he floated the wares of James Weir, a cotton and hemp merchant, from Lexington to

---

[277] William Bratton archive. William Bratton to Martin Grider letter, 10 November 1810. The Marian Morrison Local History Collection. Crawfordsville District Public Library.
[278] Ibid.
[279] Kentucky. Warren County. John Davis to John Sturgeon deed, 15 September 1847. Kentucky Department of Library and Archives.

New Orleans. He might have hurried back to Frankfort so that he could attend an important family wedding. On July 3, 1811, his brother Robert married Nancy McCoskey. She was the daughter of John McCoskey and Nancy Little.[280] They owned 200 acres near Benson Creek that was near the Hammond Creek neighborhood.[281] Like those who lived in the Hammond Creek neighborhood, their land was considered part of Mercer County until it was appropriated into Franklin County. Within days of the marriage, Robert was listed on the Franklin County tax list. He listed himself as over age twenty-one, and he owned two horses. He did not own any land at this time.[282] It is impossible to know how long Robert had been seeing Nancy McCoskey before they married but during their courtship, the entire McCoskey clan and their Little cousins were discussing a move to Indiana Territory. If the discussion had been taking place for some time, it could be why William had begun the process of buying land in Warren County, Kentucky. William was not listed on the 1811 tax list for Franklin County.

As winter approached, a catastrophe occurred on December 16, 1811 in the form of an earthquake centered near New Madrid, Missouri on the Mississippi River. William Bratton was on the river at that time according to his grandson James T. Fields. "In regard to Grandfather Bratton being near New Madrid at the time of the earthquake, he was with a boating expedition as an employee and never lived there.[283] It is unclear how close William was to New Madrid at the time of the earthquake but if he ever stayed in New Madrid for an extended time before or after the earthquake, it might have

---

[280] *Franklin County, Kentucky Marriages, 1792-1850*, United States: Researchers: 6.

[281] Kentucky. Franklin County. John McCoskey entry. 1811 Tax List, Allen County Public Library, Fort Wayne, Indiana. Microfilm, #0100, 1781-1797, 1799 – 1804.

[282] Kentucky. Franklin County. Robert Bratton entry. 1811 Tax List, Allen County Public Library, Fort Wayne, Indiana. Microfilm, #0100, 1781-1797, 1799 – 1804.

[283] James T. Fields to Eva Dye Letter. 18 November 1901. Eva Emery Dye Collection. Oregon Historical Society. Portland, Oregon.

been to visit fellow expedition member John Ordway who lived there.

One of the people feeling the first tremors of the New Madrid earthquake was Nicholas Roosevelt who was once again traveling by boat from Pittsburg to New Orleans. This time it was in a brand new steamboat, the New Orleans, and it was her maiden voyage. They were going from Pittsburg to New Orleans, and the boat was launched on October 20, 1811. By December 16, 1811, the boat was in the area of New Madrid. When the earthquake began, the boat and one of its cables shook so hard, the crew experienced motion sickness. The tremors or shocks continued all night. The Mississippi River flooded so badly it was difficult to follow the channel. The earthquake also changed the landscape causing whole river islands to disappear. When two crewmembers from Roosevelt's boat went on shore to cut wood to power the boat the next day, distraught settlers asked to come aboard to make their escape, but there was no room for them on the boat. Roosevelt had to ignore "the cries of the terrified inhabitants of the doomed town."[284] Many of them were lucky to survive with their lives. Furthermore, if they were able to salvage any belongings, they were lucky. The flooding of the river from the earthquake swept many homes and outbuildings away. In fact, the strength of the earthquake was so strong, the water switched directions and flowed upstream for a little while. South of New Madrid, one "part of the river burst and shook up hundreds of great trees from the bottom, and what is most singular, they are all turned roots upwards and standing upstream in the best channel and swiftest water, and nothing but the greatest exertions of the boatmen can save them from destruction in passing those places" said boatman James Smith in a letter to the editors of the Ohio and Mississippi Navigator."[285]

---

[284] Petersen, William J. 1995. *Steamboating on the Upper Mississippi*. New York, New York: Dover Publications, Incorporated: 64.
[285] Pittsburgh Gazette. "Mississippi Trader."13 March 1812: 3.

In most cases, the New Madrid earthquake was devastating but it inadvertently brought justice for one horrific act by Isham and Lilburne Lewis, the nephews of President Thomas Jefferson. The Lewis brothers settled near Warren County around the Green River in Kentucky in 1806. By December 1811, they had established a plantation with help from their enslaved people. It was on a December day, probably December 15, 1811, when everyone was going about their business in the plantation house when an enslaved man named George broke a pitcher. Lilburne and Isham assembled their other enslaved people in the kitchen cabin, and made them watch as the two brothers bound George on the floor. One of them then picked up an axe and decapitated him as a drastic, cruel lesson to the others. As Lilburne lectured his enslaved people on obedience, the brothers further dismembered George's body and threw him in the fireplace to burn. Shortly after 2 a.m. that night, the New Madrid earthquake occurred which caused the kitchen chimney to collapse. When the enslaved people rebuilt the chimney, they buried the pieces of George's body that were still burning but they overlooked the decapitated head. It was found by the neighbor's dog and eventually the neighbor himself. This grisly discovery was brought to the attention of a local citizen, John Gray, who was trying to get a state law passed that allowed the arrest of any citizen that treated their enslaved people with inhumanity and cruelty. The law would also forbid torture and abuse. The law had been defeated two months previously in the Kentucky court, but Gray was determined to have it reintroduced and decided to use the cruel treatment of George by the Lewis brothers as the perfect example of why such a law was needed. When Lilburne Lewis learned of Gray's intentions to indict them, he committed suicide while Isham fled.[286] It is unknown if Isham was ever prosecuted.

William and Robert Bratton traveled from Franklin County to attend the Warren County court on February 10, 1812

---

[286] Friend, Craig Thompson. 2010. *Kentucke's Frontiers*. Bloomington, Indiana: Indiana University Press: 221-222.

because they had still not been paid the money due them from their father George and Henry Grider.[287] Warrants by the Warren County courts were issued once again for George and Grider to appear but the outcome of the cases is unknown.[288]

In Franklin County, Kentucky, on April 4, 1812, William was listed on the 1812 tax list. He listed himself as over age twenty-one and he owned one horse. At this time, he was age thirty-four. He was also taxed for 200 acres in Warren County that was entered and surveyed for him by Captain John Arnold but patented by himself.[289] Robert Bratton was also listed on the 1812 tax list for Franklin County. Robert listed himself as over age twenty-one and he still owned two horses. At this time, he was age thirty-eight. He did not own any land.[290] Several months later, on August 18, 1812 he and Nancy had their first child, a boy named John after Nancy's father.[291] Their household was joyful with the new birth. Elsewhere, in households across the nation, unrest was brewing.

---

[287] William Bratton vs. George Bratton and Henry Grider. Common Law/Ordinary Cases, 1812, Box 13, Case #1573; Warren County Circuit Court. Kentucky Dept. of Library and Archives.
[288] Robert Bratton vs. George Bratton and Henry Grider. Common Law/Ordinary Cases, 1812, Box 13, Case #1574; Warren County Circuit Court. Kentucky Dept. of Library and Archives.
[289] Kentucky. Franklin County. William Bratton entry. 1812 Tax List, Allen County Public Library, Fort Wayne, Indiana. Microfilm, #0100, 1781-1797, 1799 – 1804.
[290] Ibid: Robert Bratton entry.
[291] Bratton Cemetery (Round Rock, Travis County, Texas.) John Bratton grave marker.

CHAPTER SIX
The War of 1812

While William earned his living on the river, turmoil and bloodshed were consistently erupting over land in Ohio and in both the Indiana and Michigan Territories. Emerging from a childhood of bloody warfare, the great Shawnee Chief Tecumseh and his men fiercely battled white settlers and the American militia that were trying to retain Shawnee tribal lands. Since 1805, in a strategically unprecedented campaign, Tecumseh worked to unite all receptive Native American tribes across the northern to southern areas of the United States into a united Indian Confederacy.[292] Tecumseh was no doubt frustrated that his alliance was slow in forming and did not fully exhibit the potential force it could be since some tribes refused to join. It was only after Prophetstown, his home and base of operations in Indiana Territory, was wholly destroyed by General William Henry Harrison and his soldiers in 1811 that Tecumseh finally conceded to Great Britain's pressure of formally aligning with them against the United States. He and his British allies contributed to the busy northwest theatre of the War of 1812.

The territorial tension in the Northwest was not the only issue that prompted war, but was only one of several issues the United States had with Great Britain. According to Martin D. Hardin who served Kentucky in the following capacities - as a Major First Battalion, an U.S. senator, as Secretary of State for two terms, and as a Kentucky House Representative - those reasons were "the uncertainties of our markets owing to the crooked and insidious policy of the British Cabinet; the

---

[292] Eckert, Allan W. 1992. *A Sorrow in our Heart: the Life of Tecumseh*. New York, New York: Bantam Books.

impressment of our seamen; the Henry plot (the expensive purchase by President Madison of papers of questionable value from spy John Henry); and the Native American murders daily committed on our defenseless frontiers."[293] After a formal declaration of war on June 18, 1812, President James Madison called for 100,000 militia troops from several states. About 5500 Kentuckians volunteered, and William Bratton was one of them.[294] He was one of eighty-six men from Franklin County to volunteer and form a company under Captain Paschal Hickman. Around August 12, 1812, when William left his home to rendezvous with fellow soldiers at Georgetown, Kentucky, he would have had his own flintlock gun and powder horn, and any other tools or weaponry of his choice like a hatchet or even a tomahawk. He might have brought an extra set of clothes. He would have worn a "hunting shirt made of linsey, with a slight fringe border, color either blue, such as is obtained from indigo, a pale yellow made from hickory bark, or a dingy brown obtained from the black walnut."[295] His pants would have been "Kentucky jeans, and he would have worn shoes or moccasins. Around his waist was a leather belt. On one side of the belt there was a leather pocket fastened by leaden tacks, instead of thread, and in this was placed the indispensable tomahawk. Across his shoulder was the strap that held up his powder horn, in which the strap was another leather case containing his formidable butcher knife, and another to hold his bullets. A knapsack of home manufacture contained his clothing, and the outside of it was garnished with a glittering tin cup."[296] He might have also carried his compass. Besides providing his own equipment, William was also responsible for providing his own traveling expenses to the mustering-in

---

[293] Clift, G. Glenn. 1961. *Remember the Raisin!: Kentucky and Kentuckians in The Battles and Massacre at Frenchtown, Michigan Territory, in the War of 1812*. Frankfort, Kentucky: Kentucky Historical Society: 15.

[294] Wilson, Samuel M. "Kentucky's Part in the War of 1812." *Register of Kentucky State Historical Society*, 1911. Vol. 9, No. 27: 2.

[295] Brown, Orlando. "The Governors of Kentucky." *Register of the Kentucky Historical Society*. 1951: 203.

[296] Ibid.

event. He probably traveled with his company from Frankfort to the rendezvous point of Georgetown instead of traveling on his own and meeting company members there.[297] William might have asked his brother Robert Bratton to take care of his horse while he was in service before he and his fellow company members walked to Georgetown as a unit. (No known War of 1812 service records for Robert exist although there was a Robert Bratton that served in the Indiana militia and fought at the Battle of Tippecanoe in November 1811. Time-wise, there is no other event involving Robert that directly conflicts with the possibility that it could have been him.) Although William's captain, Captain Paschal Hickman, did not furnish him with a gun during his period of service, Hickman did supply between five to eight other soldiers in Company B with rifles that cost about $40 each.[298] Before leaving Frankfort, the company made a brief visit to the home of Governor Charles Scott. The men lined up between the front steps and fence of the Governor's house and while they listened to an emotional speech by Governor Scott on bravery, two of his servants each carried a bucket and went from man to man offering whiskey and water.[299]

On August 15, 1812, William Bratton formally enlisted into Company B of the 1st Rifle Regiment of the Kentucky Volunteers militia as a private.[300] Again, the captain of his company was Paschal Hickman, Peter Dudley served as Lieutenant and Peter G. Voorhies as Ensign. Under them were four sergeants and four corporals. The commander over all

---

[297] Clift, G. Glenn. 1961. *Remember the Raisin!: Kentucky and Kentuckians in the Battles and Massacre at Frenchtown, Michigan Territory, in the War of 1812*. Frankfort, Kentucky: Kentucky Historical Society: 19.

[298] Reports of Committees of the House of Representatives. Committee on Military Affairs. Richard M. Johnson report.15 February 1833.

[299] Brown, Orlando. "The Governors of Kentucky." *Register of the Kentucky H Historical Society*. 1951: 203.

[300] Compiled service record, William Bratton, Pvt., Company B, 1st Rifle Regiment of Kentucky Volunteers, Carded Records, Volunteer Organizations. National Archive Catalog number, record group number, National Archives, Washington D.C.

companies of the 1st Rifle Regiment was Lieutenant Colonel John Allen and above Allen was General James Winchester though most of the men wanted William Henry Harrison to be their general. Because William had previously served in a military operation with honor as deemed by Meriwether Lewis, it is unclear why he mustered in as a private and not of a soldier of higher rank. Nevertheless, his previous experience undoubtedly helped him endure the upcoming hardships the men faced in fulfilling their upcoming orders to march northward to retake Detroit from the British. Some of the soldiers probably knew what this entailed though some probably did not. To reach Detroit, the Kentuckians had to cut their own road through swamps and other ground, had to transport supplies, war weapons and equipment along those rough roads, and had to protect themselves and those supplies from hostile Native Americans.[301]

On August 19, 1812, the men began their journey. They traveled eighty miles, mostly in the rain, on the Dry Ridge Road to Newport, Kentucky where they crossed the Ohio River.[302] The troops did not march as one unit from Georgetown but as separate regiments so they could move faster.[303] At Newport, they waited on the delivery of the supplies they would need for the march before crossing the river to Cincinnati, then north to Piqua towards Fort Wayne. The men were in high spirits because General William Henry Harrison was appointed command of the North Western Army and would be joining them at some point on their march. Even though most of these men as farmers or city men were new to military life and this was their first campaign, because of his military accomplishments, Harrison was their hero. General William Henry Harrison had a high opinion of Kentuckians as well. He admired their fiery bravado yet was aware they needed to be

---

[301] Clift, G. Glenn. 1961. *Remember the Raisin!: Kentucky and Kentuckians in the Battles and Massacre at Frenchtown, Michigan Territory, in the War of 1812*. Frankfort, Kentucky: Kentucky Historical Society: 21.
[302] Ibid: 22.
[303] Ibid.

shaped to make the best weapon, not unlike forging steel into a sword. "The troops which I have with me (this was the 17th United States Infantry) and those which are coming on from Kentucky are perhaps the best materials for forming an army that the world has produced," he said, "but no equal number of men were ever collected who know so little of military discipline."[304]

While the troops were marching towards Piqua from Dayton on September 1, 1812, Harrison requested that John Allen's Rifle Regiment disengage from the rest of the troops and proceed to Fort Wayne immediately. Again, Hickman's company which included William Bratton was under John Allen. At Piqua, they received reinforcements of three more companies, however, on their way to Fort Wayne, they received another order from Harrison to change their destination to St. Mary's because the British force that was making its way to Fort Wayne likely outnumbered them. St. Mary's was a village on the St. Mary's river previously known as Girty's Town, the home and location of a trading post that belonged to James Girty, the brother of Simon Girty, both long-time hostile enemies of the United States.[305] As part of the orders, the rest of the army would join them at St. Mary's.[306] Harrison put his men on half-rations for the march from Piqua to St. Mary's, a distance of thirty miles. It was hot and many of the men drank from water standing in wagon ruts if they were lucky enough to find some. They were much relieved to reach St. Mary's, and they were joined there with 300 Ohio militiamen and assembled into a battle formation. In this manner, they resumed their march to Fort Wayne.

---

[304] William H. Harrison to William Eustis. 28 August 1812. William Henry Harrison Papers, Microfilm 6, August 28, 1812 – December 19, 1812. William Henry Harrison Multi-institution Microfilm Project, Indiana Historical Society.

[305] McMurray, William J., ed. 1923. *History of Auglaize County, Ohio*. Vol. 1. Indianapolis, Indiana: Historical Publishing Company: 33-34.

[306] Clift, G. Glenn. 1961. *Remember the Raisin!: Kentucky and Kentuckians in the Battles and Massacre at Frenchtown, Michigan Territory, in the War of 1812*. Frankfort, Kentucky: Kentucky Historical Society: 22-23.

When the troops reached Fort Wayne, the smell was overwhelming. Hostile Native Americans, the Pottawatomies, who sided with the British, were killing people, burning houses and livestock yet they could not take the fort. Despite these atrocities of war, for the Kentuckians who had not been this far north, they found Fort Wayne impressive. "Fort Wayne is one the most elegant situations I ever saw and must be a most important place to the United States. Three weeks ago the neighborhood around the fort would have exhibited a pleasing prospect...a number of well cultivated farms, with neat houses, in view of the fort would have excited emotions of pleasure," said Elias Darnall who mustered in as a private into Captain Samuel Williams' company from Montgomery County, Kentucky.[307] "I suppose there were 400 acres of land in cultivation. All of the houses were reduced to ashes, together with a large quantity of small grain and hay by the savages. They also destroyed all the stock of every kind about these farms which was very considerable."[308] Harrison and his men reinforced the fort and dispersed the threat of nearby Pottawatamies. They found the fort well-fortified with 100 men who had four cannons, plenty of ammunition and food, and a well of water. Nonetheless, having stood their ground against the Pottawatomies that had surrounded the fort for two weeks, they were very glad to see Harrison's troops arrive. To the consternation of the troops, once Fort Wayne was secured, Harrison was summoned elsewhere, and his command was given to General James Winchester, which caused much rebellion. "The conduct of General Harrison at Tippecanoe, and familiarity with the troops while on their march to this place, had gained him a peculiar attachment. General Winchester being a stranger, and having the

---

[307] Compiled service record, Elias Darnall, Pvt. Darnall, Elias. War of 1812 Pension Records. Ancestry.com.

[308] Darnall, Elias. "A Journal Containing An Accurate and Interesting Account of the Hardships, Sufferings, Battles, Defeat, and Captivity of Those Heroic Kentucky Volunteers and Regulars Commanded by General Winchester In the Years 1812-1813." Paris, Kentucky: 1813.

appearance of a supercilious officer, he was generally disliked," Darnall said.[309]

The next task for General Winchester's troops was to proceed to Fort Defiance, a rundown fort roughly fifty miles northeast of Fort Wayne that sat where the Maumee and Auglaize Rivers converged. On Sept. 22, 1812, General Winchester left Fort Wayne with about 2000 men. Each soldier carried enough provisions for six days. They proceeded cautiously because intelligence revealed that the British army was headed to Fort Wayne to overtake it and they were adding small parties of Native Americans to their force along the way.[310] The British army was larger than their own force. It contained close to 200 British soldiers, and 1000 Native Americans. They also had four cannons.[311] The British soldiers were marching up the south side of the Maumee River. Their bags and artillery waited for them at Fort Defiance after being brought by boat and unloaded there. The British officers did not anticipate any problems taking Fort Wayne until they interrogated a certain prisoner, Sergeant McCoy. At the time of this interrogation, they were located about twelve miles above Fort Defiance. Sergeant McCoy told them General Winchester and his troops marched their way but he told them that Winchester had four times more men than he actually did. McCoy also said that another army was making their way down the Auglaize River to join Winchester. The British officers believed McCoy and halted any forward movement towards Fort Wayne. Also, they planned to set up a battle line around Fort Defiance. However, the next day, Sept. 28, 1812, no battle could be planned because three-fourths of their Native American allies left during the night because of the news about Winchester's troops. The British has choice but to

---

[309] Darnall, Elias. "A Journal Containing An Accurate and Interesting Account of the Hardships, Sufferings, Battles, Defeat, and Captivity of Those Heroic Kentucky Volunteers and Regulars Commanded by General Winchester In the Years 1812-1813." Paris, Kentucky: 1813.
[310] Lossing, Benson John. 1896. *The Pictorial Field-book of the War of 1812.* New York, New York: Harper & Brothers: 329.
[311] Ibid.

retreat. They moved twenty miles back up the Maumee River.[312]

During the whole business of McCoy's interrogation by the British, General Winchester sent out his own spies, Captains Hickman and Riddle. If this meant that it was not just the two of them, but with some of the men in their company, William Bratton might have accompanied Hickman to aid in gathering information. However, though their subterfuge occurred on September 26, 1812, they never saw the British. By some way, on October 1, 1812, General Winchester did know that the enemy had been in the area but had retreated. At this time, General Harrison issued new orders and maneuvered General Winchester and his troops to his left wing so they could serve as a corps of observation at Fort Defiance.[313] General Winchester and his troops set up camp near the old fort until they received word to rebuild it. Then per the orders, they were to make their way to the Rapids of the Maumee where Harrison wanted the men to build forts to lull the British into thinking they were setting up there for the winter when in fact, General Harrison still had Detroit in his sight.[314]

Within a couple of weeks, the first three-month term for the Kentuckians expired. It must have been at Fort Defiance or somewhere between there and the Rapids that William Bratton was mustered out on October 14, 1812. According to the company pay roll, he was paid $13.32 for this three-month service.[315] The next day, on October 15, 1812, William re-enlisted in Captain Hickman's Company B with many of the same men in the company but maintaining their health was a challenge. Because General Winchester's troops were the most advanced into the wilderness, they were in the most remote position and furthest from provisions. Within a couple of

---

[312] Lossing, Benson John. 1896. *The Pictorial Field-book of the War of 1812*. New York, New York: Harper & Brothers: 348
[313] Ibid.
[314] Ibid: 331.
[315] William Bratton military record. War of 1812 Military Service Records. National Archives Records Administration. Washington D.C.

weeks of re-enlisting, camp conditions worsened and three to four soldiers died of typhus fever every day and 300 soldiers were sick at any given time. William Bratton's service term was up on January 1, 1813 but he again re-enlisted into Captain Hickman's Company.[316] He and the other soldiers also had to contend with dropping temperatures. When General Winchester's troops advanced towards the Rapids, the temperatures fluctuated so much that traveling with supplies was almost impossible. The surrounding country was swampy and mud froze and thawed continuously which created a quagmire that entrapped horse and wagon alike. By January 10, 1813, they moved as far as they could up the Rapids and built small huts.[317]

It was at the Rapids that General Winchester heard about the trouble that villagers in nearby Frenchtown were receiving from hostile Native Americans. Several of the villagers themselves came to General Winchester and begged for help saying that the British and their Native American allies were threatening them and their village with destruction by fire. Winchester sent a group of soldiers under the command of Colonel William Lewis ahead of their main body to aid Frenchtown. William Bratton and the rest of Hickman's unit were part of this large rescue squad that traveled to Frenchtown ahead of the rest of the army. As they made their way there, they passed citizens of Frenchtown that fled towards the American army, and they also saw Native American scouts who were allied with the British. These scouts reported back to British militia officers who with their troops and Native American allies occupied the village.[318]

---

[316] William Bratton military record. War of 1812 Military Service Records. National Archives Records Administration. Washington D.C.

[317] Lossing, Benson John. 1896. *The Pictorial Field-book of the War of 1812*. New York, New York: Harper & Brothers: 348.

[318] Naveaux, Ralph. 2003. *Invaded on all Sides: the Story of Michigan's Greatest Battlefield Scene of the Engagements of Frenchtown and the River Raisin War of 1812*. Marceline, Missouri: Walsworth Publishing Company: 108.

When the first rescue squad of American troops advanced to within three miles of Frenchtown, they moved into battle formation. They divided into three wings, left, right, and center, and an advance guard. It was in this advance guard that William Bratton served with his fellow soldiers in Hickman's company and also with soldiers from four other Kentucky companies. Elias Darnall and the rest of his fellow soldiers in Captain Williams' company were in the left wing. Before the men moved out, they received their orders. It was three o'clock in the afternoon, and as they listened, the men stood in thick snow and were probably somewhat fatigued having walked eighteen miles to get where they stood. To inspire the men, Colonel Lewis identified the British as their ancient enemy, and that on this day, (January 18, 1813), they would inflict punishment as not just Americans, but also as Kentuckians.[319] Then, in their battle formations, they advanced towards Frenchtown. When they were a quarter of a mile away, they were shot at from a howitzer cannon. The first lobby of show went well over the heads of the men by twenty feet. Another lobby also missed the men although it landed nearer, yet the men were still scornful. Some of the men vocalized their disdain as crowing, others barked, while others shouted insults. The advance guard led by Captain Bland W. Ballard, and with William Bratton one of its number, crossed the ice of the River Raisin first. They faced a combination of British militia and hostile Native Americans that numbered about 500 men. All of the men in Captain Hickman's company walked except Hickman himself who had injured his feet or legs somehow on the march and could not walk very well. Many times, the combined weight of him and his horse completely broke the ice underneath him, and each time his men helped him back into the saddle. As the advance guard reached the nearest bank to the village, Captain Hickman was a conspicuous target and was the only man shot as they moved

---

[319] Clift, G. Glenn. 1961. *Remember the Raisin!: Kentucky and Kentuckians in the Battles and Massacre at Frenchtown, Michigan Territory, in the War of 1812.* Frankfort, Kentucky: Kentucky Historical Society: 52.

up the bank. The shot hit him in the leg, and broke the bone.[320] The advance guard quickly made their way into the village despite bullets speeding their way. Several Frenchtown residents joined them, and they ousted their enemy into a retreat. However, the fighting was not over as the enemy made a stand with their cannon against Captain Allen and 100 men. The right wing also fought intensely to keep the enemy moving backwards toward a distant wood. Hickman's company missed him pretty much from the beginning of the fighting. After he was ensconced in a nearby house in Frenchtown so that a doctor could look at him, Lieutenant Francis Chinn commanded the company, but he too was wounded in the action. Undaunted, the men who as Kentuckians had much experience fighting Native Americans, relied upon learned tactics and fought on their own, each one for himself. The men fought into the night. When all reported back to Frenchtown, and the roll was taken, it was found that twelve men had died, and fifty-five were wounded.[321] The enemy had not fared as well. They had thirty dead and fifty wounded, and three of their men were taken as prisoners. Additionally, the Americans confiscated a large number of British supplies – 2000 pounds of beef, wheat, and thirty barrels of flour. Cooked food was available too because the British had planned to have a ball that night celebrating the birth of their Queen Charlotte. Elias Darnall recounted that the men had access to "apples, cider, sugar, butter, and whiskey."[322] He also described Frenchtown as "situated on the north side of this river, not more than three miles from the place it empties into Lake Erie. There is a row of dwelling houses, about twenty in number, principally frame, near the bank, surrounded with a fence made in the form of

---

[320] Clift, G. Glenn. 1961. *Remember the Raisin!: Kentucky and Kentuckians in the Battles and Massacre at Frenchtown, Michigan Territory, in the War of 1812*. Frankfort, Kentucky: Kentucky Historical Society: 53.

[321] Ibid: 52.

[322] Darnall, Elias. A Journal Containing An Accurate and Interesting Account of the Hardships, Sufferings, Battles, Defeat, and Captivity of Those Heroic Kentucky Volunteers and Regulars Commanded by General Winchester In the Years 1812-1813. Paris, Ky. 1813: 44.

picketing, with split timber, from four to five feet high. This was not designed as a fortification but to secure their yards and gardens."[323]

General Winchester and the rest of his troops of 250 men reached Frenchtown two days later on January 20, 1813. Winchester had sent General Harrison a report of their victory on January 18, 1813 but General Harrison was still working intensely to send Winchester further reinforcements. He knew that the British stationed at Fort Malden were only eighteen miles away, and could march their soldiers there in four to five hours. Meanwhile, among the 250 men newly arrived to Frenchtown, those commanded by Colonel Wells set up camp in an open field about two hundred yards to the right of the original rescue squad. The rescue squad had set up camp directly north of the village within the garden pickets that Darnall had described. Wells' men were behind no pickets. Their camp "was laid out in orderly fashion, with three companies in line stretching north from the river, and the 4th company at right angles to those three and trailing further down the river."[324] The men lined their tents with straw appropriated from a Frenchtown resident's barn. The ground surrounding the camp was bare up to a mile in each direction except for some fencing and several buildings. Despite being mostly exposed, Wells' men felt that there were enough American troops in Frenchtown to discourage the British from attacking and retaking Frenchtown but they were wrong.

On January 21, 1813, a reinforcement of 550 American soldiers were on their way to Frenchtown sent by General Harrison, but they were still many miles away. General Harrison's courier Captain Nathanial Hart who could move at a

---

[323] Darnall, Elias. *A Journal Containing An Accurate and Interesting Account of the Hardships, Sufferings, Battles, Defeat, and Captivity of Those Heroic Kentucky Volunteers and Regulars Commanded by General Winchester In the Years 1812-1813.* Paris, Ky. 1813: 44.

[324] Naveaux, Ralph. 2003. *Invaded on all Sides: the Story of Michigan's Greatest Battlefield Scene of the Engagements of Frenchtown and the River Raisin War of 1812.* Marceline, Missouri: Walsworth Publishing Company: 133.

swifter pace arrived to obtain General Winchester's opinion and plans in regards to a fast-arising and alarming situation. Word arrived via Frenchmen living further north of Frenchtown, that the British had immobilized and were on their way to attack. Instead of Captain Hart leaving Frenchtown to inform General Harrison of the situation himself, he hurriedly wrote a note and Colonel Wells took it to Harrison. Why Wells was selected as a courier has been questioned by many. He was too valuable an officer to send as a courier when his battle expertise was needed as an officer. One account is that he kept asking throughout the day if he could leave Frenchtown to go back to their previous camp for his baggage to which General Winchester replied "The spies bring intelligence that the enemy have reached Stony Creek, five miles from here. If you are disposed to leave your command in the immediate vicinity of the enemy, when a battle is certain, you can go."[325] Another account depicts Wells' actions as more heroic, that Wells asked Winchester to distribute more cartridges to their soldiers and that encampment preparations begin immediately against the attack. General Winchester who was being housed in a Frenchtown home three-quarters of a mile from where the rest of the soldiers were encamped, supposedly objected that an attack would not occur that quickly so Wells' left camp swiftly for the Rapids for help.[326] It is unknown exactly why Winchester accepted to be housed in the Navarre residence which was so far away from where his soldiers were encamped. Maybe it was because the buildings and homes within the village were already full of wounded soldiers. Maybe he was relieved to rest in a more genteel atmosphere to which he had not been able to do in several months.

In the account by Darnall, the officers inspected the ground for where the most ideal location to erect a camp and

---

[325] Clift, G. Glenn. 1961. *Remember the Raisin!: Kentucky and Kentuckians in the Battles and Massacre at Frenchtown, Michigan Territory, in the War of 1812*. Frankfort, Kentucky: Kentucky Historical Society: 59.
[326] Ibid: 60.

breastworks. The area was inspected not only for the newly arrived 250-men reinforcement but also for all the men since the garden pickets were not a sufficient defense either. However, since the men had arrived late in the afternoon on January 20, 1813, "it was too late to remove and erect fortifications that evening," Darnall said. "Further, as they resolved to remove early next day, it was not thought worth while, though materials were at hand to fortify the right wing, which therefore encamped in the open field."[327] Regardless of the exact, short timeframe, this lack of fortifications did not go unnoticed by Frenchtown resident Jocko Lasselle. He, at age forty-seven, had torn loyalties between the Americans, the British, and the Native Americans. He was the son of a fur trader and a Native American mother. The Michigan territory had been home to the French and the Native Americans for so long, and they felt the territory was like a bone fought for between two dogs. His loyalty to the United States was weakly pitted against his loyalty to his Native American family. Ultimately, he chose to betray the Americans. He dictated a letter to British General Proctor informing him of the distance between the two camps of American soldiers, and that space was the key to winning an attack. His daughter Nannette wrote the letter, and his brother-in-law took the letter to meet with Proctor who was headed their way.[328]

    The evening of January 21, 1813 and into the next morning was a perfect storm of disaster for the American troops. Despite Colonel Lewis asking Colonel Wells' to squeeze his men in with his, Wells refused before he left camp. The evening was bitterly cold and too cold for night guards and pickets. General Winchester was still under the mistaken belief that

---

[327] Darnall, Elias. "A Journal Containing An Accurate and Interesting Account of the Hardships, Sufferings, Battles, Defeat, and Captivity of Those Heroic Kentucky Volunteers and Regulars Commanded by General Winchester In the Years 1812-1813." Paris, Kentucky. 1813: 44.
[328] Naveaux, Ralph. 2003. *Invaded on all Sides: the Story of Michigan's Greatest Battlefield Scene of the Engagements of Frenchtown and the River Raisin War of 1812*. Marceline, Missouri: Walsworth Publishing Company: 135-136.

Proctor could not move his troops that swiftly to Frenchtown despite many French citizens in the surrounding countryside warning the soldiers that they had seen the British troops, that they were close. In addition, the 550-men reinforcements sent by Harrison could not move as quickly with their oxen across the ice, and instead had to take the main road. Within Frenchtown, the approximately 930-man American army was in a very loose formation. In the area inside the pickets, William Bratton was in the right side with the rest of the 1st Rifle Regiment. Elias Darnall was on the left with the rest of his 5th Kentucky Volunteer Regiment.[329]

At 6 a.m., one hour before sunrise, the British attacked. Only a few sentry shots were heard beforehand that gave the American army any warning. The British first fired a relentless barrage from their cannon. General Winchester was still asleep at the time of the attack, and once woken up by the Navarre family, somewhat slowly headed towards the village. The American troops in the open field fared very badly amidst the cannon fire and hand-to-hand combat when it began. They were missing officers and fortifications. The British force contained the Native Americans led by Wyandot chiefs Roundhead and Split Log.[330] Chief Ogamorpenance also fought against the Americans with them, swinging his large wooden war club he called Poga Morgun (housed in the Museum of Monroe Pioneer and Historical Society. It was presented by B.O. Williams, and early Native American trader of Owosso).[331] The American soldiers in the open were fired upon from three sides, and were slowly backed up to the north side of the River Raisin. General Winchester arrived to aid in a retreat of the right wing. Colonel John Allen and Colonel William Lewis with

---

[329] Naveaux, Ralph. 2003. *Invaded on all Sides: the Story of Michigan's Greatest Battlefield Scene of the Engagements of Frenchtown and the River Raisin War of 1812*. Marceline, Missouri: Walsworth Publishing Company: 151.

[330] Ibid: 160.

[331] Elmer, Josephine D. "The River Raisin Massacre and Dedication of Monuments." Historical Collections, Vol. 35. Michigan State Historical Society: 203.

two fifty-man companies moved into open ground in order to cover this maneuver but it was a disaster. (Not being one of the men in either of those fifty-man companies saved William Bratton's life.) All of the men who were not behind the pickets were at great risk. Small groups of soldiers gave up any tries at reforming, and instead began to flee. By this time, Native Americans in the British force encircled the town and the woods. They laid a trap in which they left a lane covered in thick snow open and they picked off soldiers as they retreated through it.[332] One group of soldiers were able to retreat up to three miles from the battle, but were tracked by the Native Americans and killed. Colonel John Allen, though wounded, tried to make a stand with his troops after retreating for two miles, but exhausted sat down on a log. He too was shot by a Native American. Another group of officers including General Winchester retreated and left the Kentuckians still fighting, holding their own behind the pickets in the village. Only five of those soldiers had been killed and forty were wounded. When all became quiet, the troops were confused and incredulous to find that they were told to surrender. Only upon threats of burning the village and allowing the Native Americans to pillage combined with the information that General Winchester had been captured, did the troops within the pickets surrender. "There was scarcely a person that could refrain from shedding tears! Some plead with the officers not to surrender, saying they would rather die on the field!" recounted Elias Darnall.[333] The surrender terms that were agreed upon was that able-bodied prisoners had to surrender their arms but could keep the rest of their personal property, and that they would be evacuated immediately for Fort Malden. Additionally, sleds would be sent the next day to

---

[332] Clift, G. Glenn. 1961. *Remember the Raisin!: Kentucky and Kentuckians in the Battles and Massacre at Frenchtown, Michigan Territory, in the War of 1812*. Frankfort, Kentucky: Kentucky Historical Society: 65

[333] Darnall, Elias. "A Journal Containing An Accurate and Interesting Account of the Hardships, Sufferings, Battles, Defeat, and Captivity of Those Heroic Kentucky Volunteers and Regulars Commanded by General Winchester In the Years 1812-1813." Paris, Kentucky. 1813: 48.

transport the wounded American troops to the fort. "We marched out and grounded our arms, in heat and bitterness," Elias Darnall said. "But all the swords, dirks, tomahawks, and knives were given up, with the promise that they should be restored again. This promise was broken."[334] Almost immediately, tension rose when Native Americans began to plunder the property of the American troops taking pans, kettles, buckets, and tents, until Proctor stopped this violation.[335] Additionally, as Darnall said, their arms were never given back.

Wasting no time because he feared that General Harrison would show up at any time with more troops, Proctor ordered the able-bodied American prisoners into a line, and marched them from Frenchtown to Fort Malden eighteen miles away. After fighting for hours behind the pickets, William Bratton emerged from the battle unscathed physically, and he marched in line with the rest of his comrades as prisoners. His company officer, Captain Hickman who was wounded from the skirmish on January 18, 1813 was left behind. Though Elias Darnall was uninjured, he too stayed behind to resume his duties of helping the wounded, a task he had been doing since January 18, 1813 though he fought with his company during the battle. He probably was happy to help the wounded because his brother Allen was among them since he was shot in the right shoulder on January 18, 1813.

When the American prisoners reached Fort Malden, they saw a structure that was seventy to eighty yards square with a timber and clay wall around it. It sat about thirty feet from the Detroit River near where the river joined Lake Erie. The side of the fort that faced the river did not have a wall but a double row of pickets. The fort was tucked up against the town of

---

[334] Darnall, Elias. "A Journal Containing An Accurate and Interesting Account of the Hardships, Sufferings, Battles, Defeat, and Captivity of Those Heroic Kentucky Volunteers and Regulars Commanded by General Winchester In the Years 1812-1813." Paris, Kentucky. 1813: 48.
[335] Clift, G. Glenn. 1961. *Remember the Raisin!: Kentucky and Kentuckians in the Battles and Massacre at Frenchtown, Michigan Territory, in the War of 1812*. Frankfort, Kentucky: Kentucky Historical Society: 73.

Amherstburg that contained about 100 frame houses. Many of the American soldiers probably barely noted their surroundings; they were exhausted, dirty, hungry, and cold. Many of them still wore their summer uniforms which were threadbare and thin, and they lacked coats. According to Oliver Bellair, a boy living with his parents in Amherstburg at the time of the battle, he watched the prisoners arrive. To him, they looked utterly dejected. They were miserably cold and dusty from road travel, and they were still bloody, and smelled of smoke from the battle. "They were driven into an open wood-yard, and, without tents or covering of any kind, thinly clad, they endured the bitter cold of a long January night; but they were soldiers of the republic, and suffered without murmuring at their hard lot."[336] The prisoners were surrounded by guards to both prevent them from escaping and to form a barrier between them and the hostile Native Americans who wanted to harass, or worse, injure them further. According to Oliver, many of the citizens at Fort Malden were sympathetic to the American's plight, and they surreptitiously helped several of them escape. Oliver's father aided one soldier who was able to escape the enclosure, knocked on the Bellair house, and appealed to the Bellair family for help. Because of the danger, the soldier stayed only long enough to warm up and eat. He was then directed to another home where the soldier was able to stay and work for a few weeks before he was able to earn enough money to return home.[337] As prisoners, the American soldiers were subjected to even more horrors. The Native Americans cut off the heads of many Kentuckians who had fallen in the battle and "stuck them up in rows on the tops of a high, sharp-pointed picket fence; and there they stood, their matted locks deeply stained with their own gore." According to Bellair, the faces of the dead American soldiers exhibited a variety of expressions

---

[336] State Historical Society of Wisconsin. "Judge Witherell's Reminiscences." Wisconsin Historical Collections, Volume 3. 1857: 307. DOI: whcvIII0000.
[337] Ibid.

from agony, scowls, even smiles, that were literally frozen in place and which Bellair thought numbered over a hundred.[338] The Native Americans also displayed numerous scalps that hung twenty to a pole.

While staying in the wood-yard that first day, the American prisoners initially had fires but a hard rain early in the evening extinguished the fires and the prisoners sat wet and cold until morning. The next day the British transferred the American soldiers to a warehouse where they were at least out of the rain but they were still cold and were not given anything to start fires. Their clothes and blankets remained frozen. They were also really hungry which added to their misery.[339] They received very little bread and what little they did receive was literally and insultingly thrown at them like farmers throwing corn to pigs.[340]

Back in Frenchtown, after the able-bodied prisoners were marched away, tensions remained high. Though Elias Darnall, the wounded officers and privates would have liked to think that the British were going to keep their word and send sleds for them the next day, they were fearful that they were going to be massacred instead. The reason for this was because once Proctor left, the Native Americans began plundering the village again. They set fire to the commissary house. A British officer who was searching for more ammunition but who found wheat instead, implied to Darnall that the wheat would be lost when the Native Americans burned the house. As the evening progressed, the British did not leave a guard to protect the wounded prisoners and everyone knew that the Native

---

[338] State Historical Society of Wisconsin. "Judge Witherell's Reminiscences." Wisconsin Historical Collections, Volume 3. 1857: 307. DOI: whcvIII0000.

[339] Darnall, Elias. "A Journal Containing An Accurate and Interesting Account of the Hardships, Sufferings, Battles, Defeat, and Captivity of Those Heroic Kentucky Volunteers and Regulars Commanded by General Winchester In the Years 1812-1813." Paris, Kentucky. 1813.

[340] Atherton, William. 1842. *Narrative of the Suffering and Defeat of the North-Western Army Under General Winchester*. Frankfort, Kentucky: A.G. Hodges, publisher.

Americans would celebrate their victory by drinking liquor that could send them into an even more vindictive mood. The night passed peacefully but when morning arrived, no sleds were delivered. Just as the Americans feared, the Native Americans returned painted for war, and were shrieking for vengeance. They stripped the wounded prisoners and made them get out of bed and go outside even if they could only crawl, and then the Native Americans set the houses on fire. The prisoners that could not move at all were burned alive in the fires. "Now the scenes of cruelty and murder we had been anticipating with dread, during last night, fully commenced," Darnall said. "The savages rushed on the wounded and in their barbarous manner, shot and tomahawked, and scalped them; and cruelly mangled their naked bodies while they lay agonizing and weltering in their blood."[341]

American soldier Thomas Parker Dudley was in a house formerly used as a tavern and specifically in a room with Captain Paschal Hickman, Captain Nathaniel Hart and Major Benjamin Graves when the carnage began. He witnessed the fate of William Bratton's company leader. In less than six feet from where Dudley stood, Captain Hickman was tomahawked. Dudley immediately left the room to stand outside on the porch. Within a few minutes, the Native Americans dragged Hickman out between them, and deposited him on the porch where they stripped everything off him except for his flannel shirt. They then tossed him off the porch into the snow which was a foot and a half deep. Hickman only breathed once or twice before he died.[342] This massacre of wounded American soldiers became known as the River Raisin Massacre.

The Native Americans then lined up the American soldiers who were yet alive and began marching them to Fort Malden.

---

[341] Darnall, Elias. "A Journal Containing An Accurate and Interesting Account of the Hardships, Sufferings, Battles, Defeat, and Captivity of Those Heroic Kentucky Volunteers and Regulars Commanded by General Winchester In the Years 1812-1813." Paris, Kentucky. 1813: 54.

[342] Clift, G. Glenn. 1961. *Remember the Raisin!: Kentucky and Kentuckians in the Battles and Massacre at Frenchtown, Michigan Territory, in the War of 1812*. Frankfort, Kentucky: Kentucky Historical Society: 82.

Many of them could not move fast enough to please their captors, and they were slaughtered. "The road was, for miles, strewed with the mangled bodies, and all of them were left like those slain in battle, on the 22nd, for birds and beasts to tear in pieces and devour," Darnall said. His brother Allen was among those who were struck down. Allen had difficulty marching as swiftly as the Native Americans demanded, and he walked only two to three hundred yards when Elias watched with horror when the Native Americans murdered him. One Native American guarded Darnall for the eighteen-mile march to Fort Malden and Darnall feared that instead of being able to join the other prisoners, he might be adopted into a Native American tribe. He did get a chance to ask a British soldier on the edge of Amherstburg where the other prisoners were and discovered they were still in the woodyard. Darnall was determined to join them but had to bide his time after his captor marched him to another residence three miles outside the town. Darnall's chance to escape occurred two nights later. Darnall crept out of the house he was in, and without a coat or even shoes, he ran three miles through snow back to Amherstburg. He located the house where the other prisoners were, and a British sentinel allowed him to enter and join them.[343]

After two days and three nights, the prisoners were divided up into two units, each one with about 253 men. Each unit left Fort Malden marching eastward a day apart. It is unknown which unit William Bratton was assigned to, but Darnall was assigned to the unit that left first on a forced march on foot to Fort George on January 26, 1813. They followed the Detroit River seventeen miles to the town of Sandwich where about 300 people lived. It was located about one-mile south of Detroit. Here, the 253 prisoners were divided into smaller units for the evening and billeted with different households where they were happy to warm

---

[343] Clift, G. Glenn. 1961. *Remember the Raisin!: Kentucky and Kentuckians in the Battles and Massacre at Frenchtown, Michigan Territory, in the War of 1812*. Frankfort, Kentucky: Kentucky Historical Society: 59.

themselves at a fire.[344] The next day, the prisoners were given bread and fresh beef but no salt and no way of cooking the beef. Nonetheless, they were forced to begin marching again by 1 p.m. They marched ten miles some of which was on the frozen surface of Lake St. Clair. At the end of the march, they collapsed in cold barns without fires.[345] The next morning, January 28, 1813, it was the coldest that Private Elias Darnall had ever encountered. It was a miserable twenty-four mile march again on Lake St. Clair, and at the end, soldiers experienced another lodging in a cold barn with no fire. For those American soldiers who did not fit in the barn, they spent the night outside under guard camping in the woods. The next day, January 29, 1813, the cold continued as did the marching, the distance took them to the mouth of the Thames River. The temperatures were so cold, the prisoners had to run in order to prevent themselves from freezing.[346] Even though the men expended an enormous amount of calories marching, they did not receive another portion of food since they had received bread and meat two days prior. Some of the prisoners were desperately hungry. "Some of the prisoners were driven to the necessity of picking up frozen potatoes and apple peelings that had been thrown out in the yard," Darnall said.[347] It was this particular hardship that might have stuck with William over time because much later in his life he was described by his family as not wanting to waste anything to the point in which he would pick up scattered grains of corn at a corn husking. When he was teased about it, William replied that he had experienced a time when a few grains of corn would have been

---

[344] Darnall, Elias. "A Journal Containing An Accurate and Interesting Account of the Hardships, Sufferings, Battles, Defeat, and Captivity of Those Heroic Kentucky Volunteers and Regulars Commanded by General Winchester In the Years 1812-1813." Paris, Kentucky. 1813: 60.
[345] Ibid.
[346] Ibid.
[347] Darnall, Elias. "A Journal Containing An Accurate and Interesting Account of the Hardships, Sufferings, Battles, Defeat, and Captivity of Those Heroic Kentucky Volunteers and Regulars Commanded by General Winchester In the Years 1812-1813." Paris, Kentucky. 1813: 61.

a welcome sight.[348] On January 31, 1813, the prisoners again marched twenty-four miles, and again were put in a barn. They were wet and cold but at least they had been given a stingy two-day ration of food the day before. "Going to a barn to lodge on so cold an evening, was like approaching a formidable enemy, for we expected to perish with cold in the dreary dwelling," said Elias Darnall. "Many got their feet frostbitten. We tried in vain to keep our shoes from freezing, by putting them under our heads."[349] It would be two more days before they received food again, a vicious act of cruelty towards them because the soldiers still marched over twenty miles a day in terrain that was sometimes covered in two feet of snow.

By February 10, 1813, the prisoners reached Fort George which was near the town of Newark, but had recently been referred to as Niagara West since it was on the Niagara River, west of Fort Niagara (called Niagara-On-the-Lake today). It was platted out over a square mile and contained two stone churches, a jail, a courthouse, a Native American council house, six taverns, a printing establishment, and an academy. Citizens of Newark, estimated at over 500 people, inhabited over 100 homes, many of them neatly painted or made of stone or brick. Bare ground about a mile in length, used as common ground, separated the town from Fort George. British subject Sir George Prevost described Fort George as "an irregular fieldwork consisting of six small bastions faced with framed timber and plank, connected by a line of palisades twelve feet high, and surrounded by a shallow dry ditch."[350] The fort contained blockhouses large enough to house 220 men, and another sizable building for its officers. Some thought went

---

[348] Chesterson, Maud J. Bratton. "William Bratton: His Service in the Lewis and Clark Expedition, 1804-1806 and in the War of 1812." Indiana Pamphlet-00000106839277, Indiana State Library.

[349] Darnall, Elias. 1813. *A Journal Containing An Accurate and Interesting Account of the Hardships, Sufferings, Battles, Defeat, and Captivity of Those Heroic Kentucky Volunteers and Regulars Commanded by General Winchester In the Years 1812-1813*. Paris, Kentucky: 62.

[350] Cruikshank, Ernest. "The Battle of Fort George." Niagara, New York: Niagara Historical Society: 9, 10.

into the construction of the magazine for it was an attractive building, built of stone with an arched roof. Fort George itself had its problems though. It was rundown and some of it needed to be repaired. When the prisoners arrived, they might have noticed a stone lighthouse that was built nearby, on Mississauga Point. It was built in 1804.[351] The Americans might have also learned that General Winchester and twenty officers had arrived at Fort George two days prior and that all but Winchester, his personal staff and a few of the field officers had already been paroled and sent to the American lines. They did not let Winchester go just yet, nor his personal staff or those few field officers that remained with him. They were taken further north to Quebec City and retained until spring 1814.[352] British officers did not waste time paroling William and his fellow prisoners. They were paroled the same day they arrived at Fort George on Feb. 10th and 11th. After signing parole documents, British soldiers rowed the Americans across the channel to Fort Niagara.

No reference to the River Raisin POW parole records for these two units of men exists, besides the references made by the men themselves, since the parole records were filled out in 1813. (More than one search for the parole records was made by the author at the Library and Archives Canada in Ottawa, Ontario. Though the main body of parole records for prisoners of war from the War of 1812 are housed there, it is possible that the parole records for the approximately 500 American soldiers from the Battle of River Raisin taken across to Fort Niagara on February 10, 1813, and a day before or after, do not exist today. It is the collective belief of several historians from the Niagara area and the author that if the parole records stayed at Fort George for a while, then they might have burned up with the rest of the fort when it was overtaken by Americans two months later in May 1813.) When the British

---

[351] Cruikshank, Ernest. "The Battle of Fort George." Niagara, New York: Niagara Historical Society: 10.

[352] DeWitt, John H. "General James Winchester, 1752-1826." Tennessee Historical Magazine. Vol. 1, No. 2: 103-104.

soldiers paroled soldiers, they used a form similar to a census form, divided into columns with each column recording a category of data. Each soldier was recorded on a line, and in column 1, a number was issued for that line. Column 2 denoted how the POW was captured which was usually depicted by land or water, or if at sea, the name of a ship. The third column asked Time When and denoted the date of capture. Column 4 asked Place Where and denoted the place of capture. The fifth column asked in what ship or how taken and the sixth column asked whether it was in a man of war, privateer, or merchant vessel. These columns of course did not apply to the River Raisin POWs. Column 7 recorded the prisoner's name. Column 8 asked the quality of prisoner which denoted the rank of the prisoner. Column 9 asked for the date the prisoner was received into custody. Column 10 asked from what ship or from where received. Beginning with Column 11, a more personal description of the men was recorded. In Column 11, the men were asked for their place of nativity. In Column 12, they were asked their age. In Column 13, they were asked for their height. In Column 14, they were asked about their body and it was denoted if the men were heavy, slender, stout, thin, or medium-sized. In Column 15, it was denoted what kind of complexion the men possessed and what the shape of their face was. In Column 16, their hair color was recorded. In Column 17, their eye color was recorded. In Column 18, the men were asked to identify any marks or wounds. Columns 19 - 32 recorded what supplies or provisions had been provided to each man.[353] They also had to swear they would not serve again against the British and their allies during the war.

The Pittsburg Mercury newspaper reported that many River Raisin POWs had reached Pittsburg by foot from Fort Niagara by the beginning of March 1813. There, many of them caught a ride to Kentucky by water.[354] So strongly did many of

---

[353] Dye, Ira. Introduction. Records Relating to America Prisoners of War, 1812-1815. British Records Relating to America in Microform (BRRAM) Series. London, England. 1980.
[354] Niles' Weekly Register. 6 March 1813: 10, col. 2.

the men feel the outrage and sorrow of their ordeal, several surviving officers did not wait until they reached Kentucky to convene a meeting. At Erie, Pennsylvania, the following men passed several resolutions – Captains Uriel Sebree, Samuel L. Williams, Richard Bledsoe, Coleman Collier, and Henry James; Lieutenants Lyndon Comstock, Higgins, Ensigns Thomas W. Chinn and James L. Harron. "That in consideration of the high respect we hold both officers and soldiers who were thus cruelly murdered by permission of the British commander Col. Proctor and his subalterns – and of those who gloriously fell in the field defeating the only free government on earth, that each of us wear crepe on our hat and left arm for ninety days."[355] General Harrison sent Colonel Wells to Frankfort to inform Governor Shelby about the massacre. When the news initially reached Frankfort, many of the citizens were attending the theater, including the governor. After the third act, people went home. "Here you see fathers going about half distracted, while mothers, wives, and sisters are weeping at home."[356] Governor Shelby also received a letter from Major Martin D. Hardin who reported that "the stroke has been so severe that my feelings are perfectly deadened."[357] Governor Shelby was able to confront Proctor himself six months later at the Battle of the Thames. As over 600 Kentuckians charged Proctor and his soldiers and Native American allies across the swampland, they intensely cried with overwhelming wrath "Remember the Raisin" and vengefully thrashed them. The number of wounded American prisoners thought to be massacred in Frenchtown numbered about sixty-five. On their return from the Battle of the Thames, the Kentuckians returned to Frenchtown to bury their dead.

    Like many of the River Raisin POWs, William most likely traveled down the Ohio River from Pittsburg to return home, a journey that took at least two weeks at that time. Upon entering Kentucky, it is unclear whether he went home to the

---

[355] Niles' Weekly Register. 6 March 1813: 13, col. 1.
[356] Weekly Aurora. (Pennsylvania.) Letter extract. 23 Feb. 1813.
[357] Martin D Hardin to Governor Isaac Shelby. 24 January 1813.

Hammond Creek neighborhood in the southern half of Franklin County. His name was not on Franklin County's list of survivors from the River Raisin Massacre.[358] His military record showed that he was engaged in service until February 14, 1813 but his pay ended on March 5, 1813. This was probably the day he arrived back in Kentucky. William was paid for his service for the duration of two months and five days at $6.66 dollars per month for a total of $14. 39.[359] He traveled to Frankfort to receive his discharge signed on March 27, 1813 by Major Martin D. Hardin, Commandant at that time for the 1st Rifle Regiment of the Kentucky Volunteer militia.[360] William was one of only thirteen from Hickman's company to survive fighting at River Raisin, and again, the only one whose name was not included on the survivor's list. The other twelve men who straggled in after parole were "Lieutenant Peter Dudley, Alexander Renick, Joseph Clark, Lewis Fennick, Elisha Herndon, John A. Holton, Zachariah B. Lewis, Francis Mayhall, John Mayhall, John Richardson, Alexander Robertson, and James Wilson." [361]

---

[358] Clift, G. Glenn. 1961. *Remember the Raisin!: Kentucky and Kentuckians in the Battles and Massacre at Frenchtown, Michigan Territory, in the War of 1812*. Frankfort, Kentucky: Kentucky Historical Society.
[359] William Bratton military record. War of 1812 Military Service Records. National Archives Records Administration. Washington D.C.
[360] William Bratton military discharge. Aldrich autograph collection. Iowa Historical Society.
[361] Johnson, L. F. "Franklin County, Kentucky, Chapter VI: A.D. 1810-1820." The Register of the Kentucky Historical Society, Vol. 7: 49.

CHAPTER SEVEN
Warren County, Kentucky

When William Bratton returned from the war, it is unclear if his brother Robert still lived in Franklin County. Robert was not listed on the Franklin County, Kentucky tax list for 1813. It is possible that if William stopped in Franklin County before traveling on to Warren County, that when he arrived there, he found his brother away on a land speculation trip in the Indiana Territory with his wife's relatives. In another possible scenario, Robert may have already lived in the Indiana Territory "improving" a piece of ground there even though his official paperwork was not filed yet. William was not listed on the 1813 tax list for Franklin County, Kentucky either. It is also possible that William did not stop in Franklin County, Kentucky at all because he already knew Robert was not there which would account for why he was not listed on the survivor's list. Regardless, William traveled further west to Warren County to join his parents and siblings living there.

If William arrived in Warren County before May 8, 1813, then he probably attended the wedding of his younger brother Archibald who married Elizabeth Maxwell.[362] It could have been the first time he met Elizabeth, her sister Polly, and the rest of the Maxwell family. Other Bratton family members who attended the wedding besides Archibald was William's father George Bratton, his stepmother Susanna, his brother Adam, his brother George Jr., his sister Jenny with her husband Aaron Lewis and their children, and his youngest sister Nancy.

---

[362] Archibald Bratton marriage record. Kentucky Marriages, 1802-1850, database, Ancestry.com.

William was not listed on the Warren County 1813 tax list either and the date for when his father and the rest of his brothers were listed is illegible.[363]

If William returned to Kentucky by July, he was no doubt stirred by the rousing call to arms by Governor Isaac Shelby on July 31, 1813. However, he adhered honorably to the terms of his parole with the British government and did not re-enlist in the Kentucky forces. His brother Adam did answer the call to service and joined the 10th Regiment of the Kentucky Mounted Volunteer Militia under the command of Captain George Baltzell. His official muster was on September 22, 1813 at Put-in-Bay, Ohio where the Kentucky soldiers rendezvoused.[364] His regiment participated in the Battle of the Thames. Archibald had already served a term in Nicholas Miller's 3rd Regiment Kentucky Militia as a private in Captain Alexander Stuart's Company.[365] George Jr. waited until 1814 to serve when he joined William Mitchusson's 14th Regiment Kentucky Militia and served as a private in Captain Thomas Sterrett's Company.[366] George and his fellow soldiers participated in the Battle of New Orleans.

As 1813 progressed, Robert Bratton and his family solidified their claim to land in the Indiana Territory. On October 14, 1813, Robert traveled to Jeffersonville, Indiana and made the final payment on a patent claim for 160 acres in

---

[363] Kentucky. Warren County. George Bratton entry. 1813 Tax List, Allen County Public Library, Fort Wayne, Indiana. Microfilm, #0373, 1809, 1811-1813, 1815-1826, 1828.

[364] Compiled Service Record, Adam Bratton, Private, Boswell's Co., 10th Regiment, Kentucky Militia. Kentucky Carded Records, Volunteer Organizations, War of 1812; Records of the Adjutant General's Office, Record Group 94, National Archives, Washington D. C.

[365] Compiled Service Record, Archibald Bratton, Private, Miller's Co., Third Regiment, Kentucky Militia. Kentucky Carded Records, Volunteer Organizations, War of 1812; Records of the Adjutant General's Office, Record Group 94, National Archives, Washington D. C.

[366] Compiled Service Record, George Bratton, Private, Sterrett's Co., 14th Regiment, Kentucky Militia. Kentucky Carded Records, Volunteer Organizations, War of 1812; Records of the Adjutant General's Office, Record Group 94, National Archives, Washington D. C.

the SE1/4 of Section 11 in Township Two North, Range 4 West in Washington County, Indiana.[367] His interest in this area was also shared by his wife's parents, siblings and her Little cousins, particularly her uncle Alexander Little who's land bordered Robert's land. Unfortunately, the excitement for Robert and Nancy in moving their family north to Indiana Territory was dampened by the death of Nancy's father John McCoskey in November 1813 in Franklin County, Kentucky. McCoskey must have been having health problems because he wrote his will on September 21, 1813 and it was probated only two months later in November. He left one dollar to his daughter Nancy Bratton to be received one year after the date of his death per his instructions.[368] Nancy Bratton's parents, John McCoskey and his wife Nancy Little McCoskey, had been planning to move to Indiana Territory as well. McCoskey bought 160 acres of ground in Harrison County, Indiana but with county lines shifting, his land was soon re-allocated as part of Washington County. He bought it sometime in 1812 or early 1813 because he was listed on the 1813 Washington County, Indiana tax list for it.[369] Robert Bratton was taxed for 160 acres in Harrison County, Indiana as well.[370] Now a widow, Nancy Little McCoskey, as matriarch of twelve children and many of their spouses, traveled with them together as a large group to that land in Indiana Territory to join the Brattons and her brother Alexander Little. (This is the same Alexander Little who's ciphering notebook survived as discussed in Chapter 2.) Some of the McCoskey boys received some of the Indiana land from their father in his will, and other siblings bought other

---

[367] Indiana. Washington County. Robert Bratton land certificate #303, Bureau of Land Management. http://glorecords.blm.gov.
[368] Kentucky. Franklin County. Will Books. John McCoskey will, November 1813. Book 1: 206.
[369] Beanblossom, Walter S. 1975. *Early Records of Harrison County, Indiana, Copied from the Originals Found in the Court House at Corydon.* 1813 Tax List. Film#007831753, Image #293. FamilySearch.org.
[370] Ibid: image #287.

land, and although not all of their land parcels bordered each other, they were not very far away from each other.[371]

Alexander Little had been living in Indiana Territory with his family for quite some time. He moved there around 1808. At that time, Washington County had not been formed yet, and his land was part of Clark and Harrison Counties. If the tools he owned were indicative of what many settlers possessed, and similar to what George Bratton had possessed when he was a pioneer in 1790, Alexander Little had a cross-cut saw, a broad-ax, a chopping ax, a frow, a one-inch and two-inch auger, and a drawing knife.[372] With these tools, he built a double-room log house, and the construction of it was probably not much different than the methods used twenty-five years earlier in the Pisgah neighborhood in Kentucky. Little would have built each room with a space of four feet between them and a six-foot wide square hole in each wall on either side of the four-foot gap. Then he built a double fireplace with a chimney so that back to back, each one faced into each room. One of his rooms contained the kitchen, a place to eat, and a bed or two, and he and wife possibly might have used the other room as a parlor when company visited.[373] His floors were probably puncheon floors made of tree logs split in half with the flat side facing up and the bark side facing down where it could not be seen. Like many Indiana Territory pioneers living in a hostile environment, Little built port holes into each room of his cabin so that he could shoot at Native Americans if they came to attack him and his family. He also made a gun rack and attached it over the front door.[374]

Alexander Little was a man of service. He served in the Indiana Legislature many times. His first term was in 1810.

---

[371] Kentucky. Franklin County. Will Books. John McCoskey will, November 1813. Book 1: 206.

[372] Stevens, Warder W. 1916. *Centennial History of Washington County, Indiana: Its People, Industries, and Institutions*. Indianapolis, Indiana: B. F. Bowen and Company, Incorporated: 161.

[373] Ibid.

[374] Little, James A. History of the Little Family. Publishing Association of Friends. Plainfield, Indiana.

Overall, he served in the first, second, eleventh, twelfth, and fourteenth Legislature sessions.[375] He also served in the Indiana militia as a lieutenant in the 2nd Battalion of the 1st Regiment.[376] He was mentioned several times in a journal kept by General John Tipton. The War of 1812 was just beginning. From an entry on June 8, 1812, General Tipton gave the following description "a cloudy day. Myself and some of the Rangers went to shooting, then I went with Lt. Alexander Little to the place where Capt. Zenor was stationed. Found that they called their fort Fort Recovery. Took some whiskey then return'd home in the time of a hard wind. One of my men killed 2 deer."[377] Ten days later, he again spent some time with Alexander Little when they went fishing together. Little also served in the position of "county lister" for Washington County after it was established on January 7, 1814.

The land that Robert Bratton bought in Washington County was adjacent to Alexander Little. Maybe they were good friends besides being extended family. Little was technically Robert Bratton's uncle by marriage but Robert was actually older than Alexander by five years despite their generations. This sometimes happened when couples had ten or more children and the oldest children began having families and their babies could end up being the same age or older than siblings that their parents were still having. This happened in this instance. Robert was the eldest child of his family and Alexander was the youngest of his. Their land was in Section 11, and was a rolling terrain (today it would be in the eastern part of Posey Township of Washington County).[378] One of

---

[375] Hadley, John Vestal. 1914. *History of Hendricks County, Indiana: Her People, Industries, and Institutions.* Indianapolis, Indiana: B.F. Bowen & Co., Incorporated: 263.

[376] *Executive Journal, Indiana Territory 1800-1816.* Indiana Historical Society Publications, Vol. 3, No. 3. Indianapolis, Indiana, 1900: 210.

[377] Facsimile of John Tipton journal. John Tipton Collection, Box 18, Folder 9.
Rare Books & Manuscripts. Indiana State Library.

[378] Wright, Andrew. Pen name of Dudley Drewwright. blog titled "200 Years Ago in Washington County." blog entry, 14 Oct. 2014.

their neighbors, William Lindley, owned additional ground where he built a two-story double log cabin in 1811. He also built the first water mill near Salem but the mill was built before Salem was established, specifically three years before the lots for Salem were even laid out.[379] Washington County commissioners and the circuit court both used the Lindley house to conduct county business. In 1814, they sold contracts to have a courthouse and jail built in Salem.[380] Maybe Robert and Nancy Bratton liked what they saw happening in Salem because they did not stay on their rural land in Washington County long. On November 19, 1814, they sold 100 acres of their patent land to Jacob and Miriam Bogue Morris for $100. On the same day, they sold the rest of the land, sixty acres, to Robert Telford for $130. Robert Telford was their brother-in-law, the husband of Nancy's sister Sarah Ann who went by Sally. The Brattons then put down a twenty-five percent down payment on two lots, lot 159 and lot 160, in Salem.[381] The courthouse and jail were not built yet in Salem, but there were a handful of log cabins of varying sizes. Some were single log cabins and others were double-room cabins.

In Warren County, Kentucky, in 1814, the other Bratton brothers made transactions in their own land and business deals. William's brother George Jr. entered into a real estate transaction with William Nash on April 20, 1814 involving Town Lot No. 23 in Bowling Green. Nash paid George Jr. $138.00 for part of it. This lot was located on the south side of the public square.[382] Archibald did not buy land but he

---

[379] Stevens, Warder W. 1916. *Centennial History of Washington County, Indiana: Its People, Industries, and Institutions.* Indianapolis, Indiana: B. F. Bowen and Company, Incorporated: 543.
[380] Ibid: 92.
[381] Wright, Andrew. Pen name of Dudley Drewwright. Blog titled "200 Years Ago in Washington County." Blog entry, 14 Oct. 2014.
[382] Kentucky. Warren County. Warren County Deeds, George Bratton deed. Book 6: 329.

attended an estate sale in October 1814, one for John W. Craig. The items he bought were not listed but he spent $1.40.[383]

William was involved in a different kind of business, a county proceeding on July 11, 1814 that reflected the high regard that Warren County men had for his opinion. The Warren County clerk Jonathan Hobson requested via letter that the Sheriff of Warren County assemble a panel of twelve upstanding male citizens that lived in the Big Barren River area near the island below Stuart's Ferry. Hobson wanted the panel to meet on the property of Simon M. Hubbard at the spot where Alexander Graham wanted to erect a grist mill to examine the area thoroughly.[384] Hobson wanted the panel present to help determine "what lands may be overflowed and what damages the several proprietors adjacent thereto will sustain and whether the mansion house of any such proprietors or the offices, gardens or orchards therein will be immediately overflowed.[385]" Additionally, Hobson wanted to know their opinion as to the potential obstruction of fish and the change in their navigation of the water that would be caused by the mill and its dam and if stagnation from the water there would be a detriment to the surrounding neighborhood. Besides William, the panel consisted of his brother Adam, Benjamin C. Johnson, James Keel, W. Stephens, Warner Stephens, Samuel Stone, David Hudspeth, C. M. Lansdell, and A. Rollerdice. The panel was in favor of the grist mill and heartily assigned one acre of Hubbard's land for where Graham's mill could be built. They also approved a ten-foot high dam to be extended across the north shoot of the river with an abutment on the island. It might at first appear unseemly that one man's mill would be built on his neighbor's land, however, Hubbard was Graham's brother-in-law. Alexander Graham married

---

[383] Craig, John W. Probate. Loose Papers for Vol. A-C, Warren County. Kentucky Wills and Probate Records, 1774-1989. Ancestry.com.
[384] Kentucky. Warren County. Mill Sites microfilm, mill record, Alexander Graham. Mill Sites. Warren County, Kentucky. University of Kentucky Special Collections Library, Lexington.
[385] Ibid.

Nancy Hubbard on July 2, 1802 in Warren County. It is unclear whether this land was part of Hubbard's 200-acre land grant or a parcel that Nancy inherited from her father a few years earlier.

Their neighborly regard was further extended to the Brattons after another wedding occurred among the Bratton siblings on March 25, 1815. This time, William's brother Adam Bratton married Rebecca Graham, sister to Alexander Graham.[386] Due to the 1815 tax list, a financial portfolio can be assessed for Adam to see exactly what kind of catch Rebecca nabbed. Adam owned a 120-acre parcel of land that was originally entered by J. O. Lewis. The value of his land was deemed $5 per acre with a net worth of $680. That amount is equivalent to close to $10, 000 now. Some of his neighbors were John McGraw, Henry Ewing, Jacob Smith and Elihu Carter. Besides listing himself as over twenty-one, Adam also owned one horse. On the same 1815 tax list, George Bratton, Jr. was taxed for a 135-acre parcel of land that was patented by Adam. It was valued at $2 an acre. George Jr. still owned the town lot in Bowling Green too; both properties combined for a value of $270. George Jr. listed himself as over age twenty-one and he owned two horses. Their brother Archibald Bratton was taxed for a 90-acre parcel of land that was valued at $3 an acre for a total worth of $390. He listed himself as over the age of twenty-one and he owned three horses.[387]

On the same tax list for Warren County in 1815, William owned three parcels of land – a ninety-acre parcel, a fourteen-acre parcel, and a 200-acre parcel. The 200-acre parcel is the land aforementioned that was entered for him by Captain John Arnold in 1810. It was surveyed by Henry Lyons and patented by William himself. It was valued at $1.50 an acre. The fourteen-acre parcel was surveyed by Samuel Goode and

---

[386] Adam Bratton marriage record. Kentucky Marriages, 1802-1850, database, Ancestry.com.
[387] Kentucky. Warren County. Archibald Bratton entry. 1815 Tax List, Allen County Public Library, Fort Wayne, Indiana. Microfilm, #0373, 1809, 1811-1813, 1815-1826, 1828.

valued at $3 an acre as was the ninety-acre parcel adding up to $662. He also listed himself as over age twenty-one and he owned one horse.[388] In September 1815, William made some extra cash selling peaches. Then, beginning in November, he sold plank and sheeting. He kept an account book to record to whom and of what he sold (see Appendix A).[389] Due to the nature of the items he sold over several years, it was clear he ran a grist mill on the north side of the Big Barren River. His neighbors were Alexander and Charles Stuart. This was the same Alexander Stuart who was the captain of Archibald Bratton's company in 1812. The Stuart brothers inherited the property from their father James and it is likely that they sold the mill or the property to William or they were all in business together.[390]

Real estate business continued for the Bratton brothers. On January 1, 1816, George Bratton, Jr. and William Nash sold part of a Bowling Green town lot to James Morehead who was also a citizen of Bowling Green. Morehead paid George Bratton, Jr. $625 and paid William Nash $1.00.[391] On August 17, 1816, Adam Bratton entered a real estate deal with Isaac O. Lewis and his wife Fanny. They sold Adam 135 acres that bordered the waters of Ray's Branch for $600. The border of the land began near the road that led to the Stuart Ferry. This acreage was part of an original patent of land made by Lewis.[392] There were no official witnesses represented in the transaction.[393] On the 1816 tax list for Warren County, William was taxed for two

---

[388] Kentucky. Warren County. William Bratton entry. 1815 Tax List, Allen County Public Library, Fort Wayne, Indiana. Microfilm, #0373, 1809, 1811-1813, 1815-1826, 1828.

[389] William Bratton Account Book. The Marian Morrison Local History Collection. Reference Department. Crawfordsville District Public Library. Crawfordsville, Indiana.

[390] "Stewarts in Warren County, Ky." *Stewart Clan Magazine*, Vol. 18, August 1940.

[391] Murray, Joyce Martin. *Deed Abstracts of Warren County, Kentucky, 1812-1821*. Ericson Books, Nacogdoches, Texas, 1986: 45.

[392] Ibid.

[393] Kentucky. Warren County. Equity deed. Isaac and Fanny Lewis to Robert Bratton: 58.

parcels, both tallied as third-rate land. The closest watercourse was the Big Barren River. William was the only person in his household and he had no horse. His land was valued at $3.50 an acre per parcel.[394] He was taxed a total of $7.29. William's brother Adam was listed directly above William on the tax list. He was taxed for 120 acres, also third rate, near the Big Barren River. He claimed himself and he had two horses.[395] William's brother Archibald was listed directly below William on the tax list. He was taxed for ninety acres, third rate, and for three horses.[396]

Other Warren County business in 1816 involved George Bratton, Jr. who was sued for slander by Robert Bryant. Bryant asserted that George Jr. publicly accused him of stealing his grindstone. According to Bryant, during the slanderous conversation, George Jr. said "God damn you, you stole my grindstone" and "you and McConnell stole my grindstone" and "my grindstone was stolen and found in your possession."[397] Bryant stated that not only was he falsely accused, but that the "false, scandalous, malicious and defamatory words" had ruined his reputation of being a good and upstanding citizen. After the suit was filed, according to George Jr., he and Bryant met at a public establishment in Bowling Green to further discuss the issue and tried to settle it between themselves. George Jr. said that Bryant was so well satisfied with the result that he ordered wine and brandy and they all drank to Bryant agreeing to dismiss the suit. After that, according to another man named William Steward, Robert Bryant and George Jr. approached him at the location where he worked and asked him to join John Bryant and others to be witnesses to their agreement. The formal agreement was that George Jr. would go

---

[394] Kentucky. Warren County. William Bratton entry. 1816 Tax List, Allen County Public Library, Fort Wayne, Indiana. Microfilm, #0373, 1809, 1811-1813, 1815-1826, 1828.
[395] Ibid: Adam Bratton entry.
[396] Ibid: Archibald Bratton entry.
[397] Kentucky. Warren County. George Bratton vs. Robert Bryant, Suit 156 on Reel 11, Suit 90 on Reel 13. Warren County. Kentucky Department of Library and Archives.

into court, acknowledge that he "wrong'd Robert Bryant, that he did not believe him guilty of the charge he had made against him," and that he would pay all court costs. Once George Jr. did that then Bryant would dismiss the suit. After the agreement, George Jr. had to leave town on urgent business. He had not yet paid the court costs and it is unclear when he planned to do this. While he was away, Bryant pursued the suit. George Jr. who expected to pay the costs when he returned, and also expected the suit to be dismissed, was caught unaware that the suit was progressing and then was unprepared to defend himself with proof in a court trial. The court judged the situation in favor of Bryant, and charged George with $500 in damages. George Jr. promptly appealed. Included in an affidavit prepared by Justice of the Peace William R. Payne, George Jr. felt that Bryant bamboozled him with a show of meeting with him for the sole purpose of lulling him into a false security that the matter was otherwise settled. George Jr. claimed that he could prove that his grindstone was found in the possession of Bryant. At the very least, he wanted time to obtain the proof he needed. He asserted that he was always ready and willing to pay the court costs and still was. There were many reasons why George Jr. wanted a re-trial. It was alleged that one of the jury members at the original trial, Isaac Rude, was very intoxicated and not in a fit state to judge, and that another juror, Bunnell Geeter, was not a homeowner and ineligible to serve as a juror. Overall, George Jr. urged the court to overrule the verdict of the first trial and just make him accountable for court costs. The final decision of the court was not included in the court papers so the final outcome is unknown.[398]

Meanwhile, William's brother Robert Bratton was on the move again. The statehood of Indiana in 1816 triggered an ongoing public land sale in Vigo County on September 13-14,

---

[398] Kentucky. Warren County. George Bratton vs. Robert Bryant, Suit 156 on Reel 11, Suit 90 on Reel 13. Warren County. Kentucky Department of Library and Archives.

1816 at the Vincennes, Indiana land office. [399] Within two weeks, Robert traveled to Vincennes to apply for land in Vigo County. In three different transactions, he applied for two 160-acre parcels and an 111-acre parcel in sections twenty-two, twenty-seven, and thirty all in Township 11 North. [400] He, along with many of his wives' relatives, claimed many patents in Honey Creek Township in Vigo County.

The year of 1816 was also a very weird year, not just for the Brattons, but for everyone across the nation. The weather was not normal and summer never arrived. It was referred to as the "summerless" year. Such a phenomenon was a hardship for people who could not grow a garden, who depended on that food to get through the next winter, and to not only feed themselves but also their livestock. One diarist left behind this account "That year they had snow and ice in the east in June, and in July ice was thick as a windowpane throughout New England, and New York and in parts of Pennsylvania. August was cooler still and before it ended almost every green thing was killed. Many people would have starved had it not been for the fish and wild game. The same cold was experienced in Europe."[401] Such weather did not deter Robert Bratton from visiting the land office again, this time on September 16, 1816. He executed many business transactions, all located in Honey Creek Township in Vigo County. He filed a patent application for 160 acres described as the northwest quarter in section twenty-seven of Township 11 North, Range 9 West. He filed a claim for 111 acres in Honey Creek Township, Vigo County, in section thirty, in the southwest quarter in Township 11 North, Range 9 West. He filed a patent claim for 160 acres; however, this land was located in the northwest quarter of section thirty-five in Township 11 North, Range 10 West. Additionally, on the same day, Isaac Lambert and John Dickson (sometimes

---

[399] Bradsby, Henry C. 1891. *History of Vigo County, Indiana*. Chicago, Illinois: S. B. Nelson & Company: 96.
[400] Indiana Public Lands Collection, Indiana State Digital Archives, http://www.indianadigitalarchives.org/.
[401] Sarver, Bina Thompson. 1976. *Memories 1816-1819*, n. p.: 15.

spelled Dixon) were assignees for Robert for another 160 acres in Township 11 North, Range 9 West but in section twenty-two.[402] Lambert and Dickson were brothers-in-law to each other and co-owners of a mill on Honey Creek.[403] They were very active in land transactions and very prosperous gentlemen. Besides the mill, they both built impressive brick homes.[404] They were both neighbors to Robert Bratton. Furthermore, both parcels of Robert Bratton's land in section twenty-two and section twenty-seven in Township 11 North, Range 9 West bordered each other and combined became a full 320 acres. In each section, a branch of the Honey Creek rambled through. Two weeks later, Robert's mother-in-law Nancy Little McCoskey filed a claim for her own two parcels of land, both 160 acres, and both bordered Robert's land. They were the northeast and southwest quarters of section twenty-seven in Township 11 North, Range 9 West.[405]

On the 1817 tax list in Warren County, Adam Bratton was taxed for the same 135 acres, each valued at $7 per acre. He was also listed for another 125-acre parcel of land that was surveyed by a Mr. Campbell but patented by Adam. These acres were valued at $6 per acre, with a total value for the acreage at $1795.00. Adam listed himself as over age twenty-one and he owned two horses.[406] Archibald Bratton was listed on the same tax list and he owned eighty-five acres that were originally patented by L. J. Sharp and surveyed by Samuel Goode. The acreage was valued at $4 per acre for a total value of $490.00. He listed himself as being over age twenty-one and he owned

---

[402] Indiana. Vigo County. Robert Bratton land certificates #2612, #2613. Bureau of Land Management. http://glorecords.blm.gov.
[403] Scovell, J. T. *Fort Harrison on the Banks of the Wabash*, 1812-1912. Terre Haute, Indiana: Fort Harrison Centennial Association: 30.
[404] Bradsby, Henry C. *History of Vigo County, Indiana*. Chicago, Illinois: S.B. Nelson & Company: 648.
[405] Indiana. Vigo County. Nancy McCoskey land certificates #58, #230. Bureau of Land Management. http://glorecords.blm.gov.
[406] Kentucky. Warren County. Adam Bratton entry. 1817 Tax List, Allen County Public Library, Fort Wayne, Indiana. Microfilm, #0373, 1809, 1811-1813, 1815-1826, 1828.

two horses.[407] George Bratton, Jr. was also taxed for 10 acres of land that was surveyed by J. Campbell and valued at $5 per acre for a total of $50.00. He listed himself as over age twenty-one and owned no horse.[408] William Bratton was again taxed for three parcels of land, but he must have sold ten acres. He was again taxed for the 200-acre parcel, the 90-acre parcel and a 4-acre parcel. His value of land totaled $1616.00. He listed himself as being over age twenty-one and owned one horse.[409]

In 1818, William was again involved in some Warren County court business. He sued a man named William Simpson.[410] A search for the suit was unfruitful so it is unclear what the issue was between them. In further court business but in an unrelated issue, William submitted a petition in December 1818 to the Kentucky Senate addressed as a "petition of William Bratton, and sundry citizens of Warren County, praying that he may be authorized to erect a dam with locks, across Big Barren River, where he has erected a grist mill." William was doing quite a brisk business grinding corn into meal and bran. (To see who his customers were and what they were buying, see Appendix A). Archibald Bratton also appeared in court for his own business on August 13, 1818, in which he bought 180 acres of land on the north side of the Big Barren River for $500 from Solomon P. Sharp of Bowling Green.[411]

The next year, 1819, brought huge changes to the Bratton family and to William Bratton especially. First, in an early transaction, William bought a tract of land, 200 acres, near the

---

[407] Kentucky. Warren County. Archibald Bratton entry. 1817 Tax List, Allen County Public Library, Fort Wayne, Indiana. Microfilm, #0373, 1809, 1811-1813, 1815-1826, 1828.
[408] Ibid: George Bratton entry.
[409] Kentucky. Warren County. William Bratton entry. 1817 Tax List, Allen County Public Library, Fort Wayne, Indiana. Microfilm, #0373, 1809, 1811-1813, 1815-1826, 1828.
[410] Kentucky. Warren County. William Bratton vs. William Simpson. Suit 109, Reel 16. Kentucky Department of Library and Archives.
[411] Murray, Joyce Martin. *Deed Abstracts of Warren County, Kentucky, 1812-1821*. Ericson Books, Nacogdoches, Texas, 1986: 45.

Big Barren River for $5. It began at the sinking spring and ran to William Chapline's property line.[412] In the fall, William's father George Bratton, Sr. died. Archibald Bratton executed a $600 bond with the courts to administrate his father's estate. Francis Johnson and Daniel Stone were his securities.[413] It is believed that George Sr. was buried at the Mount Olivet Cumberland Presbyterian Church cemetery in Warren County. Next, on a happier note, William married Mary "Polly" Hutton Maxwell on November 25, 1819. He applied for a license the previous day, and his friend John W. Powell served as his surety. William was well over the age of twenty-one at age forty-one, and Polly was over the age of twenty-one as well at age twenty-three but her father James Maxwell still appeared at the Warren County clerk's office and gave his consent to the marriage.[414] Polly's sister Elizabeth was already married to William's brother Archibald. The Maxwell sisters moved to Warren County, Kentucky in 1811 from Washington County, Virginia with their parents James and Grisal Berry Maxwell. Their siblings were David C., Harriet, Sarah who went by Sally, Martha who went by Patsy, Malinda, John, and Prudence. When the Maxwell family arrived, their father bought 100 acres on the Big Barren River from Nicholas and Jane Quisenberry for $800.[415]

In 1820, the federal census provided another snapshot of William's household and those of his family and extended kin. William lived with his wife Polly and their newborn son James Maxwell Bratton named for Polly's father. Archibald lived with his wife Elizabeth, their daughters Grizzilla Jane and Harriet Ann, and their sons James Maxwell Bratton and William B. Bratton. Archibald also owned an enslaved girl under the age of fourteen. In Adam's household, he lived with his wife

---

[412] Murray, Joyce Martin. *Deed Abstracts of Warren County, Kentucky, 1812-1821*. Ericson Books, Nacogdoches, Texas, 1986: 106.
[413] Kentucky. Warren County. Court Order Books, 1815-1824. Book E: 221.
[414] William Bratton marriage license. Kentucky County Marriages, 1783-1965. Ancestry.com.
[415] Kentucky. Warren County. Deed Abstracts of Warren Co., Kentucky. 1797-1812, Nicholas Quisenberry to James Maxwell deed: 102.

Rebecca and his sister Nancy. He also owned two enslaved people, a boy under fourteen and a woman between thirty to forty-four. George Bratton, Jr. lived by himself. He lived but a few houses down from William. In their sister Jenny's household, she lived with her husband Aaron Lewis, with her two sons both under age ten, and her three daughters both under age ten.[416]

In 1820, Robert Bratton and his family was also listed in the federal census. Living in the household was Robert, age forty-six; his wife Nancy, age thirty-six; their eldest son John, age eight; their son William, age six; daughter Jane, age four; and the baby, George, age one. Also living in the household was Nancy's mother Nancy McCoskey, age sixty-two; her son Thomas Campbell McCoskey, age nineteen; and her youngest son Joseph, age seventeen. Two males were listed as being involved in agriculture which I believe are Robert with the help of Thomas. More of the McCoskey family lived nearby in Honey Creek Township in Vigo County, Indiana. There was Robert McCoskey; Margaret "Peggy" McCoskey Young and her husband Samuel Young; and Anna McCoskey Soesbe and her husband Daniel Soesbe. Many of the other McCoskey siblings still lived in Washington County except daughter Mary Jane "Jenny" McCoskey Latta, who lived in Owen County, Indiana with her husband John Latta.

Also in 1820, William Bratton filed another lawsuit. He went to the Warren County, Kentucky courthouse where he and his brother George Bratton, Jr. sued Thomas M. Neale.[417] William also sued Robert Briggs and Alexander Graham.[418] (These court cases are referenced in the 1970s finding aids at the archives of the Kentucky Department of Library and Archives but they did not turn up in a search. Consequently, it

---

[416] 1820 United States Census, Warren County, Kentucky. Bratton households.
[417] Kentucky. Warren County. William and George Bratton vs. Thomas M. Neale, Suit 110, Reel 16. Kentucky Department of Library and Archives.
[418] Kentucky. Warren County. William Bratton vs. Robert Briggs and Alexander Graham, Suit 119, Reel 16. Kentucky Department of Library and Archives.

is unclear why William Bratton took these men to court.)

Through another Maxwell wedding on April 20, 1820, William and Archibald Bratton became further connected to their neighbors, the Stuart family, when their sister-in-law Sally Berry Maxwell married Charles Stuart. William Bratton and Sally's brother David C. Maxwell served as witnesses when Sally's father James Maxwell submitted a written consent to the Warren County clerk for Charles to procure the marriage license.[419] Charles and Sally might have become acquainted through the marriage of Sally's sister Harriet to Simon M. Hubbard in 1813.[420] Simon M. Hubbard had been married to Charles' sister Nancy Stuart before she died and then Harriet Maxwell became his second wife. On September 11, 1820, William sold land to Charles Stuart for $20, identified as being from the southeast corner of the survey completed by Reed and Ford.[421] The tract was "on the north side of the Barren River, adjoining Jonathan Baker, and on the same day he bought of Alexander Graham, two and a half acres on the Barren River, including all of Mill Island."[422] William in turn paid Archibald $250 on November 24, 1820 for 132 acres on the north side of the Barren River.[423]

A land deed between Alexander Stuart and his brother Charles referred to William's grist mill business during a transaction on April 26, 1821 between the Stuart brothers and Ephraim Hubbard of Gallatin County, Illinois. They deeded approximately 152 acres that they inherited from their father James Stuart to Ephraim for $1. The land adjoined "Bratton's mill yard," and was on the Big Barren River. The deed was

---

[419] James Maxwell marriage consent. Kentucky County Marriages, 1783-1965. Ancestry.com.
[420] Simon M. Hubbard to Harriet Maxwell marriage. Kentucky County Marriages, 1783-1965. Ancestry.com.
[421] Murray, Joyce Martin. *Deed Abstracts of Warren County, Kentucky, 1812-1821*. Ericson Books, Nacogdoches, Texas, 1986: 143.
[422] "Stewarts in Warren County, Ky." *Stewart Clan Magazine*, Vol. 18, August 1940.
[423] Murray, Joyce Martin. *Deed Abstracts of Warren County, Kentucky, 1812-1821*. Ericson Books, Nacogdoches, Texas, 1986: 146.

witnessed by George Bratton and Robert Graham.[424] Though William was still running his grist mill business, he was probably already thinking about what kind of prospects might await him in Indiana. He might have been receiving letters from his brother Robert about how prosperous Robert was becoming north of Terre Haute in Vigo County, Indiana. Moving north would certainly be another adventure for William except this time he had a wife and son to consider. All of Polly Maxwell's family lived near she and William and if they left, she would not see them in person very often. Nevertheless, they decided to go.

---

[424] "Stewarts in Warren County, Ky." *Stewart Clan Magazine*, Vol. 18, August 1940.

CHAPTER EIGHT
Terre Haute, Indiana

William Bratton, his wife Polly, and their one-year-old son James Maxwell Bratton left Warren County, Kentucky by summer 1821 to join his brother Robert Bratton in Vigo County, Indiana. Robert's farm was east of the village of Prairieton in Honey Creek Township, and six miles south of the county seat of Terre Haute. Polly was expecting their next child and was five months pregnant at the time of their departure. For the first part of their journey, they probably loaded up their property in a horse-drawn wagon and headed north to Louisville. William might have looked up old friends there. At the very least, if he had not been to Louisville in a while, he was probably curious about what changes had taken place. He and Polly's journey could have been similar to that of William Newnham Blane's, an Englishman who traveled from Frankfort, Kentucky to Vincennes, Indiana in late autumn in 1822. For the part of his journey where he landed in Indiana, Blane rode on horseback from Louisville to a ferry below the rapids to cross the Ohio.[425] William and Polly could also have done this and it would have been a familiar procedure for William. He did this plenty of times in preparing for the Lewis & Clark Expedition about fifteen years earlier, although this time, he moved their household goods so it was probably a bit more time-consuming transferring everything and everyone across the river. For Blane, the weather was the biggest nuisance. He was deeply chilled from a hard frost and days of cold rain when he

---

[425] McCord, Shirley S. 1970. *Travel Accounts of Indiana, 1679-1961.* Indianapolis, Indiana: Indiana Historical Bureau: 117-120.

crossed the Ohio River, and he found the roads on the Indiana side almost impassable even on horseback. He traveled about eighteen to twenty miles a day and sometimes had to walk and lead his horse by the bridle.[426] He traveled from where he landed in Indiana, which was most likely Jeffersonville or Clarksville, and he traveled to Greenville, then to French Lick, than west across the White River to Vincennes.

William Bratton might have decided to go another way. He and his family could have descended the falls by boat and sailed down the Ohio River to the mouth of the Wabash River, and sailed up the Wabash River to a river port close to Honey Creek Township. Descending the falls would have presented the largest difficulty on this route but then it was mostly smooth sailing. Again, descending the falls was something William was very familiar with from his time working as a boatman on the Ohio River. Also, William might have wanted to stop at Vincennes to see where the land office was located on their way up the river. If they unloaded at the closest river port and did not bring any horses with them, William would have had to buy or rent one or two to make their way several miles to Robert's farm. Or, perhaps Robert met them at the river. Regardless, when they reached Robert's home, they were greeted by Nancy McCoskey Bratton and their children. Robert and Nancy had four children - their eldest son John was age nine, their son William, named after his uncle William Bratton, was age seven, a daughter Jane Frances was age 5, and little George named for his grandfather was age two. Nancy was also pregnant with another child. By August 4, 1821, William was receiving letters at the post office in Terre Haute.[427] It was clear he and Polly were settling in.

The origin of the name of their new home, Honey Creek Township, possibly came from one of two theories. Indiana soldier Thomas H. Files who served in a company of soldiers

---

[426] McCord, Shirley S. 1970. *Travel Accounts of Indiana, 1679-1961.* Indianapolis, Indiana: Indiana Historical Bureau: 117-120.
[427] Western Sun & General Advertiser. Vol. 12, No. 27. William Bratton letter. 4 August 1821.

defending Fort Harrison in September 1812 reported the following story - the night before an attack that occurred on September 4, 1812, the soldiers camped on the banks of a stream. Nearby, across the stream from their camp, they found a tree with a beehive that contained a large quantity of honey. The soldiers cut off the section of the trunk holding the honey, and ran a stick through the hollow so more than one soldier could help carry it. The tricky part for the soldiers was to haul the heavy section of tree back across the stream to their camp, and they chose a fallen log to assist them. Unfortunately, it did not work. They fell in and most of the honey washed downstream making it a "honey creek." Another pioneer, a Mr. Ross, personally thought that the name of Honey Creek was due to the prolific number of Honey Locust trees that grew along the stream.[428]

According to Vigo County pioneer Joseph Liston, he and his father Edmund, with men Martin Adams, Reuben Moore, William Drake, and William Greer Adams were the first men to farm in Vigo County. He said that they planted seventy-five acres of corn in 1811, then grew it, harvested it, and then sold it to nearby soldiers who belonged to William Henry Harrison's army who were busy building Fort Harrison. The name Honey Creek Township did not officially exist at that time and was called Fort Harrison Prairie instead. By the time Robert Bratton and his extended family of in-laws arrived there five years later in 1816, William Bratton might have been interested to hear that Robert's neighbors, Isaac Lambert and John Dickson built the first mill in the county on Honey Creek. This was a big deal for pioneers in the area. Before the mill was built, the settlers traveled to Vincennes for mill services or they used a mortar they had at home to pound their corn into meal. Unfortunately, Lambert's and Dickson's mill did not stand in one piece for very long because they built its foundation upon ground that was too sandy and it eroded

---

[428] Fogg, Ella Marea Meehan. Thesis titled "A Survey of the Schools of Honey Creek Township, Vigo County, Indiana. Indiana State Teachers College. 1931: 5.

away in raging floodwaters. Dickson and Lambert repaired it often until they did not think it was worth their efforts. A Major Markle on Otter Creek built another mill in Otter Township of Vigo County in 1817.[429] Lambert and Dickson had better luck with their houses and as mentioned previously, each of them built a substantial brick home in 1817. Also, they were each involved in the first Methodist Church in the area and were host to the first meetings.[430]

Both William and Polly Bratton might also have been interested to hear where their three nephews and niece attended school. The earliest school in Honey Creek Township was established by a man named Lucius H. Scott in 1817. He was inspired to start the school after meeting John Dickson and Isaac Lambert at Fort Harrison, according to a letter Scott wrote to a friend. "This meeting led me, soon after, for the want of something better to do, to take a small school in Honey Creek. The citizens built me a log cabin, and I opened my school in the latter part of July, but was soon afterward taken sick, and with such violence that nothing under the providence of God, but the kindness of the Dickson family and the skill of my physician, Dr. McCullough, saved my life. I lingered with various relapses until late in October, when I went to Vincennes to recruit my shattered health," Scott said.[431]

Sickness like Scott experienced was common in the area. By the end of spring in 1822, William and Polly might have been questioning their decision to leave Warren County, Kentucky for Indiana. Their journey the previous fall occurred after an extraordinary and unusual amount of rain had fallen in Indiana where people reported that it rained every day through June, July, and August. The rain brought disease and

---

[429] Fogg, Ella Marea Meehan. Thesis titled "A Survey of the Schools of Honey Creek Township, Vigo County, Indiana. Indiana State Teachers College. 1931: 16.

[430] Beckwith, B. W. 1880. *History of Vigo and Parke Counties*. Chicago, Illinois: H. H. Hill and N. Iddings, Publishers: 479-480.

[431] Fogg, Ella Marea Meehan. Thesis titled "A Survey of the Schools of Honey Creek Township, Vigo County, Indiana. Indiana State Teachers College. 1931: 18-19.

people died by the hundreds through the fall of 1821 and into the spring of 1822.[432] Although people knew how to treat consumption, the flux and "childbed fever," they did not know how to combat it. "Some thought it was inhaled with the night air, so closed all doors and windows at night. Others felt it was caused by stirring up too much fresh soil that might be fever-ladened," recalled Indiana pioneer girl Bina Thompson Sarver. "Medicine was hard to come by but there were many home remedies that people used - three large balls of cobwebs were taken for the shakes, mustard plasters, saltpeter, split open live chickens applied to the bottoms of the feet were good for cholera morbus. Wear a flannel shirt and long, red flannel drawers, and yarn stockings. Eat no fresh vegetables or fruit, they are poison. Take sulphur and molasses, undergo bleeding, take sassafras tea, wear a bag of asafetida around your neck to ward off germs," Sarver said.[433] The specific widespread disease and panic in 1821 and 1822 resulted in governmental action by Governor Jonathan Jennings. It was passed into legislature that the second Friday in April would, "be appointed and observed by proclamation as a day of fasting and prayer to Almighty God that he in his mercy would avert these judgments that have impeded our land, and that He in His mercies would bless our country with fruitful seasons and our citizens with health... and it is so proclaimed by my hand and seal this March 12, 1822, (signed) Jonathan Jennings." He also urged citizens to not labor strenuously at anything on that day.[434]

During this unusual weather, William traveled back to Warren County, Kentucky and filed a complaint against Martin Grider for trespass on February 6, 1822. Grider owed him $86.72 and Grider refused to pay him. William probably felt that he had no other choice but to take Grider to court. The

---

[432] Sarver, Bina Thompson. 1976. *Memories, 1816-1916*. n. p.: 14.
[433] Ibid: 15.
[434] Indiana Historical Commission. 1924. *Governors Messages and Letters*, Vol. 3. Indiana Historical Collections, Vol. 12. Indianapolis, Indiana: Wm. B. Burford: 255.

court found in favor of William Bratton but with Grider's refusal to pay him, it is unclear if the courts used some kind of pressure to enforce the ruling.[435] While Polly might have wanted to visit her family in Warren County, Kentucky, William probably made this trip alone because Polly was eight months pregnant. William and Polly's second son George was born March 6, 1822 in Honey Creek Township, most likely at the Robert Bratton homestead.[436] With so much death around them, they were probably extra vigilant in their care of him, and watchful of their son James who was age two.

Honey Creek Township in Vigo County by this time was home to churches of several denominations, not just Methodist. Hugh Judge, a Quaker, visited the Friends meetings in Honey Creek Township in late April 1822. Spring showers were so prevalent that it was very difficult to travel. "Here we attended their first-day meeting which was small, for the creek dividing Friends' settlements, was so high that none could cross it." The nearby Wabash River was also flowing high. "The water being so high, we waited a day and visited some families; then attempted to cross the river which was falling, yet high. In going along the shore in order to get to a ferry, we were interrupted by great sluices of water that flowed out of the bed of the river on the low lands. Having crossed some of them, we came to one that appeared to be very deep, and our guide turned out into the woods where the water spread wider; we followed him, and after getting through two or three miserable places of mud, or farther, quicksands and water, we came to one still worse, with limbs of trees in it. Our guide ventured in and got safe through, my companion also got through, taking care not to stir up the quick sand, but my creature sank among the limbs and sticks, threw me off, and in struggling to get out, fell on me and buried me under the water. Thomas returned in

---

[435] Kentucky. Warren County. William Bratton vs. Martin Grider suit. Kentucky Department of Library and Archives.
[436] George and Cynthia Moore Bratton Bible. William Bratton Archive. The Marian Morrison Local History Collection. Reference Department. Crawfordsville District Public Library, Crawfordsville, Indiana.

the slough to my assistance, and helped me out; but I was much hurt, and apprehensive that some of my ribs were broken. We found a log on which we crossed the remainder of this quicksand, but soon found there was another before us. Thus we were hemmed in, on every side; to attempt to go back the way we came was dreadful, and to go forward seemed impracticable. At length, we concluded to get near the bank of the river, and return if we could. Here we found a log that appeared to reach nearly across the main sluice that we had crossed. So we got on it, and our guide, Moses Hogget, on one side, Thomas on the other, endeavored to steady me across on this log; but I fell off, the log being small and wet, and I sweat also, they, however, caught me and with difficulty got me on the log again, and thus we got over safely. Thomas returning for the horses drove one through, and rode the other; and though the water was deep, it was not so bad as the sloughs."[437]

In November 1823, a farmer wrote a letter to the editor of the Western Register describing the potential of Terre Haute despite potential sickness and challenging roads. "On a late visit to your Village, the writer was much struck with its present improving state, and hopes sincerely the citizens may reap the benefit of their industry and perseverance. Travelers and strangers have always predicted, notwithstanding its heavy and distressing losses that the town must at length become a place of considerable importance. The local situation of the place is certainly as handsome and convenient as any other town in the Western country; compared to its sister towns on the Wabash, it is superior. The gentle descent from the prairie to the river, and the ease with which good roads can be made from the landings to any part of the town, are advantages denied to those below. The beauty of the surrounding country and the extensive prospect over which the eye delights to rove, strikes the attention of the traveler

---

[437] Heiss, Willard, compiler. 1961. *The Honey Creek Monthly Meeting of Friends, Abstracts of Records Vigo County, Indiana. 1820.* Indianapolis, Indiana: John Woolman Press: 1-2.

with surprise, and pleasure: it is however the fertility of the soil, and the facility with which it may be cultivated, that will most excite the attention of the emigrant farmer. Why Terre Haute should be unhealthy is a question not easily answered as it enjoys all the advantages of a healthy situation - there are no marshes or stagnant water... The farmer further said that lots were exorbitantly priced and county taxes were too high thereby obstructing people from moving there, people who would be good citizens to have. If these things could be addressed than "the manufacturer will have sufficient inducement to employ his capital, nor will the laborer seek employment in vain; the man of literature will be delighted to find a handsome and valuable library open at his command and the merchant pleased at the numerous customers that enter his shop."[438]

The exorbitant prices, taxes, or unhealthiness of the area could explain why William went to the land office in Terre Haute at the beginning of July 1823, and filed a patent claim for eighty acres in nearby Vermillion County, the west half of the northwest quarter of section twenty-one in Township 17 North, Range 9 West. He bought the land but the county itself was not officially established until 1824. His land was north of Vigo County above Parke County. Vermillion County was the fiftieth Indiana county to be formed.[439] William also purchased another eighty acres in soon to be Montgomery County, and it was the west half of the southeast quarter in section nineteen of Township 19 North, Range 5 West. His residence on the patent certificate was listed as Vigo County. [440] The land office in Crawfordsville decreed that the land will be "sold in tiers of townships, beginning at the southern part of the district and continuing north until all has been offered at public sale. Then private entries can be made at $1.25 per acre, of any that has been thus publicly offered. This rule, adopted by the officers,

---

[438] Western Register. Letter to the Editor. 26 November 1823: 2, c. 2.
[439] Indiana. Vermillion County. William Bratton land certificate #658, Bureau of Land Management. http://glorecords.blm.gov.
[440] Ibid: William Bratton land certificate #988.

insures great regularity in the sale but it will keep many here for several days who desire to purchase land in the northern portion of the district."[441] In September 1823, William returned to the Terre Haute land office and filed a patent claim for another eighty acres in Montgomery County, but this time it was the east half of the southeast quarter of section nineteen in Township 19 North, Range 5 West. He also filed an additional claim for another eighty acres for the west half of the southeast quarter of section nineteen in Township 19 North, Range 5 West.[442] Even though he bought parcels in both Montgomery and Vermillion counties, it was to Montgomery County where William chose to move his family and farm. After William and his family departed for Montgomery County, Robert and his family remained in Honey Creek Township in Vigo County for a while before moving to Austin, Texas.

The Rest of Robert Bratton's Story -

In January 1826, Vigo County officials appointed Robert Bratton along with James C. Turner and Daniel T. Pinkston as supervisors over the erection of a bridge over Honey Creek. The bridge was built near the mill of R. W. Spear.[443] Several months later, in June 1826, Robert's mother-in-law Nancy Little McCoskey sold part of her land to her son-in-law Daniel Soesbe and her daughter Anna. It was the west half of the southwest quarter of section twenty-seven. The next day, she sold the rest of her land to her sons - the east half of the southwest quarter in Section twenty-seven to her son Robert McCoskey; the north half of the northeast quarter in Section twenty-seven to her son Joseph McCoskey; and the south half of the northeast quarter in section twenty-seven to her son

---

[441] Cox, Sandford C. 1860. *Recollections of the Early Settlement of the Wabash Valley*. Lafayette, Indiana: Courier Steam Book and Job Printing House: 18.

[442] Indiana. Montgomery County. William Bratton land certificate #987, #988, Bureau of Land Management. http://glorecords.blm.gov.

[443] Bradsby, Henry C. *History of Vigo County, Indiana*. Chicago, Illinois: S.B. Nelson & Company: 298.

Thomas Campbell McCoskey.[444] It is unclear if she was living with one of her children at this time, or if she lived alone, but she stayed busy. "She was endowed with excellent business faculties, and succeeded in rearing the large family respectably and prosperously....as evidence of her active vitality, it was told that she walked a mile to visit a neighbor within four weeks of the day of her death."[445] Another story about her is that "she attended a church meeting where she went three-quarters of a mile to hear preaching, and the weather was so bad that only two or three came. The good Brother, after waiting, concluded that he would not preach, and so announced, but Grandmother McCoskey told him that she had come to hear preaching, so the minister took his text and preached the usual sermon. She was a devout Christian."[446]

In March 1829, Robert Bratton sold eighty acres to Samuel Moore. The land was the north half of the southwest quarter of section thirty in Township 11 North, Range 9 West. This parcel was not part of his farm.[447] In December 1829, Robert hosted his extended Bratton family for Christmas. It is not exactly certain that Adam, George Jr. and Archibald Bratton brought their families north to his home but members of his sister's family were there. His sister Jenny Bratton Lewis had the eldest children in the extended Bratton family as some of them were teenagers by now. In addition to her family, it is likely that William Bratton and his family were there since they lived somewhat nearby in Montgomery County. Specifically, he and Robert's sixteen-year-old nephew George Lewis was present and his life would tragically change forever that holiday morning. In following a tradition in which a popular man received a respectful Christmas salute with guns, a group of young men gathered at the front of Robert Bratton's house

---

[444] Bradsby, Henry C. *History of Vigo County, Indiana.* Chicago, Illinois: S.B. Nelson & Company: 210-211.
[445] Ibid.
[446] Ibid.
[447] Bradsby, Henry C. *History of Vigo County, Indiana.* Chicago, Illinois: S.B. Nelson & Company: 222.

Christmas morning. George Lewis was in the front of a group of young men opposite the front door of the house where some of the boys were either standing or were on top of a horse. After George discharged his gun, he turned around only to be accidentally shot in the face by another boy who had shot his pistol from atop a horse. George's injuries were extensive. "The upper part of his mouth & part of his cheek bone were shot away – his nose remaining suspended merely by a piece of skin attached to his forehead which it was found necessary to cut off; his under lip and chin shockingly mutilated."[448] He lived after the injury, but he died six years later in 1835 at age twenty-two.

In April 1830, Robert Bratton sold eighty acres to John F. Cruft. The land was the south half of the southwest quarter of section thirty in Township 11 North, Range 9 West. This was the other half of his acreage in section thirty.[449] In the summer, the 1830 Federal Census reflected that the Robert Bratton household contained Robert, age fifty-six; his wife Nancy, age forty-six; son John, age eighteen; son William, age sixteen; daughter Jane, age fourteen; son George, age nine; another son, around age six; son Joseph, age four; and son Robert, age two.[450]

In other business, Robert witnessed and signed a sworn declaration in Terre Haute on May 7, 1833 that stated that he was an acquaintance and believer of the age and testimony of Daniel Soesbe, Sr. about Soesbe's service in the Revolutionary War. Robert was a neighbor to Daniel Sr. when Daniel Sr. and his wife Rachel joined their son Daniel Jr. in Honey Creek Township. (Daniel, Jr. as stated previously was married to Robert's sister-in-law Anna McCoskey.) Robert Bratton signed his name exactly as it consistently appeared in court cases. He always signed his name and there was no "x" mark between his

---

[448] The Register. Terre-Haute. Robert Bratton article. 31 Dec. 1829.
[449] Bradsby, Henry C. *History of Vigo County, Indiana*. Chicago, Illinois: S.B. Nelson & Company: 222.
[450] 1830 United States Census. Honey Creek Township, Vigo County, Indiana. Robert Bratton entry.

first and last name, so if he was not fully literate, than he could at least sign his name.[451] Because William was literate, and Robert was age fourteen when his family moved to Kentucky, it is likely that he was literate as well.

Just one month later, in June 1833, William Earl, a teenage boy living in Vigo County, left an account of his journey through Honey Creek Township as it looked from the road as he crossed it heading south to Vincennes. Earl had the distinction of being the first white male child born in Terre Haute, but he became an orphan as a young child. On this summer day in June, he conducted business for a Mr. Probst who sent him with $100, sewed into Earl's vest, to enter an eighty-acre parcel of land for him. When Earl traveled between what he considered Old Terre Haute and the bridge over Honey Creek, he saw five houses. One belonged to the Clem family, which sat next to the bridge, and after passing about a mile of prairie land, he saw two frame houses located on his left and two frame houses on his right. Next, on his left, he saw some woods and the Honey Creek Quaker meetinghouse. The road then sloped slightly downward through the bottoms and there he saw Moses Hoggatt's farm on his left. He then saw Robert Hoggatt's farm on his right as well as Robert Hoggatt's brick store. As the road began to rise again, he saw a grog shop run by Peter Agney. Then the Honey Creek prairie started up again and the road became more wild.[452]

When 1839 arrived, Robert Bratton and his family made an important decision to move across the country and preparations began. Robert placed an ad on March 1839 in the Wabash Courier newspaper to sell his farm. He described it as a 140-acre parcel six miles south of Terre Haute with "an excellent good-hewed log house, good springs, and many other conveniences not necessary to enumerate." He said it contained fifteen acres of meadowland, an apple orchard, and

---

[451] Daniel Soesbe, Sen. Application. Revolutionary War Pension and Bounty Land Warrant Applications: 32. www.Fold3.com.
[452] Bradsby, Henry C. *History of Vigo County, Indiana*. Chicago, Illinois: S.B. Nelson & Company: 277-278.

many maple trees for sugar. He stated that he would sell it by partial payment and partial credit.[453] Also in March, Robert's son John Bratton sold the parcel of land that he bought from his father in 1834 to Daniel Pound.[454] By April or May 1839, they moved. They headed south all the way to Austin in the Republic of Texas via Louisiana. This was such a drastic move, that it was possible that one of the family members traveled down there before to speculate as to where exactly in Texas they should move. Or, they had read quite a few sources to decide. William and James Latta, nephews to Robert and Nancy, accompanied the Bratton family south. William was age twenty, and James was age eighteen. At the time of the move, Robert was age sixty-five; Nancy, age fifty-five; John, age twenty-seven; William, age twenty-five; Jane, age twenty-three, George, age twenty; Elizabeth, age eighteen; Margaret, age sixteen; Joseph, age thirteen; Robert, age eleven; Nancy Eunice, age seven, and Annie who went by the nickname Lady, was age five. It is assumed that Nancy was still alive and made the move because no grave has been found for her in Vigo County, Indiana. She would have been a huge component to their trip running smoothly because their family group also included grandchildren. She and Robert's eldest son John had been married for five years to Martha Jane Lane, and they had a son William Henry who was age three. Martha was also heavily pregnant and gave birth to their daughter Annetta at the beginning of June in Louisiana. Despite Martha's condition, the group proceeded onward and reached Texas, specifically Austin, by the end of June 1839.[455] The Austin area was still considered part of Bastrop County then, but in 1840, it became the county seat of the newly formed Travis County. It also served as the government seat of Texas. Many large extended

---

[453] Wabash Courier. Robert Bratton advertisement. 2 March 1839: 2.
[454] Indiana. Vigo County. Vigo County Deed Records, 1818-1886. John Bratton to Daniel Pound deed. Vigo Special Collections Microfilm, 929.377245V, Reel 108. Vigo County Public Library.
[455] 1840 Bastrop Returns, Clerk Returns. Texas General Land Office Land Grants.

family groups were greatly motivated to move to Texas before the beginning of 1840 because of the huge incentive Texas mandated. "By act of congress passed 4 January 1839, all free white emigrants (heads of families) arriving between the 1st of October 1837 and January 1st 1840, with a family, are entitled to six hundred and forty acres on paying the usual fees. The emigrant to perfect his title to his land under this act, must reside in Texas for three years, and perform the duties of a citizen, when he will receive an unconditional title, and no legal alienation of the land can be made until the title is perfected by the government. A single man emigrating to Texas, above the age of seventeen years, is entitled to 320 acres, under the same conditions. This also extend to males (residents) who may reach the age of seventeen, between the dates above-mentioned; but this does not apply to females."[456] The Bratton family made it before the deadline, and the male members of their extended family group were issued hundreds of acres of land after they gave the Republic of Texas their oath of allegiance and formally filed their affidavit for the land. According to Texas guidelines, Robert Bratton was issued 640 acres as well as his eldest son John. The two other Bratton boys over age seventeen – William and George – received 320 acres each, and their cousins William and James Latta were also issued 320 acres each.[457]

Bastrop County, Texas officials issued Robert Bratton a conditional certificate for his 640-acre headright on November 15, 1839. However, he did not receive an unconditional certificate until September 1842 when he had lived there for over three years and completed the duties of a citizen which might have meant that he improved his land by building a homestead and outbuildings on it. Part of his land was located on the west bank of the Colorado River and one mile from the mouth of Sandy Creek. It contained pecan and hackberry

---

[456] Maillard, Nicholas Doran. 1842. *The History of the Republic of Texas*. (accessed 2 June 2017: 389). FamilySearch.org.
[457] 1840 Bastrop Returns, Clerk Returns. Texas General Land Office Land Database.

trees.[458] John Bratton received a conditional certificate to his 640-acre headright in December 1839. His acreage bordered the west side of the Colorado River and bordered the northeast corner of his father's land. It also contained pecan trees.[459] Likewise, the rest of the boys received their conditional certificates in December 1839, and their land bordered the other Bratton parcels near Sandy Creek and the Colorado River.[460]

The Brattons also bought city lots in Austin. On April 28, 1841, Robert Bratton paid the final installment of money for lot thirty of division O which he purchased in February at a land sale. He also authorized to have the patent to this lot transferred into the name of his son George.[461] On the same day, Robert's son William was issued a patent as an assignee of his father for lot fourteen in Division O, a tract that adjoined the City of Austin.[462] Further proof of Robert Bratton's residence in Austin was confirmed by letters that arrived for him at the Austin post office. In July 1841, the post office notified Robert by newspaper that he had a letter to pick up. They would hold it until October but if it were unclaimed at that time, it would be reclassified as dead and sent to the General Post Office, location unspecified.[463]

One man passing through Austin in 1844 described the city's location as east of the Colorado River. The city was dominated by a new white building still in the construction phase that was to serve as the house for the President of the Republic of Texas. It sat on a rounded hill. On the right side of the house, there was a broad road running north and south called Congress Avenue. Another white house close to the new

---

[458] Texas. Bastrop County. Robert Bratton, File 86, Cert. 149. Texas General Land Office Grants Database.
[459] Ibid: John Bratton, File 38, Certificate 204.
[460] Texas. Bastrop County. George Bratton, File 19, Cert. 225; William Bratton, File 92, Cert. 162. Texas General Land Office Grants Database.
[461] Texas. Travis County. Austin City Lots, Robert Bratton, file#000168, Texas General Land Office Land Grants Database.
[462] Ibid: William Bratton, File#000170.
[463] Austin City Gazette, 14 July 1841: 4.

white presidential mansion sheltered more governmental bodies such as the attorney general, supreme court justices, and military personnel. Between the two distinctive white houses were other temporary houses for officers, department heads, and secretaries. General stores and hotels and denser housing made up of log homes were located south of the government. Heaps of timbers were also deposited in various places until they were raised as more housing and businesses. Six months before, none of this infrastructure had begun nut now the growth of Austin was booming. The population of Austin in 1844 was about 1000 people.[464] A few other hills were interspersed on the city limits that made up Austin, hills that provided a beautiful view. The view "of the country for some distance on the opposite sides of the Colorado, are such as would give delight to every painter and lover of extended landscape. As the face of the country ascends by a continued succession of gentle acclivities, each somewhat higher than the last, and most of their summits crowned only with grass, while their feet are bordered by shrubbery and timber, a great distance up and down the river, and as well as at a distance from it, is presented to view."[465]

In 1845, the United States annexed Texas as its 28th state so the Brattons and the Lattas were once again United States citizens. The next year, Robert Bratton was tallied in the 1846 Republic of Texas Poll Lists as well as county lists. To be taxed, males had to be age twenty-one and older. Robert Bratton Jr. was age eighteen making him ineligible to be taxed in 1846, designating the identity of the Robert Bratton listed as Robert Bratton, Senior. The poll list contained the names of the rest of Robert's sons - John, William, and George - as well. Each of them paid the Texas government one dollar. Women who were heads of households as widows were also on the poll list and taxed one dollar.[466] After 1846, Robert Bratton was not found

---

[464] *History of Texas or the Emigrant's Guide to the New Republic.* 1844. New York, New York: Nafis & Cornish, New York: 61-62.
[465] Ibid: 63.
[466] Texas. Republic of Texas Poll Lists, 1846: 18. Ancestry.com.

in any more records. He probably died in Austin, Texas between 1846-1848. He nor Nancy Bratton were listed on the 1850 census in either Texas or Indiana, but all of their children were listed in the Travis County and Milam County area. Moreover, neither Robert nor Nancy Bratton were listed on the Federal Mortality Schedules from 1849. Gravestones were never found for either of them.

Robert Bratton's nephew William Latta did not stay in Texas. He returned to Vigo County, Indiana sometime before December 1847 when he married Barbara Mewhinney. In the 1850 census, he lived in Riley Township, Vigo County with his wife and his two-year-old son Syvanus. He worked as a cooper.[467] It was likely that he sold his land in Travis County, Texas to his brother James or to his Bratton cousins. James Latta farmed around his service as a soldier. He enrolled as a private in Company L of Captain Cady's Company on October 1, 1845 in Austin, Texas. They were a regiment of Texas Mounted Rangers and fought in the Mexican War. He served a three-month term and mustered out on Dec. 31, 1845. He enrolled again on Feb. 16, 1846 and mustered out three months later on July 4, 1846 in San Antonio.[468] He married his first wife Malinda Ann Burrows in 1847 but she died shortly afterwards. By the time the 1850 Federal Census was recorded, James was married to his second wife for six months. He worked as a farmer. Within five years, he and his wife began to have a family. It is unknown where he and his wife were buried.

Most of Robert and Nancy Bratton's children at their deaths were buried in Bratton Cemetery that is located on the border of Travis County and Williamson County. John Bratton established the cemetery on the land he owned. It is considered a pioneer cemetery, and is one-acre in size. It was marked with a historical marker. The cemetery has over 100

---

[467] 1850 United States Census. Vigo County, Indiana. digital image s.v. "William Latty," Ancestry.com.

[468] James Latta, (s.v. Latty) Company L, Cat. Cady's Co. Texas Mtd. Rangers, U.S. Compiled Military Service Records for American Volunteer Soldiers, Mexican War. Ancestry.com.

burials but only half of them are marked with stones. The earliest stone marks the grave of Mary Robey in 1847 so it is possible that both Robert Sr. and Nancy could be buried there.[469] The cemetery is not active now but Travis and Williamson Counties continue to be home to descendants of Robert Bratton today.

---

[469] Loop 1, Extension FM 734 to IH 35, Travis and Williamson Counties, Texas. U.S. Dept. of Transportation Federal Highway Administration and Texas Dept. of Transportation: 9.

CHAPTER NINE
Settling in Montgomery County, Indiana, 1823-1829

In the latter half of 1823, William and Polly Bratton and their two small boys moved to Wayne Township in the northwest quarter of Montgomery County, Indiana. At that time, Polly was pregnant again. To ease their travel, they traveled with several horses to carry their household belongings. Before they arrived on their land, but fairly close to where they finally settled, the family camped for the night. In the morning, they discovered that the horses had broken loose and disappeared. Suspecting that the horses headed back towards his brother's farm, William had Polly and the children stay in the camp while he went after them. According to one of William's great granddaughters, "by the time he gathered them up and brought them back again, the family had gotten acquainted around the neighborhood."[470] (Previous accounts of this story have William and Polly coming from Ohio but only one source puts them there, which is William Clark's account book. It is unclear where Clark received his information. Multiple other primary sources set up a very tight timeline making it impossible for William and Polly to have lived in Ohio at any time. William Clark's notation was likely based on someone telling him that they heard that William Bratton was living there but it was a different William Bratton.) When William and Polly finally reached their ground, their experience was probably similar to that of Robert Humphrey who brought his own family to neighboring Ripley Township in 1826. The Humphreys traveled on a very rough and

---

[470] Remley, David. 2011. *Kit Carson: The Life of an American Border Man.* Norman, Oklahoma: University of Oklahoma Press: 30.

unbroken road, and when they reached their own land, there was nothing there but sky and ground amidst a thick woods. They built up a stalwart campfire where they cooked their food, warmed their bodies, and kept away any larger predators such as wolves. The first shelter that Robert Humphrey built was a temporary house made of poles. Once the family ensconced themselves as comfortably as they could in the makeshift home, he then built a log cabin. He took a break every day from cabin-building and hunted in the nearby woods. He brought back meat to feed his family, that of bear, turkey, and deer.[471]

Whether William first built a temporary home of poles for his family is unknown, but there was a very large hill lying on his land, and it was there that he built a log cabin.[472] He also improved his property by planting trees and at least one of them was an apple tree. It was a feature on the homestead for over the next 100 years. In 1928, descendant Mary Maud Chesterson wrote her cousin Myrtle Fields Mariner about the family homestead. "The old apple tree, which great-grandfather set out here on the place is all gone now except some limbs. Have been thinking of having candlesticks made of it."[473]

William's cabin might have been similar to the one built by Joseph Cox, the father of Sandford C. Cox who later became a schoolteacher. Their log cabin was twelve-feet by sixteen-feet and housed seven in their family. When the public land sale opened for Tippecanoe County, the county directly north of Montgomery County, the sale ran for several days. Hopeful buyers flocked to the area. The Cox family hosted neighbors that they previously used to live by before they moved to this part of Indiana. Even though the cabin was full of family

---

[471] Crawfordsville Journal. "Brief Biography of a Remarkable Woman Related." 18 February 1916.

[472] Chesterson, Maud J. Bratton. "William Bratton: His Service in the Lewis and Clark Expedition, 1804-1806 and in the War of 1812." Indiana Pamphlet-00000106839277, Indiana State Library.

[473] Mariner, Myrtle. "William Bratton." *Heroes of 1812*. Lincoln, Nebraska: Nebraska Society of United States Daughters of 1812, 1930: 98.

members, room was created for the men by covering the floors with beds for the temporary duration.[474] When Sandford Cox was older, he had an accident in his late teenage years and needed an operation but the doctor was over sixteen miles away which was quite a long distance then. The operation to repair the damage was started by local people but they were in over their heads and waited for the doctor; the total duration of the operation occurred over a twenty-four hour period. Sandford Cox was lucky to live but the injury resulted in a serious physical handicap that still remained after an eighteen-month recovery. During his recovery, he and his family also relocated nearby to Tippecanoe County, on the south side of the Wabash River to the village of Granville. Determined to make his own way, he disappeared from his family's home by using crutches and hitching a ride in a hog trough across the Wabash River. This was when he organized and taught a log cabin school despite only having two years of limited schooling. His parents did not find out where he was until nine months later. Because of his studious habits and dependability, at age twenty Sandford Cox was appointed deputy county recorder. He did such a great job that he served in this position for twenty-two years. He was "eloquent in debate and witty in speech" so much so that he was in great demand as a "stump speaker." He studied law and eventually became a successful lawyer. His recollections were printed in a Lafayette newspaper in 1859 as extracts of the "Journal of the Black Creek School Master," and helped people visualize the conditions of pioneering in the Indiana landscape.[475]

    Sandford Cox recalled that "after the public sales, the accessions to the population of Crawfordsville and the surrounding country were constant and rapid. Fresh arrivals of movers were the constant topic of conversation. New log

---

[474] Cox, Sandford C. 1860. *Recollections of the Early Settlement of the Wabash Valley*. Lafayette, Indiana: Courier Steam Book and Job Printing House: 15.

[475] Ibid.

cabins widened the limits of the town, and spread over the circumjacent country. It is interesting how people spent their time, and what they followed for a livelihood in those early times in the dense forest that surrounded Crawfordsville. We cleared land, rolled logs, and burned brush, blazed out paths from one neighbor's cabin to another, and from one settlement to another, made and used hand mills and hominy mortars, hunted deer, turkey, otter, and raccoons, caught fish, dug ginseng, hunted bees, and the like, and lived on the fat of the land. So, not only was the area rich with wildlife for hunting, but many kinds of fish were abundant in Sugar Creek. According to Cox, "at John Stitt's mill below town, on Sugar river, there is a fish-trap, and in one night we caught nine hundred fish the first spring we were in the country, most of them pike, salmon, bass, and perch. Some of the largest pike and salmon measured from two to four feet in length, and weighed from twelve to twenty-five pounds. We carried them by skiff loads and threw them alive into the millpond hard by, which was fed by springs, and thus we had fresh fish all year. Stitt took him to the pond, and the fish were selected and the price agreed upon before the salmon was lifted from the water."[476]

    The largest town closest to William Bratton's cabin was Crawfordsville. Just seven months earlier, Major Ambrose Whitlock established the town from his one hundred plus acres he bought from the government. In designating town lots and in anticipation that Crawfordsville would be the county seat, he specified that the proceeds from every odd numbered lot should be used for school purposes except for lot forty-nine which was to be for a dog pound. As the lots were sold, a percentage of the money was set aside for a school building officially known as the main fund for a County Seminary.[477]

---

[476] Cox, Sandford C. 1860. *Recollections of the Early Settlement of the Wabash Valley*. Lafayette, Indiana: Courier Steam Book and Job Printing House: 15.
[477] Beckwith, B. W. 1880. *History of Vigo and Parke Counties*. Chicago, Illinois: H. H. Hill and N. Iddings, Publishers: 479-480.

Once established, Crawfordsville was the only town between Terre Haute and Fort Wayne for a while.[478] In 1824, the first Montgomery County courthouse, a small log structure, was built by Eliakim Ashton at the cost of $295. Major Ristine owned a two-story log home that he also ran as a tavern, and Jonathan Powers ran a little grocery.[479] It was around this time when pioneer Robert Humphrey arrived in the county and bought land in Ripley Township. On his first trip from Ross County, Ohio, he left his family back in Ohio, and traveled lightly with just his gun and his knapsack. He remembered only seeing the land office, a few log cabins, and the grocery. As previously mentioned, he did not return with his family until 1826.[480] As the community grew, Magnus Holmes and Thomas M. Curry served the community as local doctors, Providence M. Curry was a lawyer, John Wilson served as a clerk of the court, and David Vance served as sheriff. William Nicholson ran a tannery and a shoemaker shop, and George Key worked as a blacksmith. There were also a couple of cabinet shops. Men walked from up to ten to thirty miles to a grist mill and waited three to four days for mill services.[481]

    Citizens of Crawfordsville slowly established community infrastructure to fill their needs, and with each new building, they changed the landscape from wilderness to the resemblance of civilization. "Society is in a chaotic state," noted Sandford Cox, but "the Baptists talk of building a small house for worship. The Rev. Hackaliah Vredenburg, of the Methodist denomination, preached here a few Sabbaths ago, and took incipient steps for the organization of a church while the Presbyterians think strongly of building a college northwest of

---

[478] Beckwith, B. W. 1880. *History of Vigo and Parke Counties*. Chicago, Illinois: H. H. Hill and N. Iddings, Publishers: 479-480.

[479] Sarver, Bina Thompson. 1976. *Memories, 1816-1916*. n. p.: 4.

[480] "Brief Biography of a Remarkable Woman Related." The Crawfordsville Daily Journal. 18 Feb. 1916, p. 9, c. 4.

[481] Cox, Sandford C. 1860. *Recollections of the Early Settlement of the Wabash Valley*. Lafayette, Indiana: Courier Steam Book and Job Printing House: 20.

town, between Nathaniel Dunn's and the graveyard."[482] In his writings, Cox documented who lived by whom and where they were located. "Old Man Hill has a small mill on the south bank of Sugar river, north of town. West of town, in the country, there is a small neighborhood composed of the following persons and their families, viz: John Beard, Isaac Beeler, three of the Millers (John, Isaac and George), Joseph Cox, John Killen, and John Stitt who owns a little mill about two miles west of town. Southwest of town, near the Fallen Timber, live Crane, Cowen, Scott, and Burbridge. East of town reside Whitlock, Baxter, McCullough, Catterlin, and John Dewey. Further east is Jacob Beeler, Judge Stitt who owns the sawmill, W.P. Ramey, McCaffterty, widow Smith, and the Elmores. Zachariah Gapen has a little tanyard near Stitt's sawmill, and in the vicinity of Kinworthy and Lee's. On the north side of Sugar river, I know of but Abe Miller, Henry and Robert Nicholson, Samuel Brown, Farlow, and Harshbarger. Besides those named, there are but few others living in the town and country. I think I am safe in saying that half a dozen more families would embrace all, including hunters and trappers, within fifty miles around."[483] These men and their families were hard-working, lower class to middle class people. Because most of them probably wore some combination of home spun clothes, Cox was probably not the only one amused or who noticed when citizen "John I. Foster bought a new pair of silver plated spurs, and T.N. Catterlin was seen walking up the street with a pair of curiously embroidered gloves on his hands."[484]

As more people settled in Crawfordsville and the surrounding area, social opportunities increased. Church meetings was the most prominent social gathering but Cox listed many other functions of entertainment - "we had our meetings and our singing schools, sugar boilings and

---

[482] Cox, Sandford C. 1860. *Recollections of the Early Settlement of the Wabash Valley*. Lafayette, Indiana: Courier Steam Book and Job Printing House: 16.
[483] Ibid.
[484] Ibid.

weddings, hoedowns on puncheon floors, and were not annoyed by bad whiskey. As for manly sports requiring mettle and muscle, there were many wild hogs running in the cattail swamps on Lye Creek and Mill Creek, and also large boars.[485]

Amidst all the excitement of the growing community, William and Polly had another son in March 1824 whom they named John. He was their third child and third son. In the short amount of time they had been living in Montgomery County, not only was his family growing, but William Bratton began to serve in prominent roles in the community. In June 1824, he was elected as the first Justice of the Peace in Wayne Township. This township was a large chunk of northwest Montgomery County. Within seven years, two more townships were carved out of it.[486] On September 6, 1824, as part of his duty as a Justice of the Peace, he was sworn in along with Robert Johnston, Samuel McClung, Jesse Richardson, and Absalom Mendenhall to serve as a Board of Justices for Montgomery County. At that time, they elected Robert Johnston to be the president of the Board.[487]

Bratton performed marriage as part of his duties. At that time, in place of a fancy wedding, an eager couple might enthusiastically show up unannounced on the doorstep of the Justice of the Peace or a pastor for the basic ceremony. One morning, a couple showed up at William's house on the hill and Bratton loved to tell about this specific occasion, relayed by his great granddaughter Mary Maud Chesterson. "Then, the Justice never set a price for marrying a couple, but two dollars was the regulation price, so when one morning as he was performing the morning task of rinsing his face before breakfast, his expectation of a $2.00 fee was heightened upon being approached by a country swain with a rifle across his shoulder and leading a blushing maiden, who informed his

---

[485] Cox, Sandford C. Recollections of the Early Settlement of the Wabash Valley, Courier Steam Book and Job Printing House, 1860: 16.
[486] *Waynetown Sesquicentennial, 1830-1980*. Waynetown, Indiana: Waynetown Sesquicentennial Book Committee, 1980: 19.
[487] Indiana. Montgomery County. Commissioner's Book, Book 1: 17.

honor that they were to be made one. The ceremony was performed in Mr. Bratton's most happy way and after kissing the bride, he stood expecting the speedy payment of his fee but had his ardor dampened when the fellow informed him that he had no money, but right then and there made faithful promises to bring him the first pair of venison hams that he should get, and left the 'Squire. The happy couple trotted off over the hill to the south; soon the keen report of a rifle was heard and on going to investigate the cause, the groom was seen approaching at full speed and informed the Justice that his venison hams were just over the hill where a fine buck had been bagged by the happy husband who was more than pleased to be able to pay his debt so soon."[488]

In addition to his duties as a Justice of the Peace for Wayne Township, William Bratton was also appointed superintendent of schools in section sixteen of Township 20 North, Range 6 of Wayne Township on November 6, 1824 by the Commissioners of Montgomery County.[489] When the year turned to 1825, Bratton continued to serve. On January 3, 1825, he traveled to Robert Johnston's house in Crawfordsville to meet with the other members of the Board of Justices. They were still Robert Johnston, Samuel McClung, Absalom Mendenhall, and Jesse Richardson. They were joined by new member, William Moore. Robert Johnston continued to serve as president. [490] Less than two weeks later, on January 15, 1825, William documented in his account book that Andrew Crouch reported that he found a black mare and a brindle cow in Wayne Township. The mare was just over thirteen hands high, and judged to be about two-years-old. She was appraised at the price of $14.50. The cow was judged to be about eleven years and appraised at $7.00.[491]

---

[488] Chesterson, Maud J. Bratton. "William Bratton: His Service in the Lewis and Clark Expedition, 1804-1806 and in the War of 1812." Indiana Pamphlet-00000106839277, Indiana State Library.

[489] *Waynetown Sesquicentennial, 1830-1980*. Waynetown, Indiana: Waynetown Sesquicentennial Book Committee, 1980: 37.

[490] Indiana. Montgomery County. Commissioner's Book 1: 22.

[491] William Bratton Account Book. Archives, Local History Department. Crawfordsville District Public Library, Montgomery County, Indiana.

Whoever their owner turned out to be or whether they were eventually claimed was not noted.

Because William was on the Board of Justices for the county, he not only oversaw Wayne Township business as its Justice of the Peace but also helped with business that pertained to Montgomery County as a whole. Furthermore, although the Wabash River remained some distance to the west of Montgomery County in 1825, legal business pertaining to land directly west and north of Crawfordsville fell to Montgomery County officials. On March 7, 1825, William Digby submitted an application to operate a ferry on the east bank of the Wabash River, in section twenty, Township 23 North, Range 4 West. He planned to charge the following rates for his ferry services: man and horse – eighteen and three quarter cents; single horse – twelve and a half cents; single man – six and a quarter cents; a wagon with four horses or oxen – one dollar; a wagon with two horses or oxen - fifty cents; one cow – twelve and a half cents; and hogs and sheep per head – six and a quarter cents. Tavern keepers also submitted the rates they were charging for their services: wine per bottle – two dollars; brandy per half-pint - fifty cents; gin per half-pint – twenty-five cents; whiskey per half-pint – twelve and a half cents; oats per gallon – twelve and a half cents; corn per gallon – twelve and a half cents; horse per night fed prairie hay – twelve and a half cents; horse fed timothy hay – twenty-five cents; food per meal – twenty-five cents; and lodging per night – twelve and a half cents.[492]

Besides township and county business, William also conducted his own business. On February 18, 1825, he and Polly sold their two adjoining parcels of land in Vermillion County to James Hopkins of Vigo County for $237.50.[493] There is no documentation that William ever made any improvements to this land after he bought it at the land office in Terre Haute, in Vigo County in July 1823. He bought that

---

[492] Indiana. Montgomery County. Commissioner's Book, No. 1: 25-26.
[493] Indiana. Vermillion County. William Bratton entry. Deed Index Book 1: 39-40.

land parcel and the one in Montgomery County within two months of each other, and could have been undecided for a short time as to which one he would make his permanent home. Regardless, the sale of the property provided a nice boost to their finances, worth about $6000 today.

On May 10, 1825, William Bratton was elected president of the Board of Justices. Just a month later, a petition circulated through Crawfordsville in relation to an elderly man named Samuel Fields. He was a Revolutionary War veteran, and served as lieutenant in the 3rd Battalion of Northumberland County, Pennsylvania under Colonel William Hepburn. His captain had been his brother-in-law Thomas Forster. At this time in 1825, Fields was living with his daughter Sarah and her husband John Thompson in their log cabin in Brookville, the county seat of Franklin County, a county on the southeast side of Indiana. Fields was arrested for the murder of a young police officer named Robert Murphy who tried to arrest him for assaulting his neighbor, Elizabeth Rariden. The first time Murphy tried to arrest him, Fields refused to go with him but assured Murphy he would come the next morning. Apparently, Murphy was very new to his job because serving Fields a warrant and arresting him was his first act as an official. When Murphy returned home without arresting Fields, his father advised him that he had better return to do it or deal with the repercussions of being called a coward.[494] Though Fields was an elderly man about eighty-five years of age with completely white hair, it was probably his stubborn, mean, ill-tempered manner that cowed Murphy instead of his size. Consequently, Murphy returned to the cabin with several of Fields' neighbors to make the arrest, but by this time, Fields had suspected that Murphy might return, and he had stowed a large butcher knife out of sight beside the doorway in the crack of the log wall. Fields warned Murphy away but Murphy kept advancing towards the doorway. When Murphy reached the doorstep and proceeded to cross it, Fields snatched his butcher knife and

---

[494] Miller, James M. "An Early Criminal Case – Samuel Fields." Indiana Quarterly Magazine of History. 1905. Vol. 1, No. 4: 201-203.

stabbed him in the left side with it. Murphy died ten days later.[495] Fields' trial for murder commenced in March 1825 in Franklin County. He was found guilty and was condemned to die by hanging on May 27, 1825. People were torn by the situation. Some wanted Fields to be hanged to obtain justice for the murder while others wanted his age and Revolutionary War service taken into account on Fields' behalf. Petitions that supported a pardon for him began circulating urgently through many Indiana counties. After circulating, the petitions were returned to government officials, specifically for Governor James Ray to review. Over 730 signatures were collected statewide in support of a pardon. These petitions were not just important as an example of how the voice of the people was taken into consideration, but also because they became primary documents signifying who was living in what area in Indiana in a time when documents reflecting this many signatures for residents of a community was scarce. The Montgomery County petition serves as not only an early snapshot as to who was in the county, but serves as a mini census exactly halfway between the 1820 and 1830 federal censuses.[496] (See Appendix B for a full list of the men of Montgomery County who signed the petition.) William Bratton did not sign the petition, but nor did any of the current serving members of the Board of Justices. Former Justice Robert Johnston signed the petition perhaps because he was no longer on the Board and could freely sign without bias or a conflict of interest.

    After reviewing all of the petitions, the Governor James Ray granted Fields a pardon but he delivered it in a ridiculously late and dramatic fashion. The events of the day were relayed by a witness, a 13-year-old girl, who stood with the rest of the townsfolk gathered in the town square. Fields was to hang on a large sycamore tree on the riverbank at the

---

[495] Miller, James M. "An Early Criminal Case – Samuel Fields." Indiana Quarterly Magazine of History. 1905. Vol. 1, No. 4: 201-203.
[496] Samuel Fields case. Secretary of State Records. Indiana State Archives. Indianapolis, Indiana.

end of Brookville's main street. It is unclear if other obstructing branches were cut away from the sycamore for this particular hanging or whether this tree had served the town previously before for hangings, but only one large horizontal limb remained on one side where the rope was thrown over. A grave for Fields was already freshly dug not far from the tree. Twenty-five deputies sporting red flannel band of fabric on their right arms and carrying flintlock muskets accompanied Franklin County sheriff Robert John to the log jail in Brookville to fetch Fields. They placed him in a chair on a wagon with a custom platform with his coffin lying beside the chair, and then pulled the wagon underneath the sycamore tree. A minister preached a funeral service, but when it was over, the sheriff tied Fields' hands together, adjusted the noose around his neck and set a black cap on his head that would be pulled down. Sheriff John must have been part of the sympathetic party because he had tears running down his face when he climbed a ladder up the sycamore tree to tie the rope. Once he completed that task, he consulted his watch and announced that Fields had twenty-three minutes left to live. After the time expired, the wagon driver, Walter Rolf, grabbed the reins and cracked his whip for the horses to move forward, and they moved just enough for Fields to be pulled to an erect position when a shout caused Rolf to halt the horses. The Governor who had been racing from Indianapolis that day, rushed up on his horse with a hand-written pardon for Fields.[497]

Fields would eventually end up near Crawfordsville but not for several months. Once Fields was released, his daughter and son-in-law with their infant daughter Isabella took him back to their family fold near the town of Hamilton in Butler County, Ohio. This was where Samuel Fields and his wife Lovia Forster raised their family after they moved there from Pennsylvania. It was also where Lovia's only sibling, a sister, Elizabeth Forster Walker, lived after moving with them from

---

[497] Miller, James M. "An Early Criminal Case – Samuel Fields." Indiana Quarterly Magazine of History. 1905. Vol. 1, No. 4: 201-203.

Pennsylvania. When Samuel Fields, his daughter Sarah, his son-in-law John Thompson, and granddaughter Isabella arrived in Hamilton, Ohio, they found that many of their family members had already moved near Crawfordsville in Montgomery County, Indiana in the last year or so. These family members included Samuel's son Foster Fields and his family; his daughter Dorcas Fields Hahn and her family; his son Stephen Fields and his family; and his daughter Lovia Fields Powers and her family. His daughter Rachel who married first cousin James Forster Walker was still in Hamilton with the rest of the Walker clan. Maybe Samuel, Sarah and John knew that the rest of the family was no longer there and their trip was just a visit, or maybe they did not. Regardless, John and Sarah must have been very patient people, or just very loving, because they made the decision to take Samuel Fields to Montgomery County, Indiana to live with one of his children there.

None of Samuel's children settled in Crawfordsville itself but bought ground in Union Township near Wayne Township, and also in Ripley Township, west of Yountsville.[498] Most of them bought their land directly from the government at the land office, and held patent documents for it. Samuel's son Foster also worked for the local government at certain times. He was employed as a Montgomery County "lister" in 1825 to compile the county's tax lists but was also "exonerated from working on the public highway in the county of Montgomery on account of bodily disability" by the board of justices.[499] It is unclear how long Samuel Fields lived with his children in Montgomery County before he passed away, but it was not more than a couple of years. The exact location of his burial is also unknown but perhaps not totally undeterminable. Somewhat close to his death, his daughter Dorcas Fields Hahn died in 1827. It was most likely from complications from childbirth because her daughter Ann Hahn was born in 1827.

---

[498] *Family Maps of Montgomery County, Indiana*, Arphax Publishing Company, Norman, Oklahoma, 2006: 151.
[499] Indiana. Montgomery County. Commissioner's Book, Book 1: 29.

Many times, pioneers buried a family member on their land and when it grew to a handful of people, it became a family cemetery. There was no Fields or in-law family cemetery in 1825 or by 1827. If Samuel was living with Dorcas and Joseph Hahn and their family, it is possible that Samuel and Dorcas were both buried together on Joseph's patented land. When Joseph Hahn moved westward several years later, there was no description of a cemetery in the deed record for the property he sold which was the usual practice if a cemetery was there but if only two bodies were buried on the property, then perhaps a reference to them did not have to be included. If Samuel had been living with Foster at the time of his death, it is possible that he was buried on Foster's patented land, but a family cemetery was never formally established on his land. A church cemetery is the next likely place for where Samuel could be buried but it is unknown if any of the Fields family attended a specific church at this time. Their denomination of choice was probably Presbyterian because most of the Fields children were married by Presbyterian minister Rev. Matthew G. Wallace in Hamilton, Butler County, Ohio before they emigrated to Montgomery County, Indiana. In Montgomery County, in 1824, a Cumberland Presbyterian church was established one mile west of Waynetown but no physical existence of it remains today.[500] (Cumberland Presbyterian churches were a sect of Presbytery that broke from the traditional Presbytery in 1811 due to a difference of views.

    The question of where to bury a Fields family member arose again a decade later when another bit of bad luck struck the Fields family, this time to Foster Fields. He was not on good terms with his neighbor John Bloomfield due to a never-ending disagreement over a shared road or lane between their properties. One day in 1839, when Bloomfield knew Foster was temporarily away from home, Bloomfield erected a fence

---

[500] Hamil, Lura Coolley. *A Story of Pioneering*. (The Illinois Company, 1955; Internet Archive, 2018): 36-37; *Waynetown Sesquicentennial, 1830-1980*. Waynetown, Indiana: Waynetown Sesquicentennial Book Committee, 1980: 26.

over the lane blocking him from access to his home, and then hid himself nearby waiting for Foster to return. When Foster arrived and saw the fence, he dismounted from his horse and threw it to the side. Bloomfield burst out of his hiding place and engaged Foster in shouting match. It ended with Bloomfield striking Foster over the head with a stake. The blow killed him. Bloomfield though tried was acquitted due to there being no witnesses, and his pleaded self-defense. According to Ripley Township resident Robert Kennedy Krout who lived in the area at the time of the murder, Foster was buried in the Seceder Cemetery, next to the Presbyterian Seceder Church housed in a log cabin there. This church might have been another Cumberland Presbyterian church due to its name. It is unknown who else was buried in the cemetery there.

By 1835, John and Sarah Fields Thompson followed her Field siblings permanently to Montgomery County, Indiana.[501] Many Fields family members who died during and after the 1840s were buried in their family cemetery, Thompson Cemetery, located on Thompson land in Ripley Township.[502] Eliza Ayers, the wife of Foster Fields and many of their children are buried in Thompson Cemetery. However, one of Foster and Eliza's sons is not buried there. Their son Stephen Fields married William and Polly Bratton's daughter Grizzella Ann Berry Bratton and they eventually moved west to Iowa.

---

[501] McCormick, Ruth Glee and Essie Mae Potts. 1968. *Yountsville History*, n.p. Unpublished: 122.

[502] *Cemeteries in Montgomery County, Indiana*. Vol. 11, Wayne Township. Crawfordsville, Indiana: Dorothy Q. Chapter, Daughters of the American Revolution. 1973: 122.

CHAPTER TEN
Life in Montgomery County, 1825-1841

William continued to grow his farm while working as a Justice of the Peace in Wayne Township. Also, he and Polly continued to expand their family. Just before Christmas, on December 23, 1825, William and Polly were blessed with another son and they named him William after his father. He was their fourth child. A short four months after Christmas, William and Polly and their family were joined in Wayne Township of Montgomery County by most of his wife's Maxwell family. His brother-in-law David C. Maxwell bought a parcel of land about four miles away from he and Polly in April 1826. It was northeast of the Bratton farm, and legally described as the east half of the northwest quarter of section eleven in Range 6 of Township 19.[503] David arrived with his newly pregnant wife Elizabeth who went by Betsy, and their one-year-old daughter Martha; another brother-in-law John, age twenty; and sisters-in-law Patsy, age twenty-four; Malinda, age twenty-three; and Prudence, the baby of the family, age fifteen. Also traveling with them was another Maxwell sister, Elizabeth Maxwell Bratton and husband Archibald and their family of seven children, four girls and three boys. Like David's wife Betsy, Elizabeth was pregnant with another child. Maxwell sister Sally and her husband Charles Stuart also came, and brought their two daughters.

    A different accounting of the Maxwell family's arrival to Montgomery County, Indiana trickled down Malinda Maxwell's line. Primary documents such as land records, newspaper

---

[503] David C. Maxwell. U.S. General Land Office Records, 1796-1907. Certificate 3586.

accounts of postal letters and administration sales, and will administration records do not support this story but maybe there are some kernels of truth in some of it. This accounting relayed that the four oldest living Maxwell children – Elizabeth Bratton, David C., Polly Bratton, and Sally Stuart – all traveled together with their spouses to Montgomery County, Indiana from Warren County, Kentucky but that they did not leave until after their mother died. No specific death date has surfaced for their mother Grisal Berry Maxwell but she was listed on the 1820 Federal Census for the Maxwell household in Warren County, Kentucky. If there is a kernel of truth that the children did not leave until after her death, and her daughter Polly Bratton was in Vigo County in 1822, then Grisal died around 1821. The story accounted that the four youngest children stayed with their father outside Bowling Green, Kentucky until he died in 1825. It was at that point that they decided to join their siblings in Indiana. Each of the four youngest children – Patsy, Malinda, John, and Prudence each had a horse to ride for the journey during their preparations but right before they departed, John's horse died so he had to walk. At this time, Patsy was age twenty-three; Malinda, age twenty-two; John, age twenty; and Prudence, age fourteen. They traveled northward, entered Indiana, but when they came to the White River, it was late so they stayed the night in the area before attempting to ford it by ferry. They stayed with an older couple who had retired from running the ferry business. The next morning, the wife urged her husband to accompany the youngest Maxwells and see them safely across the river. She knew that the current ferryman frequently drank and she was worried something might go wrong. He was able to secure them several boats, but they were small so the Maxwells rode in the boats with their things and had the horses swim across beside them. When they reached Crawfordsville, they met several men who were headed towards Waynetown. Upon hearing of John's plight that he did not have a horse and he had walked there, they let him borrow a horse for the last leg of their journey. When they reached William and Mary's house,

William opened the door and calmly called to Polly, "Oh, Polly, the girls have come."[504] Again, primary documents such as land records, newspaper accounts of postal letters and administration sales, and will administration records do not support this account that the Maxwell children split up and came at two different times.

When everyone did arrive, no doubt William was happy to see his brother Archibald and it was possible that letters had been traveling back and forth between them precipitating the move. Again, the death of Maxwell patriarch, James Maxwell in March 1825 was most likely the reason for the timeline of the Maxwell arrival. David and Patsy were executor and executrix of his estate and held an inventory and sale the previous year in Warren County, Kentucky. When the Maxwell siblings and their families moved to Montgomery County to join their sister Polly Bratton in Indiana, the settling of their father's estate was still in process. It might have been impossible or at least a very tight squeeze but they all probably lived with William and Polly until they expeditiously built some type of housing on David's land. Only five months after their arrival, William was designated as Prudence's guardian in September 1826, and David served as surety for the legal proceeding.[505] Once settled, John, Patsy, and Malinda bought a parcel of land together. It bordered David's property in section eleven of Range 6 in Township 19 of Wayne Township. Also, the three single Maxwell girls did not waste much time before getting married and all three were married within a year and a half of their arrival. Surprisingly, it was the youngest sister Prudence who married first. She married Stephen Blackford on September 20, 1827. Malinda married Jonathan Cooley on February 19, 1828, and Patsy married Moses Harriman on

---

[504] Hamil, Lura Coolley. *A Story of Pioneering*. (The Illinois Company, 1955; Internet Archive, 2018): 36-37.

[505] Indiana. Montgomery County. Prudence S. Maxwell entry. Guardians Docket, 25 Sept. 1826. Database. Crawfordsville District Public Library. http://history.cdpl.lib.in.us/Presto.

August 19, 1828.[506] During this time, William and Polly also had another son on April 28, 1828, and they named him Robert after his uncle. He was their fifth child.

Despite the excitement and upheaval of the Maxwells arriving and settling in, according to William's account book, he also continued to be busy with township and county business as well as his own affairs for several years. One resident, Joseph Hahn who was previously mentioned as a member of the extended Fields family, filed charges on more than one occasion in 1826. He first filed against Daniel Hopkins in order to collect Hopkins debt from an overdue account. In his account book, William noted how much money it cost for the case to be prosecuted by him and other related parties. To summon him as a Justice, it was twenty-five cents; for him to issue a subpoena, it was another twenty-five cents, and to render a judgement cost over ten cents. To have the deputy constable, Henry Donahue, serve a summons to Hopkins, it cost twenty-five cents plus the mileage for four miles at four cents per mile; and to have the constable serve subpoenas to four witnesses, John Swearingen, Samuel McClung, William Crooks, and Michael Hahn, it cost fifty cents plus mileage for six miles at four cents a mile. Each witness was also paid twenty-five cents to appear. William Bratton found for Hahn but it is unclear if Hahn had to pay the court costs or if Hopkins had to pay for them.[507] In another case, Hahn filed a complaint against William Mann for trespass and damages. Again, witnesses were secured and they were Michael Harshbarger, Michael Hahn, William Crooks, and John Mann. After the allegations and evidence were submitted to William Bratton, he found for

---

[506] Indiana. Montgomery County. Marriage Records, Database, C Crawfordsville District Public Library. http://history.cdpl.lib.in.us/Presto.

[507] William Bratton Account Book. The Marian Morrison Local History Collection, Reference Department. Crawfordsville District Public Library. Crawfordsville, Indiana.

the plaintiff, and declared that William Mann had to pay Hahn fifty cents in damages and seventy eight cents in court costs.[508]

In other business, on May 21, 1827, William Talbert reported to William Bratton that he found a sorrel mare. Talbert lived on Coal Creek, about ten miles from Crawfordsville. The mare had a long star on her forehead and was about four-years-old. Joseph and John W. Washburn appraised her at $20.[509] On November 18, 1828, Daniel Mosburger paid William $1.25 for his service in some matter of controversy between Mosburger and woman, Fanny Taylor. A suit between the two occurred earlier in the year in May, and Mosburger's payment to William in November was Mosburger's final payment. On February 6, 1829, William Crooks reported to William Bratton that he found a bay mare. Crooks lived three and a half miles west of Crawfordsville which was considered Wayne Township at the time. The mare was fourteen hands and three inches high. Her horseshoes were steel-toed. She was appraised for $40 and was deemed a natural trotter.[510]

Another role that William Bratton served in was as Judge of the General Election for Wayne Township in both 1828 and 1829. He was paid seventy-five cents from the Wayne Township treasury for this one-day job in each year.[511] As Justice of the Peace, William was bombarded with a barrage of cases pertaining to single women having babies during the spring and summer of 1829. On March 20, 1829, Polly Cooper filed a complaint against Henry Donahue, stating he was the father of the male infant she delivered on March 1, 1829. Donahue agreed to pay Cooper $40 for the maintenance of the child which Cooper agreed to. Donahue also gave bond for $300 with Michael Donahue as his security, payable to the

---

[508] William Bratton Account Book. The Marian Morrison Local History Collection, Reference Department. Crawfordsville District Public Library. Crawfordsville, Indiana.
[509] Ibid.
[510] Ibid.
[511] Indiana. Montgomery County. Commissioner's Book, Book 1: 92, 102.

overseers of the poor of Wayne Township. On June 6, 1829, Jane Williams filed a complaint to William against Baldon Heaton, stating she was pregnant by him. William issued a warrant for Heaton and instructed Edwin Quick to deliver it to him. Quick returned the warrant on June 15, 1829 and said that Heaton "had made his escape and was going at large and could not be found." Just a week later on June 23, 1829, Nancy Clifton filed a complaint to William against Christopher Mann, a married man with a family. Christopher Mann was a neighbor of William's, and at the time of this two-month affair, he was age fifty-four, and married to Elizabeth Rusk, the daughter of Montgomery County pioneer David Rusk. He already had three sons under the age of five at the time, and another son between the ages of five to nine years.[512] When Nancy discovered she was pregnant, she filed a complaint with William Bratton in order to establish the paternity of her baby and to possibly receive support. Bratton issued a warrant to be delivered by Wayne Township constable Randle D. Bryant "commanding him to take the body of Christopher Mann and forthwith have him before me to be dealt with according to law."[513] The next day Christopher and Nancy both appeared before William Bratton. The case proceeded as the state of Indiana vs. Christopher Mann on complaint of Nancy Clifton, an unmarried woman, for bastardy. It was different from the other cases because William recorded the questions that Christopher Mann as the defendant asked Nancy Clifton who was identified as the complainant. Mann's motive based on the questions is not readily apparent by the answers. It is possible he tried to intimidate or shame her.

> "Be it remembered that on the examination of the said Nancy Clifton under her oath before me, William Bratton, a Justice of the Peace in and for

---

[512] 1830 United States Census. Montgomery County, Indiana. digital image s. v. "Christopher Mann," Ancestry.com.
[513] William Bratton Account Book. The Marian Morrison Local History Collection. Reference Department. Crawfordsville District Public Library. Crawfordsville, Indiana.

said Montgomery County, in the presence of the said Christopher Mann who hath been brought before me by virtue of my warrant issued upon the complaint aforesaid. The said Nancy Clifton saith that on or about the eighth day of February 1829 and at several other times since, the said Christopher Mann, and her, the said Nancy Clifton, carnally knew, whereby she, the said Nancy Clifton, is now pregnant with a child and that he, the said Christopher Mann, is the father of said child."

Question by defendant – Can you recollect the day that I carnally knew you since 8th day of February?
Answer by complainant – No.

Question by defendant – Do you know how many times since the 8th day of February?
Answer by complainant – Twice.

Question by defendant – Do you remember if one of the times was when I had been at Parker's and I came home when it snowed so fast?
Answer by complainant – No.

Question by defendant – When I went to a meeting at David Rusk's and my wife was left at her father's, was it the first time?
Answer by complainant – Yes.

Question by defendant – Was that before the 8th of February?
Answer by complainant– Yes.

Question by defendant – When was the next time?
Answer by complainant – At your house.

Question by defendant – When was the last time?
Answer by complainant – On the 8th day of May.

The result of the case was that Christopher Mann made a bond of $300 with Samuel Means Cooley as his security, that was paid to Dennis Ball and John Watts, overseers of the Wayne Township poor. Three hundred dollars in 1824 was equivalent to almost $8000 today. Wayne Township overseers administered these funds to Nancy as needed over time to support her baby. The residence that belonged to a Parker that Mann referred to might have been the home of William Parker. He lived thirteen miles northwest of Crawfordsville in Montgomery County. He reported to William Bratton that he found a stray heifer on March 28, 1829. It was appraised by Solomon Decker to be about one-year-old and worth $2.50. Samuel Means Cooley who served as Mann's security was the brother of Jonathan Cooley who was William Bratton's brother-in-law from Cooley's marriage to another Maxwell sister, Malinda.[514]

On October 29, 1829, William expanded his farm. He bought a forty-acre parcel of the northwest quarter of Section 19 in Township 19, Range 5 from Reuben and Laura Munger for $200.[515] Just a few months later, he bought another parcel in the neighboring section, section twenty, for $200 from his brother George Jr. and his wife Betsey Ann. George Jr. bought the parcel previously even though he and his wife had always lived in Warren County, Kentucky. Perhaps George Jr. thought very seriously at one time about moving north that he purchased the parcel and then determined by January 1830 that he was not going to move with his family after all.[516]

---

[514] William Bratton Account Book. The Marian Morrison Local History Collection. Reference Department. Crawfordsville District Public Library. Crawfordsville, Indiana.

[515] Indiana. Montgomery County. *Montgomery County General Index of Deeds,* William Bratton and Reuben Munger land deed, Book 1: 194.

[516] Indiana. Montgomery County. *Montgomery County General Index of Deeds*, William Bratton and George Bratton land deed, Book 1: 418.

Sometime in the late 1820s, more Maxwell kin arrived in the area. A maternal aunt, Mary Berry Hutton, her husband Leonard Hutton, and her family traveled from Washington County, Virginia. They settled in Fountain County, Indiana. Fountain County was directly west of Montgomery County, and bordered Wayne Township. Mary Berry Hutton was the aunt who Polly Bratton, officially Mary Hutton Maxwell Bratton, was named after. In addition, just like her sister, Grisal Berry Maxwell, Mary Berry Hutton named several of her daughters after her sisters as well. She named one daughter Prudence Steele Hutton after her sister Prudence Berry Steele. She named another daughter Grizella Maxwell Hutton after her sister Grisal Berry Maxwell and this daughter married George Davidson Miller in Fountain County. George Miller was a graduate in the third graduating class at nearby Wabash College in Crawfordsville, and he became a Presbyterian pastor. Mary Berry Hutton named another daughter Martha "Patsy" Wilson Hutton after her stepmother, and she named yet another daughter Sarah Dryden Hutton after her sister Sarah Berry Dryden. In the 1830 census, Leonard and Mary Hutton had seven children living with them before Leonard Hutton died in 1831. By 1850, Mary moved with two of her daughters, Prudence Hutton Miller and Grizella Hutton Miller, to White County, Indiana where she died in April 1850.[517]

During the summer of 1830, the Wayne Township census taker David Vance visited William and his family to log their information for the federal government. William was check-marked under the column of males, age fifty to fifty-nine; Polly, his wife, was tallied under the column for women, age twenty to twenty-nine; several males were also accounted for with one at age ten to fourteen; two males five to nine, and two males under five. The census taker recorded everyone almost exactly right. William was age fifty-two, but Polly was age thirty-three and should have been tallied under the column thirty to forty. A discrepancy like this was not uncommon and

---

[517] 1850 United States Census, Mortality Schedule. White County, Indiana. Mary Hutton entry. Ancestry.com.

could have happened for a variety of reasons. Either Vance accidentally tallied the wrong column, or Polly did not reveal her true age, or she was not there and someone else in the family offered information to the best of their knowledge. The Bratton children were represented true to their ages - James Maxwell was age ten; George was age eight; John was age six; William was age four, and Robert was age two.[518] William's family continued to grow. In 1831, they welcomed their sixth son, Adam, named after William's brother.

Montgomery County continued to grow and by 1831, the population was around 3000 people. The old log courthouse was no longer big enough to conduct county business, and a new one was necessary. The contract for a new courthouse was awarded to John Hughes for $3430 and he built a two-story, forty-foot square brick building with a cupola.[519] By May 1832, if the courthouse was finished, it was at the center of much hoopla. Rumors arrived in town that a band of hostile Native Americans was headed their way, that the band was near Lafayette and had already killed two men. Crawfordsville officials sent messengers to homes of county militia commanders to ready their men for war and to hasten to Crawfordsville for duty. "The colonel, major and captains were all on hand with their red and white plumes, red sashes, and shining brass buttons, and hardy settlers in homespun shirts brought their trusty rifles, powder-horns, and deer-skin bullet pouches." This patriotic fervor resulted in a recruitment of a 100-man infantry and a fifty-man cavalry.[520] The infantry and cavalry joined others that scouted the general area. At one point in the two to three-week timeframe, Crawfordsville citizens were "suddenly astounded by the arrival of a courier at full speed with the announcement that the Indians, more than a thousand in number, were then crossing the Nine-Mile

---

[518] 1830 United States Census. Montgomery County, Indiana. William Bratton family. Ancestry.com.
[519] Beckwith, B. W. 1880. *History of Vigo and Parke Counties*. Chicago, Illinois: H. H. Hill and N. Iddings, Publishers: 25-26.
[520] Ibid.

prairie about twelve miles north of town, killing and scalping all. The strongest houses were immediately put in a condition of defense, and sentinels were placed at principal points in the direction of the enemy. Scouts were sent out to reconnoiter, and messengers were dispatched in different directions to announce the danger to the farmers, and to urge them to hasten with their families and to assist in fighting the momentarily expected savages."[521] Their soldiers were elsewhere but scouts were able to report that the Native Americans had not crossed the Wabash River by sunset. In fact, the Native Americans were over 100 miles away. This kind of alarm was running through communities and counties along the western border of Indiana from Vincennes north to La Porte, Indiana. The actual action against Black Hawk and his warriors occurred in Illinois along their western border. Eventually, tension petered out, and life resumed to normal. During some of that scary year, Polly Bratton was pregnant. On April 24, 1833, William and Mary had their first daughter, Grizzella Ann Berry Bratton, named after Polly's mother.

William's neighborhood in Wayne Township continued to grow and church congregations began to form. Congregations did not have their own buildings to worship in yet, but people met in each other's homes.[522] William Bratton's brother-in-law, Jonathan Cooley was elected as trustee for Township 19 N, Range 5 West for three years from August 4, 1838. He also served as Wayne Township treasurer after he was elected May 11, 1839.[523]

Through a diary of Barton Griffith, we learn a little more about William and Polly's neighbors. Griffith was a young man from Covington, Indiana, a town located in neighboring Fountain County. Barton was the manager of the Sloan

---

[521] *The History of La Porte County*. 1880. Indiana: Chas. C. Chapman & Company: 432.
[522] Walters, Pauline Randel. 1975. *The History of Churches in Montgomery County, Indiana, 1821-1975*. Wesley Methodist Church (formerly Wesley Chapel) Indiana: CPR Walters: 183-184.
[523] Indiana. Montgomery County. School Commissioners Journal: 113.

Merchandise Store in Covington. On May 1834, Barton left Covington to travel to New Orleans. At the beginning of his journey, he stopped at the farm of Nathan Small for a meal he called "strong food" which he bought for twenty-five cents.[524] Mr. Small and Louisa, his bride of four years, were a pioneer couple working hard to clear land for a prosperous farm. The farm would eventually equal 1000 acres and be distributed among six of their nine children who survived to adulthood.[525] When Griffith visited their home, he was not very complimentary of Louisa. "My lady, in this case, was one of the most portly and boasted the most masculine arm I ever saw."[526] Griffith traveled through Crawfordsville where he stayed overnight at Ristine's. Griffith's brother lived in Crawfordsville also, but maybe he rented a room and there was no room for Barton to sleep. The two brothers ate dinner at an establishment owned by a Mr. Jones and Griffith thought the food was excellent. They then watched a scholarly exhibition at the Manual Labor College by the male students. (This would later be known as Wabash College. The school was first established in 1832.) He found that the students "acquitted themselves with credit."[527] The next morning Griffith left Crawfordsville to continue his journey but not before complaining to Ristine that the bed he was assigned was too hard and not big enough for him and the gentleman he had to share it with who was sick to boot.[528] Barton Griffith made it successfully to New Orleans but contracted dysentery there and died a few days after he arrived back home in Covington.

One of the more popular trips people undertook by the 1830s was to travel north to Lafayette, which had grown in the

---

[524] Griffith, James Barton. 1932. *The Diary of Barton Griffith, Covington, Indiana, 1832-1834*. Crawfordsville, Indiana: R. E. Banta: 2.

[525] Beckwith, B. W. 1880. *History of Vigo and Parke Counties*. Chicago, Illinois: H. H. Hill and N. Iddings, Publishers: 605.

[526] Griffith, James Barton. 1932. *The Diary of Barton Griffith, Covington, Indiana, 1832-1834*. Crawfordsville, Indiana: R. E. Banta: 2.

[527] Ibid: 3.

[528] Ibid.

ten years after William Digby platted it. In 1835, Lafayette had a population of roughly 2500 people but grew quickly due to its prime location on the Wabash River. Shipping was a big business and abounded down the river to the Ohio River and on to New Orleans. River commerce was much faster than roads in the 1830s and 40s. Crawfordsville pioneer girl Bina Thompson Sarver described travel on roads as "slow and many roads were impassable in wet weather. Various means were used to keep the wagons from becoming mired in the mud. The road from Crawfordsville to Lafayette was one of these, so someone came up with the idea of making a road of logs, laid side by side and very close together. Trees were cut, trimmed and one side hewed flat. Laid flat side up, they became a plank or corduroy road.[529] The construction and maintenance of these roads was consistently paid for every few miles through a tollhouse and a man was appointed to stay there and collect money as a toll fee from everyone who used the road.

In 1835, William and Polly Bratton lost their son Robert who died at age seven.[530] They and their Maxwell relatives also lost another one of their members, Charles Stuart, the husband of Sally Berry Maxwell Stuart.[531] It is unclear if Charles Stuart was buried in the nearby cemetery in Waynetown like little Robert Bratton or if he was taken back to Warren County, Kentucky where he still owned land. A gravestone is not found for him in either location. On November 9, 1835, a neighbor, Dennis Ball, was granted guardianship of Charles and Sally Stuart's five children, Mary E., age fourteen; Sarah Jane, age twelve; Ann Mariah, age seven; James Alexander, age five; and Harriet Amanda, age four. Ball lived south of William and Polly Bratton and was also a long-time resident of Wayne Township. He came to Montgomery County from Butler County, Ohio, and

---

[529] Sarver, Bina Thompson. 1976. *Memories, 1816-1916*. n. p.: 4.
[530] Robert Bratton gravestone. Old Pioneer Cemetery. Waynetown, Montgomery County, Indiana.
[531] Charles Stuart (s.v. Stewart) probate papers, Box 4, Order 29. The Marian Morrison Local History Collection. Reference Department. Crawfordsville District Public Library. Crawfordsville, Indiana.

bought four parcels from the government as patent ground on March 5, 1825. William served as a surety for the transaction.

By the middle 1830s, Montgomery County was the destination for many migrating from outside the state. In one letter written in 1836 by Mrs. Eliza Julia Speed Fry, she talked about a shortage of furniture due to so many people moving there. Eliza was the daughter of William Smith and Mary Speed, and she wrote from Crawfordsville to her uncle Judge John Speed at Farmington, his plantation home outside Louisville, Kentucky. Eliza with her husband Thomas Walker Fry and their younger children had recently moved to Crawfordsville to run a mill, leaving behind their own Kentucky plantation home called Spring House. They must have left their own furnishings with the house, because Eliza wrote that when writing her letter she had no table to write on or a chair to sit on. She was especially upset she did not even have a bedstead. "I can tell you the old Speed temper was so strong in me I could not write," she wrote to her uncle. As she described the furniture situation with her uncle, you can envision a glimpse of what was happening in Crawfordsville at the time. "The emigration to this place is so great, there is such a demand for furniture. It is improbable for it to be made as fast as it is called for," she wrote. "We have a tolerable good house, four rooms, a kitchen, milk house and dairy, good society, much piety, and as much industry as ever you saw in one place......we are quite well-pleased, it will be in a few years a great place."[532] Another letter written by Robert Kennedy Krout to his sister Jane in 1908, reminisced about their own journey to Montgomery County from Covington, Kentucky in 1837. "Our wagon was drawn by two faithful old horses, Tom Tinker and Fanny Fletcher." Robert's mother, Mary Hannah Kennedy Krout, died about a month after his birth, so in 1837, it was he, his father Jacob Krout, and his sister traveling in the wagon. They were accompanied by his uncle Lawson Moore and Robert's little dog Veney, both of whom traveled most of

---

[532] Eliza Julia Speed Fry letter. The Filson Historical Society. Louisville, Kentucky.

the way on foot..."Uncle Lawson to procure peaches from roadside orchards and Veney to beg a bone from kind mistresses of the houses," he wrote. The family settled in Ripley Township. "I can see the old log houses looming up before me now, with their mud and stick chimneys crowned at their tops with lumps of clay of the size and shape of huge corn dodgers. In those houses, you and I made our home for some years."[533]

In 1836, William and Polly had a houseguest for two weeks. It was a fifteen-year-old boy named Isaac Davis. He was the son of Randolph and Abigail Davis. They were originally from Butler County, Ohio and moved to Montgomery County in 1826. Isaac was one of their nine children. The reason Isaac stayed with them is unknown but he relayed the only existing physical description that we have of William Bratton today. Isaac described him as over six feet tall, "spare of build, very straight and erect." Isaac also described William as "rather reserved, but a man of great intelligence and the strictest morals, that his neighbors not only respected, but loved him." Isaac and William Bratton talked about William's experiences on the Lewis and Clark Expedition. It was from Isaac's stories about William to William's grandchildren that we learn of William's amusement of how the Native Americans always assumed York was the leader of their party, that they would put him on their shoulders, and gave their presents of skins and furs to York.[534]

In 1838, William and Polly were blessed with another daughter. They named her Eliza Jane. Perhaps they were also following the Scottish Onomastic naming pattern and named her partially after her paternal grandmother or after her aunt Jenny Bratton Lewis. Eliza Jane Bratton died as an infant and was buried in the Old Pioneer Cemetery in Waynetown next to

---

[533] Robert Kennedy Krout letter. The Filson Historical Society. Louisville, Kentucky.

[534] Chesterson, Maud J. Bratton. "William Bratton: His Service in the Lewis and Clark Expedition, 1804-1806 and in the War of 1812." Indiana Pamphlet-00000106839277, Indiana State Library.

her brother Robert.[535] Her gravestone is shared with a sibling identified only as an infant with no gender, birth or death information, only the names of her parents, William and Mary H. Bratton. Because the information for the infant sibling was chiseled exactly as hers, it was created by the same stonemason. It is possible that since they share the stone that maybe they were twins and the infant died soon after birth while Eliza Jane lived a little longer.[536]

Waynetown was originally established as Middletown by pioneer Samuel Mann in 1830. Another little community sprang up near William Bratton and his extended family called Wesley. It was located six miles west of Crawfordsville. A church was built on a hill there, on William Switzer's land. and was referred to by some people as the "Church on the Hill."[537] Another nearby church was the New Salem United Bethren Church, located one mile east of Wesley. Within two years, the Wesley community built the Wesley Academy to supply a more formal institution to educate their children. At that time, when Wesley community members traveled into Crawfordsville, they would have crossed Sugar Creek along a new bridge called Sperry's Bridge. It was named for Henry Sperry who operated a mill just north of the bridge on the east side of the road.[538]

On November 9, 1839, Dennis Ball died and a new guardian was needed for the Stuart children. By February 1840, William attended the Probate Court of Montgomery County for two days and was appointed guardian to Charles and Sally's children. The estate paid him $1.50 for his time. At this time, Mary Elizabeth Stuart was age nineteen and had married the previous May to Harvey Johnson; Sarah Jane Stuart was age seventeen; Ann Mariah Stuart was age twelve;

---

[535] Eliza Jane Bratton gravestone. Old Pioneer Cemetery. Waynetown. Montgomery County, Indiana.
[536] Infant Bratton, Old Pioneer Cemetery. Waynetown. Montgomery County, Indiana.
[537] Walters, Pauline Randel. 1975. *The History of Churches in Montgomery County, Indiana, 1821-1975*. Wesley Methodist Church (formerly Wesley Chapel) Indiana: CPR Walters: 183-184.
[538] Sarver, Bina Thompson. 1976. *Memories, 1816-1916*. n. p.: 5.

James Alexander Stuart was age ten; and Harriet Amanda Stuart was age eight. Their uncle David C. Maxwell served as surety. This guardianship and administration of Charles Stuart's estate in Warren County, Kentucky took up much of his time and became like a second job, taking a back seat only to his own affairs.[539] He made many trips back and forth to Bowling Green in Warren County, Kentucky. Once appointed, he earned fifteen cents a day from the estate. More importantly, he provided food for the Stuart family. In one specific instance, he delivered beef, flour, cornmeal and coffee. He was paid $17.33 by the estate for this food.[540] In another instance, in March 1840, he traveled to Coal Creek Township and nearby Covington, Indiana in the neighboring Fountain County on estate business and was paid $1.50 for his time. He traveled to Bowling Green, Kentucky and stayed from March 27-April 24, 1840, and for his effort and expenses, the estate paid him $40.00. On April 11, 1840, William entered the courthouse in Bowling Green and paid the county clerk there for a certificate and seal. The estate reimbursed him one dollar.

Administrating the estate of Charles Stuart lasted into the next year and as the administrator, William continued to do various tasks. He visited William Burnsides in Fountain County on estate business and delivered a money order and the estate paid William $1.50 for his service. He delivered cornmeal and flour to Sarah for her and the children and the estate paid him $3. 87. William went to Crawfordsville to pick up a money order from a man named Humphrey and took it to the Fountain County clerk in Covington and the estate paid him $1.50. William paid the postage for a letter from the Sheriff of Fountain County and the estate reimbursed him six cents for the postage. William traveled to Fountain County by horse to

---

[539] Charles Stuart (s.v. Stewart) estate. Guardian's Docket, Book 1, p. 25. The Marian Morrison Local History Collection. Reference Department. Crawfordsville District Public Library. Crawfordsville, Indiana.

[540] William Bratton Account Book. The Marian Morrison Local History Collection. Reference Department. Crawfordsville District Public Library. Crawfordsville, Indiana.

attend a sale and returned home. He was paid $2.25 by the estate so maybe some of the items he bought were for Sally and the children but the estate also paid him thirty-seven cents for his expenses while attending the sale. William went to Crawfordsville to have money changed. The estate paid him fifteen cents; and William again traveled to Warren County, Kentucky on estate business. The estate paid him $45.00.

Henry Crawford, a Waynetown merchant, was one of the proprietors who received the most business from William Bratton for the Bratton household and from William Bratton and Sarah Suart for the Stuart household. Henry Crawford arrived in Montgomery County in 1827.[541] Crawford ran his general store out of a log cabin.[542] In a two-year period, William bought the following items from Crawford – indigo (a plant for blue dye), madder (red dye), pepper, coffee, muslin, sole leather, paper, Epson salts, a spelling book, brass buttons, screws, horseshoes, flannel, other buttons, canvas, tin cups, and calico, needles, quilling, spools of thread, silk, cotton hose, and yarn. Perhaps the most curious item that William bought from Crawford was listed as brimstone. Brimstone was also known as sulfur. Sometimes it was mixed with lard to create an ointment to treat lice, and children would also wear little bags of it around their neck at school which parents believed would prevent their children from getting it.[543] William paid a quarter of his bill with chickens, feathers, apples, eggs, and returned a pair of silk gloves. In the Stuart household, in a three-year period, Sally received the following items from Crawford – yarn, blankets, sole leather, muslin, bowls, sincy which was a kind of fabric, coffee, merino, flannel, velvet, hooks and eyes, lace, tea, pepper, calico, a hair comb, side combs, black silk, ribbon, silk gloves, white satin, tuck combs, footing, edging,

---

[541] Robinson, Dick. "Henry Crawford Was an Early Merchant." Montgomery County Magazine. Dec. 1977: 17.
[542] *Waynetown Sesquicentennial, 1830-1980*. Waynetown, Indiana: Waynetown Sesquicentennial Book Committee, 1980: 15.
[543] McKnight, William James. 1905. *A Pioneer Outline History of Northwestern Pennsylvania*. Philadelphia, Pennsylvania: J.B. Lippincott Company: 400.

and ruled paper. William periodically settled her account with Crawford.

In late spring, May 2, 1840, William and Polly joyfully welcomed their daughter, Mary Etta. She was their youngest daughter and last child. Several months later, a local census taker once again visited the William Bratton household to record its occupants for the 1840 Federal Census. William was check-marked under the column for being a male, age sixty to sixty-nine; Polly, his wife, was tallied under the column, age forty to forty-nine; three males were also accounted for within the column for males fifteen to nineteen; one male was recorded in the column for males ten to fourteen, and one male was recorded for being between the age of five to nine. The census taker recorded everyone exactly right. William was age sixty-two, Polly was age forty-four, James Maxwell was age twenty; George was age eighteen; John was age sixteen; William was age fourteen, Adam was age nine, Grizzella was age seven, and the new baby Mary Etta was a few months old.

CHAPTER ELEVEN
Will the Real William Bratton Please Stand Up?

In the fall of 1832, another William Bratton was paring down his possessions in Virginia. He and his wife sorted through their household and personal items, and culled them to crucial necessities that would fit in a four-horse wagon. They planned to pull out in just a few days with their family on a journey from Augusta County, Virginia to Montgomery County, Indiana. William R. Bratton was a farmer and enslaver just four years younger than William E. Bratton. Both men were members of the same extended Bratton family of Augusta and Bath Counties, Virginia, and were first cousins. William R. Bratton was born July 3, 1782 in Bath County, Virginia, as the second son of James B. Bratton and his wife Rebekah Hogshead.[544] James B. Bratton was the eldest son of Robert Bratton and Ann McFarland of Augusta County, Virginia, and it is likely that William's middle initial R was for Robert. He married Mary Gambrel Berry, the daughter of James Berry and Jane Doak of Augusta County, Virginia.

Only William R. Bratton's mother Rebekah was alive at this time because William R. Bratton's father James passed away in 1828. She lived in the family home named Rock Rest which is still standing today. It is three and half miles east of Millboro Springs in Bath County. The home is two stories with twelve rooms. One end of the home was constructed with brick while a part of the kitchen was constructed with logs.[545] It was James

---

[544] Union Hill Cemetery Records. Database. Crawfordsville District Public Library. Porter, William Arthur. 1934. *A History of Union Presbyterian Church, 1834-1934*. Indianapolis: 19- 20.
[545] Wood, Russell G. The Bratton Home survey report. WPA Virginia Historical Inventory, Report 120. Library of Virginia.

and Rebekah Bratton's first home. Their more modest first home was nearby, about two miles west of Rock Rest. It was one and a half stories, and constructed of logs on one end and a stone chimney with a large fireplace placed in the middle to bisect each part of the house. After James and Rebekah built Rock Rest, their other home was used to house their enslaved people.[546]

When William R. Bratton's father James died, William R. served as co-executor with his brother Andrew for his father's estate, which was probated in July of 1828 in Bath County. In his father's will dated May 6, 1826, William was bestowed the tract of land where he and his family lived and 400 acres on the Big Calfpasture River. He also received $300 and the ownership of an enslaved male named Orville.

By looking at the inventory in James B. Bratton's estate, it reflected a detailed picture of Rock Rest and the kind of atmosphere in which William R. Bratton grew up. James and Rebekah Bratton owned some of the typical early 1800s items such as the house, furniture, tools, wood, crops, guns, looms, whiskey and stills, but they also enjoyed some luxury items such as three gilt mirrors, a clock, a walnut desk, a bookcase with books on geography, religion, biographies and evangelism.[547] The ownership of several enslaved people was also a reflection of their wealth. In James Bratton's will, an enslaved man named William and an enslaved woman named Mary were bestowed to William's mother Rebekah; enslaved people Anderson, Lilly, Bill, Sam and Charlotte were bestowed to William's sister Rebekah Bratton McClung; and enslaved people May, Peggy and Isaac were bestowed to William's sister Margaret Bratton Crawford. The household items listed in the estate were possibly the same kind of items that William had to sift through to decide what to pack. Because Indiana was a

---

[546] Wood, Russell G. The Bratton Home survey report. WPA Virginia Historical Inventory, Report 120. Library of Virginia.
[547] Bruns, Jean Randolph. 1995. *Abstracts of the Wills and Inventories of Bath County, Virginia, 1791-1842*. Baltimore, Maryland: Clearfield Publishing Company: 139, 148.

free state and slavery was illegal there, it is most likely that William R. Bratton left Orville behind with family but rented him out to family or friends for compensation, or sold him.

    The decision to move from Virginia to Montgomery County, Indiana might not have been very difficult for William R. Bratton and his wife Mary because several family members were already living there. William R. Bratton's sister Margaret "Peggy" Bratton Crawford and her husband William Crawford lived in the southwest portion of Union Township in Montgomery County, Indiana. In 1829, Peggy and William Crawford sold their home in Bath County, Virginia to William Crawford's sister Martha "Patsy" Crawford Burger and her husband Joseph Burger. The home, built in 1786 by Andrew Crawford, was passed down in 1803 to William Crawford's father Nathan Crawford, and then to William and Margaret Crawford. It was located two miles west of Millboro Springs in Bath County and was two stories with six rooms. The oldest part of the house was in the front which was built of weatherboarded logs. The interior of the home was sealed with boards and the exterior was finished with planed boards from a local sawmill. A large chimney with a large fireplace dominated the back part of the house.[548] Their house in Montgomery County, Indiana would not have been so large. On Thanksgiving Day in 1829, William Crawford paid David Barnes $300 for land four miles east of Crawfordsville.[549] The next summer, county officer David Vance called at their homestead to gather their demographics for the 1830 census. Some of the neighbors living close to the Crawfords were William Burbridge, Isaac Watkins, Andrew Smith and David McCabe.[550] Soon after Vance's visit, William Crawford made a

---

[548] Wood, Russell G. The Burger Home survey report. WPA Virginia Historical Inventory, Report 54. Library of Virginia.
[549] Indiana. Montgomery County. *Montgomery County General Index of Deeds*, William Crawford and David Barnes land deed, Book 1: 389; Boyd, Gregory A. 2006. *Family Maps of Montgomery County, Indiana*. Plat Map. Norman, Oklahoma: Arphax Publishing Company: 161.
[550] 1830 United States Census. Walnut Township, Montgomery County, Indiana, digital s. v. "William Crawford" Ancestry.com.

visit to the land office in Crawfordsville. He purchased another eighty acres in Union Township on February 1, 1831 and another 320 acres of land in the bordering township of Walnut Township on March 3, 1831.[551] When Walnut Township was organized in 1831, it was six miles square and was bordered by Boone County on its east side. It was covered with woodland, and settlers who came at this time cleared what land they could and erected primitive log cabins. The township was named for the numerous large tracts of walnut trees that grew along the banks of what became known as Walnut Creek that meandered through the land.[552] Later that year, William and Peggy Bratton Crawford celebrated the wedding of their son Nathan Crawford and Margaret Simpson on November 17, 1831.[553] Several months later in July 1832, William Crawford bought another 160 acres in Walnut Township.[554] William Nelson Youel, a brother-in-law to William R. Bratton's wife Mary Berry Bratton, was also living in Montgomery County, Indiana. William Youel married Jane Berry in 1816 in Augusta County, Virginia. The William Youel family lived in Rockbridge County, Virginia before making their own trip to Montgomery County, Indiana in 1830. They made their trip in the latter half of the year since they were listed on the 1830 census taken in the summer in Rockbridge County, Virginia.[555] Additionally, their daughter Mary Margaret who was born in March 1830, was born in Virginia according to later censuses. Once in Montgomery County, Indiana, it is possible that the William Crawford family opened up their home to the Youel family until William Youel bought eighty acres in Walnut Township

---

[551] William Crawford land certificates, #10016, #13270, #13251, Bureau of Land Management. http://glorecords.blm.gov.
[552] Bowen, A.W. 1913. *History of Montgomery County, Indiana: with personal sketches of representative citizens.* Vol. 1. Indpls., In,: A.W. Bowen & Co.: 439.
[553] Shanklin, Mabel V. 1971. *Montgomery County, Indiana Will and Marriage Records.* Vol. 1. Danville, Illinois: Heritage House, Danville, Illinois. Vol. 1.
[554] William Crawford land certificate, #15358. Bureau of Land Management. http://glorecords.blm.gov.
[555] 1830 United States Census. Virginia. Rockbridge County. William Nelson Youel entry. Ancestry.com.

on March 3, 1831 and another 160 acres on January 3, 1832.[556] It is also possible that the David Doak Berry family could have traveled to Montgomery County, Indiana from Augusta County, Virginia with his sister Jane Berry Youel and his brother-in-law. David was granted a land patent to two parcels of land on January 3, 1832 in Walnut Township.[557] The patent stated David's place of residence as Montgomery County so he arrived in a timeframe somewhere between July 1830 to December 1831.

John Porter, another brother-in-law to William R. Bratton, was also living in Montgomery County, Indiana at this time. He was a widower, but had previously been married to Nancy Agnes Bratton on July 4, 1811 in Bath County, Virginia.[558] Nancy died in 1824, nine days after the birth of their child, Mary Elizabeth Porter. She was buried in the family cemetery, the Bratton graveyard, six miles east of Millsboro, Virginia.[559] John Porter remarried to William R. Bratton's sister-in-law, Rachel Berry, on December 21, 1826 in Augusta County, Virginia.[560] Rachel, Mary Gambrel Berry Bratton, and Jane Berry Youel were all daughters of James Berry and Jane Doak.[561] In 1828, John Porter left his family in Virginia and rode on horseback to Montgomery County, Indiana to scout for potential land. He might have been accompanied by William Crawford at this time. Porter stored his cash of $700 into a leather pocketbook that he strapped to his waist. The

---

[556] William Nelson Youel land certificate, #13173. Bureau of Land Management. http://glorecords.blm.gov.

[557] David Doak Berry land certificates, #14463, 14464. Bureau of Land Management. http://glorecords.blm.gov.

[558] Metheny, Constance Corley. 1978. *Bath County Marriage Bonds and Ministers' Returns, 1791-1853*. Warm Springs, Virginia: The Bath County Historical Society: 41.

[559] Porter, William Arthur. 1937. *The Descendants of Peter Porter, an emigrant of 1621*. Minneapolis, Minnesota: Argus Publishing Company: 34-36.

[560] John Vogt and T. William Keithley, Jr., *Virginia Historic Marriages, Orange County, 1747-1850*. Athens, Georgia: Iberian Press.

[561] Virginia. Augusta County. Will Book 16. James Berry estate, 17 October 1827: 19-20, 97-98.

pocketbook has passed down through John Porter's son, John Reason Porter, to descendent William Arthur Porter who died in 1959 in Minnesota. Presumably, the pocketbook was inherited by one of his sons. John Porter bought land two miles west of Yountsville in Montgomery County, Indiana.[562] Two years later, in 1830, he used horses and a covered wagon to transport his second wife Rachel Berry Porter and his eight children conceived with his first wife Nancy Agnes Bratton, and brought them to Montgomery County. It is unclear as to whether he still owned the land in Yountsville or if the family stayed with the Crawfords until a home was available. John paid John Hayhurst $300 for land near the Crawfords in Union Township on December 13, 1830. However, the Porter family moved within several years to a new farm of about 80 acres in Walnut Township in Montgomery County, Indiana that he purchased on September 26, 1831.[563] Nevertheless, soon after their arrival in Indiana, romance was quick to kindle for one Porter family member, daughter Delilah, who met and married James Shanklin on June 9, 1831.[564]

On September 12, 1832, William R. Bratton and his four-horse wagon rolled out of Augusta County, Virginia. With him was his wife Mary; son James, age nineteen; son David, age seventeen; Abel, age fifteen; Charles, age fourteen; Martha, age ten; Rachel, age eight; Nancy Charlotte, age six, and Margaret, age four. Two of William R. and Mary Bratton's children died before the family's migration to Indiana. Their son Andrew died at age five in Augusta County, Virginia and was buried in the Rocky Springs church. Another daughter died young and

---

[562] Indiana. Montgomery County. Recorder's Office, Montgomery County Courthouse. *Montgomery County General Index of Deeds*, Book 2: 172.
[563] Norwalk, Jay. 1998. *Johan Jost Zimmerman: and Related Genealogies of Roth, Yaggy, Schlunegger, Bratton, Cochlin, Elliott, Campbell and McCullough*. Newcastle, Maine: Axion Press: 482-483; John Porter land certificate, #13399. Bureau of Land Management. http://glorecords.blm.gov.
[564] *Indiana Marriages to 1850*. James Shanklin to Delilah Porter. Database. Ancestry.com.

might be buried there as well.[565] The family most likely traveled along the Wilderness Road from Virginia through Kentucky and up into Indiana. The family traveled on weekdays through rough terrain and woods, and rested on Sunday, ultimately arriving in Montgomery County, Indiana on October 13, 1832.[566] They arrived in their wagon at the William Crawford farm to stay for a month until William could build his own dwelling for his family. Within eleven days, he pursued a land purchase. He paid Charles Johnson $350 for land in Union Township.[567] Although the success of land acquisition was realized in that one-month stay at the Crawford farm, tragedy struck the William R. Bratton family three weeks after their arrival when their daughter Martha died. She was buried on the Crawford farm in a place that the family later referred to as the Crawford Cemetery.[568] Soon after Martha's death, the Brattons built their own primitive cabin and moved in. Two years later, William R. Bratton traveled to the Crawfordsville land office and bought three parcels of land in Walnut Township on September 16, 1834, two 40-acre parcels and an 80-acre parcel of land.[569]

The Bratton children attended school in a log cabin that was indicative of many rural schools in that it had greased paper for windows and puncheon benches for the children to sit on.[570] They attended the school with their cousins, the Crawford children, the Porter children, the Youel children, and

---

[565] Crawfordsville Weekly Journal. "History of William Bratton Family." 27 July 1917: 3, c. 2.

[566] Bowen, A.W. 1913. *History of Montgomery County, Indiana: with personal sketches of representative citizens*. Vol. 2. Indianapolis, Indiana: A.W. Bowen & Company: 1112.

[567] Indiana. Montgomery County. Recorder's Office, Montgomery County Courthouse. *Montgomery County General Index of Deeds*, Book 3: 5.

[568] Crawfordsville Weekly Journal. "History of William Bratton Family." 27 July 1917: 3, c. 2.

[569] William R. Bratton land certificate, #17839. Bureau of Land Management. http://glorecords.blm.gov.

[570] Bowen, A.W. 1913. *History of Montgomery County, Indiana: with personal sketches of representative citizens*. Vol. 2. Indianapolis, Indiana: A.W. Bowen & Co.: 1112.

the Berry children. The school was located on the John Porter farm in Walnut Township, northwest of Porter's spring.

In 1834, death again claimed one of William R. Bratton's daughters. Margaret died and was also buried on the Crawford farm beside her sister Martha. She might or might not have been alive when the Union Hill Presbyterian Church was organized by numerous people in her neighborhood on August 30, 1834. They gathered at this initial meeting to establish their own church at the schoolhouse. The people who attended this meeting were - Joseph and Hannah Henderson and their daughters Elizabeth and Matilda; Rebecca Porter; John H. and Jane Pogue and their daughters Hannah and Cynthia Ann; Delilah Porter Shanklin; Joshua McDaniel; William and Jane Youel; John and Rachel Porter; Silas and Elizabeth Pogue; David D. and Elizabeth B. Berry; Mary Ann Foster; Margaret Bratton Crawford; Margaret Evans; William G. McCutcheon; and William Zimmerman. The three elders elected for the congregation were Joseph Henderson, John H. Pogue and William Youel.[571] Though William R. Bratton and his wife Mary were not listed as present at the initial meeting, they were members of this congregation. On March 28, 1835, William R. Bratton was appointed as a Trustee of the congregation along with John Porter and John Walkup.[572] Later in July, William's wife Mary and their son James were received into the congregation on certificate which means that their membership transferred from Rocky Springs Presbyterian Church. William and Mary's son David Bratton was received into the congregation upon examination which means he successfully answered questions before the congregation that are designed by elders to assess an individual's religious faith.

While public records were the foundation for an accurate picture of life for the William R. Bratton family before 1835,

---

[571] Union Presbyterian Church. *Minutes of the Session of the Presbyterian Church of Union.* Vol. 1, 1834-1858: 1. The Marian Morrison Local History Collection. Reference Department. Crawfordsville District Public Library. Crawfordsville, Indiana.

[572] Ibid: 2.

William R. Bratton himself left actual details of his life in 1836 and beyond through his surviving letters. His letters to Bath County, Virginia resident, Michael Wise, are not just a lens into his family life and but also for issues at the community, county, state and federal levels. He regularly corresponded with his friend Wise because though Wise bought a forty-acre parcel in Walnut Township in Montgomery County, Indiana that bordered William's on the north, Wise never settled it but stayed in Virginia. Besides being a prolific pen pal, Wise was a landowner and a carpenter. He was compensated by the James Hodge estate in Bath County for a coffin he made on August 10, 1830. His carpentry work was again mentioned in September 1836 when he was paid out from the Samuel Blackburn estate for his work on Blackburn's house in Staunton, Virginia.[573]

In a letter dated January 16, 1835, William R. Bratton wrote to Robert Graham but perhaps it was never delivered by Wise since it was included in the Michael Wise papers. Bratton wrote "the boys have got clear of the chills and fevers about Christmas, they had a long and tedious spell of it. There never was as much sickness known in this section of country since the first settlement of it as was this last season, and it may be a long time before there will be as much again." Also in his letter to Graham, he compared the fertility of Indiana to Virginia. "I would be glad to hear that you were about to move to this country where you could raise as much corn off of five to six acres as you would of all your old place. I raised as good corn last season and gave it a but one plowing as I ever raised in Virginia with all the labor I could bestow and you may probably dispute this but if you do, I refer you to Mr. Wise for the truth of it."[574]

Sickness struck the William R. Bratton household again when the three youngest living children, Charles, Rachel and

---

[573] Bruns, Jean Randolph. 1995. *Abstracts of the Wills and Inventories of Bath County, Virginia, 1791-1842.* Baltimore, Maryland: Clearfield Company: 139, 148.

[574] William R. Bratton to Michael Wise letter, 16 January 1835. The Papers of Michael Wise. Library of Virginia.

Nancy Charlotte, had the whooping cough, but their cases were not severe. In a letter to Michael Wise dated May 15, 1836, William R. Bratton wrote "First, I will inform you that we are all well at present excepting our three youngest children. They have the whooping cough though not bad for which we ought to be very thankful to the bountiful Giver of all of our mercies...I will next inform you that last winter was very sickly and more deaths occurred last fall then there had been put them altogether to that last time since I came to the country, the sickness was principally measles and whooping cough together. We have escaped the measles though they were all around us within ¼ of a mile of us." William R. Bratton next related to Michael Wise how life in Montgomery County was booming since Wise's visit in 1835. "You have been here, you can have an idea how land has risen value in this country about Crawfordsville; land is from thirty to fifty dollars per acre. There has some town lots sold as high as $160 dollars per acre and that in the woods. Crawfordsville is improving very fast, you would hardly know any of the places that you knowed when you were here. Now there are so many attractions. I was in there yesterday and I counted the stores and there is 18 dry goods stores, and one book store, one apothecary shop, 7 groceries, two tan yards, and five saddlers."[575]

In other news, William R. Bratton described a lot that he bought recently in 1836 for $400. It was located three-quarters of a mile from where he lived and it already had a house and stable on it, information that he asked Wise to relay to his brother John Bratton. The land William was referring to in his letter was a parcel he bought from Henry Long in section seventeen in Walnut Township on January 23, 1836.[576] It is clear from William's letter that for several years, John Bratton planned to follow his brother William to Montgomery County, Indiana. "You may tell him that I will keep the house that is on

---

[575] William R. Bratton to Michael Wise letter, 15 May 1836. The Papers of Michael Wise. Library of Virginia.
[576] Indiana. Montgomery County. Recorder's Office, Montgomery County Courthouse. *Montgomery County General Index of Deeds*, Book 5: 194.

it for him to go into when he comes to this country next fall as I understood he is about to come next fall and the boys say they will plant him some cabbage there so that he may have some sauce when he comes." In fact, John Bratton was granted a patent for eighty acres of land in Montgomery County, Indiana on September 16, 1835 but he and his family did not migrate to Indiana in 1836 but left most likely in the spring of 1839. John Bratton's wife Polly gave birth to their son Charles Andrew Bratton on February 4, 1839 in Virginia, and then they moved to Montgomery County, Indiana by the summer of 1840 when the 1840 Federal Census was taken. John Bratton married Mary "Polly" Gambrel Berry on September 17, 1818 in Bath County, Virginia and had a large family. Polly had the same exact name as William R. Bratton's wife Mary, and was her first cousin, but she was the daughter of John Berry and Eleanor Jamison.[577] Their other children included James Berry Bratton, John Gamble Bratton, Rebecca Ellen Bratton, Margaret Ann Bratton, Robert Lewis Bratton, Nancy Jane Bratton, Mary Charlotte Bratton, Adaline Ruth Bratton, William Crawford Bratton, and Samuel Brown Bratton.[578]

In Bath County, Virginia, Michael Wise was single but actively interested in securing a suitable wife. In a letter dated May 15, 1836, William R. Bratton described the ripe marital opportunities that were available in Montgomery County, Indiana. He hoped to entice Wise to travel from Virginia for another visit. "I will just mention to you that if you cannot get a wife in that country, if you will come out here, I will recommend you to some of the handsome girls and if you get one of them, you need not be afraid of her running off to that country." Michael Wise still had not married a year later in 1837 but Bratton thought Wise's opportunity had passed him

---

[577] Berry Family Bible Record, 1765-1883. *The New Testament of our Lord and Saviour Jesus Christ.* Philadelphia: Mathew Carey, 1813. Online images of family pages. *The Library of Virginia.* http://image.lva.virginia.gov/Bible/25548/index.html.

[578] Norwalk, Jay. 1998. *Johan Jost Zimmerman: and Related Genealogies of Roth, Yaggy, Schlunegger, Bratton, Cochlin, Elliott, Campbell, and McCullough.* Newcastle, Maine: Axion Press: 484.

by. In a letter dated May 22, 1837, Bratton wrote to Wise, "You wrote to me that if you don't get a wife there, soon you will put what we have here but my advice to you is to try and get one there as they are marrying very fast here. There was two weddings on Thursday last up the creek above us, Mr. Wright's daughter Jane to a Mr. Griffin from Rockbridge and a Miss Airhart to a Mr. Wisehart and every week more or less weddings."[579] In one wedding he referred to, Jane E. Wright married Thomas Griffin in Montgomery County and Polly Airhart married John Wisehart in Boone County, both marriages occurred on the previous Thursday, May 18, 1837.

William R. Bratton expressed several issues of concern in his 1837 letter, the most important one involved financial matters. "I think that times will take a turn shortly for the worse as I have just heard that all the banks in this state have refused specie payment. The merchants in Crawfordsville are all very much down in the mouth about it and I have no doubt it will affect the prices of all kind of property." William R. Bratton referred to the Panic of 1837, a financial crisis that rocked the whole nation in May when the United States government did not renew its charter with the Second Bank of the United States in Philadelphia. The Bank was initially created to help the federal government finance its military operations of the War of 1812, which had been difficult to do before then because of severe inflation. Bratton stated that the banks were refusing specie payment. This happened after the announcement that banks would only accept specie payment of gold and silver, but then banks could not fulfill the demand for it. New York banks were the first banks to suspend payments to people and other state banks soon followed. Depreciated currency soon followed and the nationally financial panic triggered a five-year depression in which prices soared.[580]

---

[579] William R. Bratton to Michael Wise letter, 22 May 1837. The Papers of Michael Wise. Library of Virginia.

[580] McWilliams, James E. "The Panic of 1837." *The American Economy: a Historical Encyclopedia,* California: ABC-Clio, Inc. 2003: 221.

"I will next inform you that there are about 30 miles of the Canal finished and it is generally thought that the whole line will be finished in three years…The people in this country had got in a great spirit of internal improvements. They have made up in Crawfordsville and Montgomery County about 270 shares of railroad to Indianapolis to Lafayette which is 70 shares more than the charter called for."[581] The building of canal infrastructure was actually an ongoing issue in Indiana since before 1817 when Governor Jonathan Jennings addressed the Indiana House of Representatives on the importance of canals to connect the northern lake waters to the Ohio and Mississippi Rivers.[582] In 1827, the federal government deemed that a western artificial waterway was still of national importance and granted Indiana substantial money to be used in the specific location of the Fort Wayne portage to link the Maumee and Wabash Rivers.[583] A problem arose however when a state survey revealed that a portion of the projected canal would lie in Ohio. Representatives met in Cincinnati in 1829 to discuss the issue but Ohio officials were reluctant to allow the Indiana government to build on their land. Ohio was already constructing two canals of its own, one from Lake Erie to southern Ohio towns and another to connect Cincinnati to Toledo. If Indiana were to finish their canal, it could possibly divert commercial trade into Indiana and out of Ohio. It took Ohio five years to grant Indiana permission to finish their canal. In the meantime, Indiana's first portion of the Wabash Canal, a thirty-mile section from Fort Wayne to Huntington, was ready for travel on July 4, 1835. Transportation infrastructure remained a principal political issue in elections when a proposal was presented to Indiana legislature that requested that six million dollars be used

---

[581] William R. Bratton to Michael Wise letter, May 22, 1837. The Papers of Michael Wise. Library of Virginia.
[582] Indiana General Assembly. 1817. *Journal of the House of Representatives of the State of Indiana*: Corydon, Indiana: state printer: 8-9.
[583] Dunbar, Seymour. 1937. *A History of Travel in America*. New York, New York: Tudor Publishing Company: 828.

toward an extensive system of canals, railroads and turnpikes. Public opinion was in favor of the proposal and it passed overwhelmingly.

In 1840, another snapshot of the William R. Bratton family is accessible through the federal census. William R. Bratton and his wife Mary lived with their sons David and Charles, and their daughters Rachel, and Nancy Charlotte.[584] William and Mary's son James was married and in his own household, and Abel was single but listed as his own head of household. In a letter dated September 27, 1840, William R. Bratton wrote to Michael Wise about the health of his family. Everyone was well though Mary sustained an injury from a horse which strained her knee. This injury inhibited her from getting around for several weeks but once she was healed she began visiting neighbors again.[585] At the exact time William wrote the letter, Mary visited her sister Rachel Porter. William did not write to Wise about any tension between the Porters, the Youels, the Brattons or the Berrys but by May 8, 1841, scandalous rumors about Rachel and her stepdaughters erupted in the community. The Union Presbyterian elders met in a session to address the rumors officially titled "common fame" that Rachel was verbally and possibly physically abusing her stepdaughters Margaret and Nancy Jane Porter. Nathan Crawford, son of William and Peggy Crawford, served as clerk of this session and he issued a formal citation for Rachel to appear on May 25, 1841 at the schoolhouse to defend herself against this charge of unchristian conduct. On May 25, 1841, they interviewed three witnesses about their knowledge of the situation, John Bratton, Rachel Lockridge and Elizabeth C. Lockridge.[586] John Bratton reported that he personally heard Rachel use

---

[584] 1840 United States Census. Walnut Township, Montgomery County, Indiana, digital s. v. "William Bratten" Ancestry.com.

[585] William R. Bratton to Michael Wise letter, September 27, 1840. The Papers of Michael Wise. Library of Virginia.

[586] Union Presbyterian Church. *Minutes of the Session of the Presbyterian Church of Union.* Vol. 1, 1834-1858: 17. The Marian Morrison Local History Collection. Reference Department. Crawfordsville District Public Library. Crawfordsville, Indiana.

slanderous language toward Margaret Porter and that it was generally believed in the community that she hit the girls. At the time that he witnessed Rachel verbally abusing Margaret, he felt Rachel was in such a great rage that she would have struck Margaret if Rachel's husband John Porter had not interfered. After his testimony, Rachel asked John Bratton if he knew that Margaret had struck her over the head before and he replied that he had not heard that information.[587]

Before or after these charges, Rachel became afflicted with episodes of palsy which affected her motor skills and caused her body to shake or become too weak to support her. Around the end of March or beginning of April in 1842, during one episode of palsy, John Porter tied Rachel to a chair and left her alone next to the fireplace. Either Rachel struggled furiously to get out of the chair or her body shook so agitatedly that her chair tipped over towards the fire and she was burned badly. She became bedridden to heal. This situation greatly distressed Rachel's sisters and brothers and they felt that John Porter and his daughters Margaret and Nancy Jane treated Rachel very badly, and at times neglected her in her rehabilitation.[588] Consequently, on June 6, 1842, John Porter and his daughters Margaret and Nancy Jane were charged by "common fame" of unchristian conduct towards Rachel and were asked to appear before church elders to answer to this charge. Many witnesses were interviewed.

Rachel's sister Jane Youel said that Rachel complained to her of being put out of her kitchen and that the girls had bruised her. Rachel also complained to Jane that the girls refused to wash her clothes, that she had not been given winter clothes soon enough, and that she was not given enough food. Specifically, Rachel told Jane that on one occasion she did not receive food until 9:00 p.m. and that all she received to eat was

---

[587] Union Presbyterian Church. *Minutes of the Session of the Presbyterian Church of Union*. Vol. 1, 1834-1858: 19. The Marian Morrison Local History Collection. Reference Department. Crawfordsville District Public Library. Crawfordsville, Indiana.
[588] Ibid: 71.

cold milk and cornbread, and that on another occasion she only received some coffee and bread. "I was there in the spring when the weather was cold and there was no fire in the house and she was very wet and had to be up in that situation. The girls were washing that evening. I asked them to bring in some wood and help to lift her but neither of them came near," testified Jane Youel. "Another evening this spring, the time of Presbytery, as I was going to the house, before I got near, I heard her crying. When I went to the house, she was alone and in a very bad fix as her clothes were much torn and dirty as though they had been wore two weeks. At the same time, she had on his big coat. Shortly after I went in, Jessy Golen's wife came here and we lifted her and examined her and found her all golden so that she could hardly sit."[589] Jane also tended to Rachel's burns with an oak bark poultice but when a local doctor, Dr. T. W. Fry, finally treated Rachel's burns, he did not like the oak bark poultice and regarded it as an "injurious application." He felt that John Porter should have called him earlier to treat Rachel. He treated her for six to eight weeks for her burns and administered medicine to her and also instructed that she be fed a light diet. In his testimony, in his overall opinion, he did not find anything amiss in regards to abusive treatment towards her.[590]

A Mrs. Dorsy was interviewed by John Porter before the church elders in regard to his treatment of his wife but though her testimony was not flattering about him, it is evident by the line of his questioning that he tried to show the church elders that Rachel's brother David Berry was stirring up trouble about him in the community. [591]

John Porter: What did you tell Mr. Berry?
Mrs. Dorsy: I told him that half of the confusion about the

---

[589] Union Presbyterian Church. *Minutes of the Session of the Presbyterian Church of Union*. Vol. 1, 1834-1858: 57. The Marian Morrison Local History Collection. Reference Department. Crawfordsville District Public Library. Crawfordsville, Indiana.
[590] Ibid: 48-49.
[591] Ibid: 54.

	house could not be told.
John Porter:	Did not Mr. Berry tell you about my wife being tied to a chair and the flies being very thick over her?
Mrs. Dorsy:	Mr. Berry tell me that he hear her crying and he went to the house and found her tied in a chair and he never seen so many flies since he been in this country.
John Porter:	Did you ever hear Mr. Berry say that I would fret her and get her irritated and then call in some person to quiet her and then look very mild like a saint?
Mrs. Dorsy:	He said they would all irritate her and get her in a rage and then send for some person to quiet her and then they would all be very mild and pleasant.

Andrew Loop, who had been boarding with the Porters for four months also testified to church elders about what he observed in the household. He did not notice any neglect of the girls towards their stepmother but did witness some difficulties between them. "She (Rachel) would give them a short answer and on the day that she was struck (with palsy), as I returned to dinner, I saw that something had happened and I met one of the girls going to the spring crying," Loop said. "I went in to the house where (Abel) Washington Bratton was. The old lady had got into one of her ways that day. He said that she went from house to house tearing things and quarrelling with him, W(ashington) Bratton, sometime, and then went into the kitchen and commenced quarrelling about the weaving of her flannel dress and picked up a chair to strike one of them. At this time she was struck with palsy. Five minutes after she was struck, I came in, she was being in the kitchen and I saw the old man carry her in the house."[592] Loop referred to William and Mary's son Abel Bratton whose middle name was Washington who was probably called by his middle name and not his first name. Abel Washington Bratton died within a year, in 1842, and was buried at the Crawford farm cemetery. Rachel died on March 18, 1843 and exactly six months later, John Porter married a third time to Charlotte McWilliams in Montgomery County, Indiana.[593]

William R. Bratton wrote Wise a letter on December 13, 1842 but did not mention anything about Abel's death or the previous upheaval in his extended family. He informed Wise that he was plagued with a pleurisy attack that kept him confined to his house for three to four weeks. William said that his brother John was also attacked by the same sickness at the end of November but did not rest enough and was not fully recovered at the time of the letter though William stated that John was not at death's door. William and Mary's daughter Nancy Charlotte was very sick during the summer months and into fall with a bad cough, weak spells and shortness of breath but was doing better by December. William also mentioned that his nephew Nathan Crawford was sick as well with fever but had recovered. Others were not so fortunate. William's brother-in-law William Crawford died before September 8, 1842.[594] In his letter, William lamented the absence of William Crawford and Crawford's sound advice in regard to Wise's business matters, and especially the land that Wise owned as an absentee landowner. William advised, "I do not know what to do with the place as it is…If you never intend coming to this

---

[592] Union Presbyterian Church. *Minutes of the Session of the Presbyterian Church of Union.* Vol. 1, 1834-1858: 71. The Marian Morrison Local History Collection. Reference Department. Crawfordsville District Public Library. Crawfordville, Indiana.

[593] John Porter and Charlotte D. McWilliams marriage record. 18 March 1845. Crawfordsville District Public Library. Database. http://history.cdpl.lib.in.us/Presto.

[594] Indiana. Montgomery County. Recorder's Office, Montgomery County Courthouse. *Montgomery County General Index of Deeds*, Book 10: 445, 601-602.

country to live, I would advise you to sell it as it as it cannot be valuable to you in the situation it is. I feel at a great loss about your place since Wm. Crawford died as I have no one to consult with about it."[595]

William revealed the dear price the migration to Indiana cost him in his letter of condolence to Wise on July 7, 1845 when he heard of the death of Wise's wife. "We have had several afflictions in our family since we came to this country by the loss of five of our children which you no doubt have heard of but these afflictions are but light to what it is to lose the dear partner of their bosom."[596] Also, though William's service to his local church seemed light over the years, it is clear he was a religious man when he urged Wise to "not murmur or complain but to submit to God in all his dealings with us." In other news, William informed Wise that his brother John Bratton and his wife Polly were planning a trip to Virginia for the first week of August if Polly was well enough to go. Her health had been declining the last two years. Though the health of William's family was good, it seemed smallpox was present in Lafayette. It killed several people and there were rumors that it was in Crawfordsville too but no deaths had occurred there yet from it or at least William had not heard of any cases yet.

In a very brief letter to Wise in January 1850, William R. Bratton wrote many things about his brother John Bratton's family. John's son and William's nephew Robert Bratton was engaged to marry William Youel's youngest daughter within the week on a Wednesday, and then John's daughter and William's niece Margaret was to wed the next day to a Mr. Martin. He also informed Wise that John Bratton, Jr., his brother John's son and William's nephew, had lost his second wife and that the young child from this union was being raised by yet another

---

[595] Virginia. Augusta County. William R. Bratton to Michael Wise letter, December 13, 1842. The Papers of Michael Wise. Library of Virginia.
[596] Virginia. Augusta County. William R. Bratton to Michael Wise letter, July 7, 1845, The Papers of Michael Wise. Library of Virginia.

member of the family, John's daughter Rebeckah E. Bratton.[597]

Another snapshot of William R. Bratton's household was captured through the 1850 Federal Census. William R. and Mary lived in the same home with their two children David and Rachel.[598] They all lived together in 1860 too.[599] William R. Bratton died on March 20, 1862 in Walnut Township of Montgomery County, Indiana and was buried with his wife in the Union Hill Cemetery.

---

[597] Virginia. Augusta County. William R. Bratton to Michael Wise letter, January 1850. The Papers of Michael Wise. Library of Virginia.

[598] 1850 United States Census, Walnut Township, Montgomery County, Indiana, digital image s. v. "William Bratton," Ancestry.com.

[599] 1860 United States Census, Walnut Township, Montgomery County, Indiana digital image s. v. "William Bratton," Ancestry.com.

CHAPTER TWELVE
The End of an Adventure

As the new decade progressed, William E. Bratton continued to be quite busy. At the end of February 1841, William spent a lot of time administrating Stuart guardianship business. On February 24, 1841, William met with Harvey Johnson, the husband of Mary Elizabeth Stuart Johnson, to have him sign a receipt acknowledging that he and Mary received $74.50 from him. This was their portion of money owed to them from an individual paid for the work of two enslaved men still owned by the Stuart family. The enslaved men named Nat and Lewis lived in Bowling Green, Kentucky and probably lived on the property of one of Charles' siblings. The hiring out of enslaved people was a common practice at the time. It was popular because owners could hire out their enslaved people to other employers and receive twelve to fifteen percent per year in payment of what the owner deemed an enslaved person was worth if sold.[600] Likewise, the next day, William visited Abraham Zuck, the husband of Sarah Jane Stuart Zuck, to have him sign their note acknowledging that he and Sarah received $74.50 from him, their portion from the hiring out of Nat and Lewis. On February 26, 1841, William visited Sally Stuart. Perhaps William felt that Sally was frivolously spending some of the money that William was doling out to her for the maintenance of her household from her husband's estate. He had Sally sign a note that was her agreement to use the $18.75 he was giving

---

[600] Clement, Eaton. "Slave-hiring in the Upper South: A Step toward Freedom." *The Mississippi Valley Historical Review* 46, no. 4 (March 1960): 663.

her "to furnish Ann Maria, James Alexander, and Harriet Amanda, minor heirs of said Charles Stuart, with sufficient boarding, lodging, clothing, washing, and mending from this date until the 25th of May."[601] Her portion of the hiring out of Nat and Lewis was also $75.50, and her three minor children would have received a portion as well. William probably added the amount, $298, to the estate funds.

    In May 1841, the youngest Stuart children attended school and received instruction by schoolmaster John G. Kerr. William paid him $4.00 for his teaching services and for paper, an arithmetic book, and a slate. The children probably attended a log schoolhouse similar to the nearby log house that Robert Kennedy Krout attended in the bordering township of Ripley Township. The schools were log cabins with puncheon floors. As previously explained in chapter two, puncheon floors were constructed from logs in which only one side of the log was flattened, and then placed flat side up to become the floor. When the walls of the school were constructed, they left a log out of the wall for light and when the weather was cold, they would cover it with greased paper. While learning from Kerr, students sat upon benches made from split logs with a flat side facing upward, and attached and supported with pegs also made from wood.[602] It is unclear if the Stuart children attended school with the Bratton children or not. It is equally unclear in which school John G. Kerr was a teacher. He could have taught in the schoolhouse on the property of neighbor Elias Moore, who lived near Dennis Ball, the former guardian of the Stuart children who had died two years before. The schoolhouse was built in 1828 so it was firmly established by 1841. Or, they might have attended a school just north of the cemetery in Waynetown that was built in 1832. The teacher was Samuel Means Cooley, brother to Jonathan Cooley who married their

---

[601] William E. Bratton Account Book. The Marian Morrison Local History Collection. Reference Department. Crawfordsville District Public Library. Crawfordsville, Indiana.

[602] *Waynetown Sesquicentennial, 1830-1980*. Waynetown, Indiana: Waynetown Sesquicentennial Book Committee, 1980: 37.

aunt Malinda Maxwell.[603] By 1841, it is possible that Cooley was no longer teaching and perhaps Kerr took over that school.

When summer was in full swing, the Bratton household suffered more loss. William and Polly's eldest son, James Maxwell Bratton, died on July 1, 1841, at age twenty-one. Although he was not a minor, as documented by the 1840 Federal Census, he still lived at home and was single, and did not own any land of his own. He did not leave a will nor was there any probate proceedings to disperse his personal belongings. His death accounted for the third child his parents had lost. He was buried to the left of his sister Eliza Jane in the pioneer cemetery in nearby Waynetown.[604]

On August 12, 1841, William's job as guardian to Ann Maria Stuart, James Alexander Stuart, and Harriet Amanda Stuart was transferred to their brother-in-law Abraham Zuck.[605] Maybe Sally was not happy about money matters with William since February and persuaded Abraham over five months to take over the guardianship, or maybe it was a mutual agreement for all parties. In relation to the situation, possibly due to the timing, William owed the Stuart estate $20.97. He signed a note on September 16, 1841 promising to pay back the amount plus ten percent and that he would pay it by Christmas. When William visited Sally Stuart three weeks later, his business with her was also probably related to this matter. On October 6, 1841, he asked her to sign a note acknowledging that an order that Sally placed with her son-in-law Abraham Zuck for $5 was lost or mislaid but that William had paid for it. This $5 could have been a reimbursement for the money Zuck spent in securing the guardianship.

Several days later, on October 11, 1841, William served as

---

[603] *Waynetown Sesquicentennial, 1830-1980.* Waynetown, Indiana: Waynetown Sesquicentennial Book Committee, 1980: 37.

[604] *Cemeteries in Montgomery County, Indiana.* Vol. 11, Wayne Township. Crawfordsville, Indiana: Dorothy Q. Chapter, Daughters of the American Revolution. 1973: 138.

[605] Indiana. Montgomery County. Guardian's Docket. Abraham Zuck entry. 19 Aug. 1841. Database. http://history.cdpl.lib.in.us/Presto.

a grand juror. He was paid $10.00 for eight days in the September term of the circuit court.[606] Just a couple of weeks later, unexpectedly, William began to feel ill. Polly summoned Dr. Albert McClelland to come look at him. Dr. McClelland prescribed some medicine but it did not help and the worst-case scenario unfolded. William died on November 11, 1841 at age sixty-three. Like his children that had died before him, he was buried in the Old Pioneer Cemetery in nearby Waynetown.

    Even though William was over age sixty, he must have enjoyed overall good health before he died because he did not leave a will. He, probably like most people, did not expect to die so quickly. His lack of a will was called intestate which meant that his property and belongings as part of his estate had to be inventoried, and if he owed any debts or if people owed him money, they had to be paid and collected. This process took time and each step was accounted for through the local courts. As Polly mourned his passing, she leaned on their friend and neighbor John Sanford Gray to administrate the estate. In July 1842, Polly signed a declaration that John prepared in which she would "renounce, release, and forever quitclaim all my right and title to the administration of the estate of the said deceased; and I desire that the same may be committed to my friend John S. Gray."[607] It looked like it was prepared by John S. Gray and Polly signed it. The same day, John Gray paid $2.00 to a local newspaper to publish a notice for the sale of William's estate which was held on July 30. He sold the following items - old irons, a broad axe, a grubbing hoe, a lock and chain, wagon irons, bench planes, a coffee mill, a gray horse, a brown mare, a sorrel horse, sheep, a calf, steers, a heifer and calf, a sow and her pigs, shoats, other livestock, acres of oats and corn, four bee hives, clover hay, wheat, a saddle, a wheel, a mantle clock, a rifle gun and pouch, a

---

[606] Indiana. Montgomery County. Register of County Orders. 1841.

[607] Indiana. Montgomery County. William E. Bratton probate papers, Box 12, Order 8. The Marian Morrison Local History Collection. Reference Department. Crawfordsville District Public Library. Crawfordsville, Indiana.

cupboard and ware, a log chain, a crosscut saw, meal bags, a candle stand, a small bedstead and bedding, three larger beds and bedsteads, and cooking utensils. Polly bought the gray horse, and her son John bought the sorrel horse. John Gray bought the grubbing hoe and one acre of corn. Many other family members attended the sale and bought items.

After John Gray administered William's estate, he continued to look after Bratton affairs. In 1843, he paid the Montgomery County treasurer and collector $8.85 for taxes on the Bratton land.[608] On April 3, 1845, he paid the sum of $4.00 towards the building of a schoolhouse in District No. 5 in Wayne Township. And much to Polly's grief, John Gray also administrated the estates of several of William and Polly's children in the next several years. William and Polly's son John Bratton died in 1846 following his service in the Mexican War. He served as a private in Captain Allen May's company in the Montgomery Volunteers in the First Regiment Indiana Volunteers.[609] His mother Polly was his heir, and as such she received 160 acres of land in 1851 located in nearby Warren County, Indiana that came to John as payment for his service.[610] She sold the land to Levi Moore. Her son George Bratton also served in the Mexican War but he survived. In 1850, William and Polly's son William died from consumption.[611] In his will, he stipulated that he wanted his siblings to receive a Bible, one to his brother George, one to his

---

[608] Indiana. Montgomery County. William E. Bratton probate papers, Box 12, Order 8. The Marian Morrison Local History Collection. Reference Department. Crawfordsville District Public Library. Crawfordsville, Indiana.

[609] Perry, Oran. 1908. *Indiana in the Mexican War*. Indianapolis, Indiana: Wm. B. Burford Printing and Binding: 109.

[610] John Bratton land warrant, #8725. Bureau of Land Management. http://glorecords.blm.gov.

[611] 1850 United States Census, Mortality Schedule, Wayne Township, Montgomery County, Indiana, digital image s. v. "William Bratton," Ancestry.com.

sister Grizzella, and one to his sister Mary Etta.[612] His death on May 21, 1850 occurred before the 1850 Federal Census so he was not listed with the rest of his family. Polly was age 53 and listed as the head of the household. Her son Adam was age nineteen, Grizzella Ann was age seventeen, and Mary Etta was age ten. The farm at this time was valued at $4000.

In 1851, Adam Bratton was ill as well and John Gray petitioned the court for guardianship of him and his estate on August 31. Adam at age twenty was considered a minor. He needed John Gray as his guardian to sell his forty-six acres of land for him. This was land he received from his father's estate. Adam wanted to leave the area on the recommendation of his doctor who thought a different climate would restore his health.[613] John Gray stated in his petition that Adam "at this time has been for many months so severely afflicted and in bad health that he is entirely unable to labor or do anything towards his own support – that his afflictions are such that one of his arms is entirely disabled which prevents him labor or making suitable sustenance and support and owing to his sickness and disability, he has been forced to go in debt for medical attendance and other necessities for his comfort and he has no way of making any money except by sale of his said real estate." John Gray further informed the court that if the guardianship could be granted, that he and Adam had already found a buyer, Garrett Harlow, who would buy the land for $600 in which he would pay $300 cash out right, and pay the remaining amount in two IOUs of $150 each. Harlow would pay one IOU in six months, and the other one in twelve months in addition to interest that accrued from the date of the sale.[614]

---

[612] Indiana. Montgomery County. William Bratton probate papers, Box 26, Order 24. The Marian Morrison Local History Collection. Reference Department. Crawfordsville District Public Library. Crawfordsville, Indiana.

[613] Indiana. Montgomery County. William Bratton probate papers, Box 26, Order 24. The Marian Morrison Local History Collection. Reference Department. Crawfordsville District Public Library. Crawfordsville, Indiana.

[614] Ibid.

The guardianship was granted, and the land was sold, but Adam Bratton did not live past the upcoming winter. He died on February 4, 1852 and was buried in the Old Pioneer Cemetery in Waynetown with his father and siblings.

At his death, his sister Grizzella had been wed for six months to Stephen Fields. She was probably a solace to her mother who must have been devastated to lose so many of her sons so soon. Moreover, Polly's sorrow no doubt grew in 1854, when she lost a sister, not to death, but to Illinois. Her sister Malinda Maxwell Cooley and her husband Jonathan joined their own sons and their families who had moved to the previous year to Douglas County, Illinois near the town of Newman. Land was cheap and their boys bought neighboring parcels at an affordable price from the government. Their main reason for moving was that Jonathan worried that he and Malinda would be alone when their two youngest sons became men and he suspected they too would move to Illinois with or without them. Both of Jonathan Cooley's parents were dead, and though he still had a brother and sister in Montgomery County, he felt stronger familial ties pulling him to Illinois. As a farmer and pastor, he recreated their life in Illinois by buying eighty acres of land from his son John, and by founding the Fairfield Presbyterian Cumberland Church by July 1855.[615]

Polly Maxwell Bratton also became an owner of land to the west. In 1855, the U.S. Congress approved an Act called "An act in addition to certain Acts granting Bounty Land to certain officers and Soldiers who have been engaged in the military service of the United States. Thus, in 1859, Polly received bounty land for William's service in the War of 1812. It was eighty acres located in St. Peter, Minnesota.[616] She sold it to George W. Harding. In 1860, her sister Elizabeth Bratton, widow of Archibald Bratton, also received bounty land for Archibald's service in the War of 1812. It was 120 acres

---

[615] Hamil, Lura Coolley. *A Story of Pioneering*. (The Illinois Company, 1955; Internet Archive, 2018): 42, 45.
[616] William Bratton land warrant, #21805. Bureau of Land Management. https://glorecords.blm.gov.

located in Council Bluffs, Iowa. She sold it to Branch Miller.[617] Polly and Elizabeth's sister-in-law Elizabeth Bratton still lived in Warren County, Kentucky, and she had already received bounty land in 1859. As the widow of George Bratton, Jr. she received eighty acres of bounty land in Stillwater, Minnesota Territory. She sold it to Erastus Edgerton.[618] George Bratton, Jr. also received bounty land before he died in 1853 for his War of 1812 service in Captain Sterrett's Company, 14th Regiment of the Kentucky Militia. He received eighty acres near Milan, Missouri. He sold the land to Edmund P. Steele.[619] William E. Bratton's brother Adam, still lived in Warren County, Kentucky as well, and he also received bounty land for his War of 1812 service. In 1853, he received eighty acres of bounty land near Batesville, Arkansas. He sold the land to James A. Hooper.[620]

In 1860, Polly Bratton was once again recorded on the federal census. Her daughter Mary Etta was not listed with her because Mary Etta married Milton J. Switzer on August 2, 1859. He was a neighbor who lived just a couple of farms away with his parents James and Ann Switzer. Sadly, Mary Etta did not live long past the recording of the 1860 Federal Census, and she was buried with her father and siblings in the Old Pioneer Cemetery in Waynetown. On the 1860 Federal Census, Polly was listed as age sixty-four. She lived with her son George, his wife Cynthia, and their young daughter Malissa, and their young son George Washington Bratton. As the only son left alive, George helped his mother run the farm. He and Cynthia had had a tough time growing their family and had lost several children. They were buried in the Potts cemetery nearby with members of Cynthia's Moore family.[621] In another household, William and Polly's daughter Grizzella and her husband

---

[617] Archibald Bratton land warrant, #57635. Bureau of Land Management. https://glorecords.blm.gov.
[618] Ibid: George Bratton land warrant, #13115.
[619] George Bratton land warrant, #16713. Bureau of Land Management. https://glorecords.blm.gov.
[620] Ibid: Adam Bratton land warrant, #14980.
[621] 1860 United States Census, Wayne Township, Montgomery County, Indiana, digital image s.v. "George Bratton," Ancestry.com.

Stephen Fields had made quite a start to their large family by 1860. According to the census, they lived on Fields land in neighboring Ripley Township in Montgomery County, Indiana and had four young children, George, age seven; John, age five; Mary, age three; and James, age two months.[622]

About three years later, Polly lost another child. Her son George died on May 15, 1863. He too was buried in the Old Pioneer Cemetery. It is unclear if her son-in-law Stephen began running the farm or if Polly rented it out. It is also unclear if Polly continued to live with Cynthia and the children, however, change was in the near future. Letters were probably flying back and forth between Douglas County, Illinois and Wayne Township in Montgomery County. The Cooleys were quite happy in their new situation and might have relayed what fine land they farmed. In November 1866, Stephen Fields approached Polly to ask her for a loan of $1000 and she agreed to loan it to him on the terms that he pay it back to her in five years plus ten percent interest, and the interest was to be paid to her annually. This loan could have been to secure land in Douglas County, Illinois because sometime before July 1868, Stephen and Grizzella Fields joined the Cooleys in Illinois and took Polly Bratton with them to live.

Polly's business affairs must have been fairly comfortable because she loaned $100 to Douglas County resident J. R. Page with the terms that it would be repaid within a year plus ten percent interest. Maybe he attended the same church as Polly. It is unclear if Polly joined the Fairfield Presbyterian Church where her brother-in-law Jonathan Cooley was a pastor, or if she attended another church. Stephen Fields was one of the first trustees of the Pleasant Ridge church that was located six miles northwest of the town of Newman in Douglas County and it is conceivable that Grizzella and their children attended it as well. The church congregation was Methodist and the first building for it was built in 1870. At this time, Stephen was age forty; Grizzella, age thirty-six; and their children were the

---

[622] 1860 United States Census, Ripley Township, Montgomery County, Indiana, digital image s.v. "Stephen Fields," Ancestry.com.

following ages: George Washington, age seventeen; John, age fifteen; Mary, age thirteen; James, age ten; Abbie Jane, age two. Polly Bratton also lived with them and was age seventy-three.[623]

Stephen again borrowed money from Polly in September 1871. He borrowed $987.82. This time, the terms stated that he would pay it back in three years plus ten percent interest to be paid back annually. Also at this time, Polly loaned $97.29 to a James McIntire with ten percent interest. He was a Scottish farmer, age sixty-five, living near Newman with a large family.[624]

Polly traveled back and forth between Douglas County, Illinois and Wayne Township in Montgomery County, Indiana to visit her grandchildren and nieces and nephews. She stayed for weeks at a time. She was on one of these visits when she was struck with symptoms of palsy that afflicted her for six weeks. She stayed with her daughter-in-law Cynthia Bratton who nursed and cared for her. Cynthia had not remarried and was still raising her three children on her own. Polly probably knew Cynthia's money was tight because once she recovered, Polly paid Cynthia $15.00 to offset the costs of caring for her. At some point, Mary returned to Douglas County, Illinois but was back by the end of February 1874 when she became sick again. This time, she stayed with George and Grizzilla Jane Bratton Philips. Grizzilla was Polly's niece and the eldest daughter of Polly's sister Elizabeth and Archibald Bratton. The Philips did not have any children of their own but they opened their home to many of their family members who needed a home. They raised their orphaned nephew Archibald Bratton Philips. Archibald was a full nephew to both of them because his father was George's younger brother, and his mother Mary was Grizzilla Jane's younger sister. When Polly Bratton lived with them in 1874, George and Grizzilla Jane were raising

---

[623] 1870 United States Census, Douglas County, Illinois, digital image s.v. "Stephen Fields," Ancestry.com.
[624] 1870 United States Census, Douglas County, Illinois, digital image s.v. "Jas Mcintyer," Ancetry.com.

Archibald's daughter Minnie who was age 5. Tragically, history had repeated itself. Just as Archibald had been orphaned due to both of his parents dying during his first year of birth, so too did this happen to Archibald's daughter Minnie. Both Archibald and his wife Serada died within months of Minnie's birth. According to the 1870 census, George and Grizzilla Jane also had a housekeeper and a farm hand.

Polly stayed with George and Grizzilla Jane Philips from February 27, 1874 through April 25, 1874. She stayed with someone else for the month of May and she might have made a trip back to Newman, Illinois. Regardless, by June 2, 1874 she returned to stay with the Phillips' for twelve and a half weeks. During the month of September, she stayed with her daughter-in-law Cynthia Moore Bratton. In the middle of the month, she became sick again and a Dr. Hipes and Dr. Anderson took turns treating her. After one month, still ill, she returned to stay with George and Grizzilla Phillips again, and the doctors began to treat her there.

It was during this time that Polly's nephew James Maxwell Cooley, son of Jonathan Cooley and Mary's sister Malinda, began making trips to see Polly from Newman in Douglas County, Illinois. He did this at Polly's request. She wanted his advice with her business affairs and she wanted him to be the executor of her estate when she died. She also talked to him about a special request that she wanted in her will. She wanted him to select and purchase land in Missouri for her daughter Grizzella Bratton Fields and her family. Cooley described the request as "his duty to select suitable real estate in which to invest a large part of her assets for the use of her daughter, Mrs. Fields and her children."[625] In February 1875, Polly was afflicted with severe paralysis, so much so that the local newspaper, the Crawfordsville Weekly Review, reported that she was "at the point of death" but Polly rallied somewhat and remained with George and Grizzilla Jane Phillips until her

---

[625] Indiana. Montgomery County. Mary H. Bratton probate papers. Box 76, Order 33. The Marian Morrison Local History Collection. Reference Department. Crawfordsville District Public Library.

death on November 19, 1875.[626] She was buried in the Old Pioneer Cemetery in Waynetown beside her husband William E. Bratton and their children.

In Polly's will, she wanted her estate to reimburse George and Grizzilla Jane Philips and Cynthia Bratton for their care of her. She wanted them to have $5 for her room and board for each week they cared for her. To George A. Phillips, she reimbursed him and Grizzilla Jane for the washing they had done for her while living and upon her death, for putting up her tombstone, for collecting her rents and paying her taxes while she was ill. She paid him $150.00 while she was still alive, and her estate paid him an additional $189.98. Per Polly's special request, Stephen and Grizzella Bratton Fields selected their own land in Page County, Iowa instead of sending James Cooley to do it. Polly also made provisions in her will for her grandchildren Malissa, George, and Warren Bratton, children of her son George Bratton and his wife Cynthia.

Only two of William and Polly Bratton's nine children married and had children of their own and it is through these lines that their heirlooms have traveled. The wooden block that housed William Bratton's compass was last accounted for in the early 1900s in the hands of his grandson, Grizzella's son, James T. Fields. He lived in Buda, Illinois in 1930. His niece, Myrtle Fields Mariner, daughter of Grizzella's son George relayed this information for her membership into the Nebraska Society of United States Daughters of 1812.[627] William's great-granddaughter Mary Maud Chesterson inherited a cherry table that belonged to William and Polly.[628] Mary Maud also showed a young neighborhood boy, David Remley, a beaded rosette from a shot pouch bag that belonged to William, but the location of the rosette if it still exists today is unknown. Finally,

---

[626] Crawfordsville Weekly Review. Mary H. Bratton article, 6 February 1875: 8, c. 1.
[627] Mariner, Myrtle Fields. "William E. Bratton" *Heroes of 1812*. Nebraska Society of United States Daughters of 1812; (Omaha, Nebraska, 1930): 96.
[628] Ibid: 98.

there is a captivating picture donated to the William Bratton archive in Montgomery County, Indiana by Bratton descendants of a powder horn. It depicts a hunter after a deer.[629] Like the remnants of the compass, the picture of the powder horn raises some tantalizing questions. Where is the powder horn today? Was it carried by William E. Bratton on his adventures with Lewis and Clark? Did he use it into the wilds of Indiana? Like his pocket compass, it might have been cherished by him as an old friend and a reminder of his adventures for the rest of his days.

---

[629] Indiana. Montgomery County. William Bratton archive. The Marian Morrison Local History Collection. Reference Department. Crawfordsville District Public Library. Crawfordsville, Indiana.

PICTURES

William E. Bratton tombstone, front
Photo by Amie Kunkle Cox

William E. Bratton tombstone, back
Photo by Chris Light, Creative Commons

William E. Bratton tombstone, close-up
Photo by Chris Light, Creative Commons

Photos by Amie Kunkle Cox

Bratton archive, Marian Morrison Local History Collection
Crawfordsville District Public Library, Crawfordsville, IN

Bratton archive, Marian Morrison Local History Collection
Crawfordsville District Public Library, Crawfordsville, IN

William Bratton's grandson George Bratton with his daughter Maud Bratton; Bratton archive, Marian Morrison Local History Collection, Crawfordsville District Public Library, Crawfordsville, IN

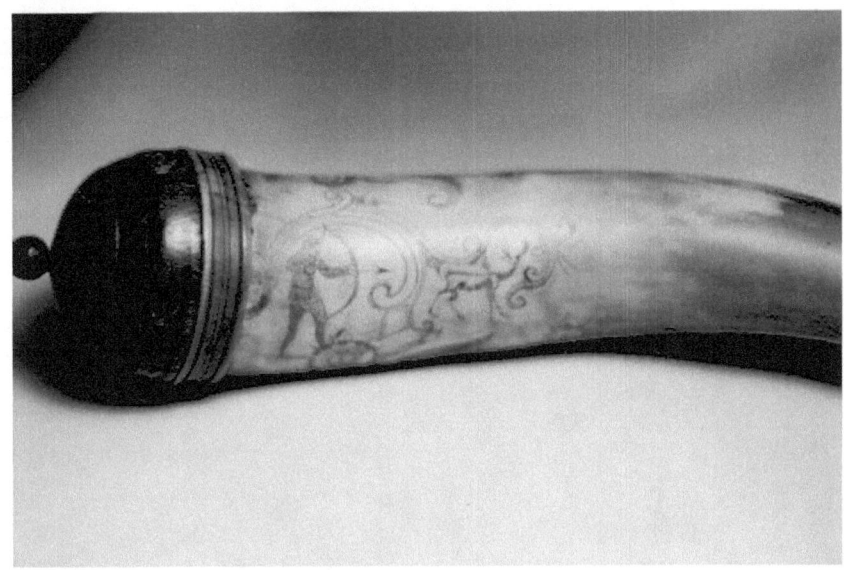

William Bratton's powder horn; Bratton archive, Marian Morrison Local History Collection, Crawfordsville District Public Library, Crawfordsville, IN

APPENDIX A
William E. Bratton's Account Book

Name	Date	Item	County
Stephens, Thomas L.	__ Nov. 1815	plank	Warren Co., Ky.
Beauchamp, Dr.	18 Nov. 1815	sheeting	Warren Co., Ky.
Beauchamp, Dr.	24 Nov. 1815	plank	Warren Co., Ky.
Beauchamp, Dr.	06 Nov. 1815	sheeting	Warren Co., Ky.
Sterrett, Thomas	23 Nov. 1815	plank	Warren Co., Ky.
Lucas, Sary	18 Dec. 1815	plank	Warren Co., Ky.
Work, Samuel	22 Dec. 1815	plank	Warren Co., Ky.
Hogsett, James	22 Dec. 1815	plank	Warren Co., Ky.
Small, Mrs.	12 Jan. 1816	plank	Warren Co., Ky.
Isbell, Livingston	01 March 1816	plank	Warren Co., Ky.
Brooking, Samuel	12 March 1816	plank	Warren Co., Ky.
Maxey, John	27 March 1816	scantling	Warren Co., Ky.
William R. Payne	16 May 1816	shtg., plk	Warren Co., Ky.
Hogsett, James	17 May 1816	plank	Warren Co., Ky.
Brant, Henry	04 Aug. 1816	_____	Warren Co., Ky.
Howarth, Lawrence	07 Sept. 1816	meal	Warren Co., Ky.
Hay, James	16 Sept. 1816	meal	Warren Co., Ky.
William R. Payne	21 Sept. 1816	pd. cash	Warren Co., Ky.
Howarth, Lawrence	01 Oct. 1816	meal	Warren Co., Ky.
Howarth, Lawrence	07 Dec. 1816	meal, flr	Warren Co., Ky.
Cunningham, Bracket C.	14 Dec. 1816	meal	Warren Co., Ky.
Graham, Alexander	18 Dec. 1816	meal	Warren Co., Ky.
Howarth, Lawrence	19 Dec. 1816	meal	Warren Co., Ky.
Cunningham, Bracket C.	19 Dec. 1816	meal	Warren Co., Ky.
Cunningham, Bracket C.	23 Dec. 1816	flour	Warren Co., Ky.
Castilow, John	23 Dec. 1816	meal	Warren Co., Ky.
Graham, Alexander	23 Dec. 1816	meal	Warren Co., Ky.
Grider, Henry	24 Dec. 1816	flour	Warren Co., Ky.
Sheldon, Charles	23 Dec. 1816	flour	Warren Co., Ky.
Mitchell, Asa T.	23 Dec. 1816	bran	Warren Co., Ky.
Castilow, John	31 Dec. 1816	meal	Warren Co., Ky.
Cunningham, Bracket C.	31 Dec. 1816	meal	Warren Co., Ky.
Howarth, Lawrence	02 Jan. 1817	meal	Warren Co., Ky.
Mitchell, Asa T.	02 Jan. 1817	bran	Warren Co., Ky.
Donaldson, Louis	02 Jan. 1817	bkwht flr	Warren Co., Ky.
Castilow, John	02 Jan. 1817	bail box	Warren Co., Ky.
Graham, Alexander	03 Jan. 1817	meal	Warren Co., Ky.
Castilow, John	07 Jan. 1817	meal	Warren Co., Ky.

Name	Date	Item	County
Cunningham, Bracket C.	11 Jan. 1817	meal	Warren Co., Ky.
Castilow, John	24 Jan. 1817	meal	Warren Co., Ky.
Castilow, John	01 Feb. 1817	cash	Warren Co., Ky.
Howarth, Lawrence	01 Feb. 1817	plank	Warren Co., Ky.
Castilow, John	06 Feb. 1817	cash	Warren Co., Ky.
Castilow, John	08 Feb. 1817		Warren Co., Ky.
Maxwell, James	10 Feb. 1817	walnut plk	Warren Co., Ky.
Castilow, John	15 Feb. 1817	cash	Warren Co., Ky.
Castilow, John	21 Feb. 1817	meal	Warren Co., Ky.
Long, Reuben	21 Feb. 1817	cash, meal	Warren Co., Ky.
Cunningham, Bracket C.	24 Feb. 1817	meal	Warren Co., Ky.
Cunningham, Bracket C.	04 March 1817	meal	Warren Co., Ky.
Graham, Alexander	05 March 1817	meal	Warren Co., Ky.
Castilow, John	17 June 1817	meal	Warren Co., Ky.
Graham, Alexander	21 June 1817	meal	Warren Co., Ky.
Howarth, Lawrence	23 June 1817	meal	Warren Co., Ky.
Castilow, John	23 June 1817	meal	Warren Co., Ky.
Vanlandingham, Wm.	24 June 1817	meal	Warren Co., Ky.
McGraw, John	24 June 1817	meal	Warren Co., Ky.
Castilow, John	27 June 1817	meal	Warren Co., Ky.
Graham, Alexander	27 June 1817	meal	Warren Co., Ky.
Castilow, John	01 July 1817	meal	Warren Co., Ky.
Middleton, Mathias	01 July 1817	meal	Warren Co., Ky.
Lucas, Bennet	01 July 1817	meal	Warren Co., Ky.
Vanlandingham, Wm.	01 July 1817	meal	Warren Co., Ky.
Middleton, Mathias	04 July 1817	meal	Warren Co., Ky.
Cunningham, Bracket C.	05 July 1817	meal	Warren Co., Ky.
Vanlandingham, Benj.	05 July 1817	meal	Warren Co., Ky.
Campbell, John	07 July 1817	meal	Warren Co., Ky.
Maxwell, James	14 Aug. 1817	meal	Warren Co., Ky.
Neal, R(ichard) D.	15 Aug. 1817	wheat	Warren Co., Ky.
Cunningham, Bracket C.	15 Aug. 1817	meal	Warren Co., Ky.
Stuart, A(lexander)	16 Aug. 1817	wheat	Warren Co., Ky.
Magness, Joseph	16 Aug. 1817	wheat	Warren Co., Ky.
Lewis, Arch	18 Aug. 1817	meal	Warren Co., Ky.
Graham, Alexander	19 Aug. 1817	meal	Warren Co., Ky.
Spalding, Charles	19 Aug. 1817	flour	Warren Co., Ky.
Stuart, A(lexander)	03 Sept. 1817	wheat	Warren Co., Ky.
Howarth, Lawrence	06 Sept. 1817	meal	Warren Co., Ky.
Lewis, James	09 Sept. 1817	meal	Warren Co., Ky.
Graham, Alexander	10 Sept. 1817	meal	Warren Co., Ky.
Howarth, Lawrence	11 Sept. 1817	meal	Warren Co., Ky.
Howarth, Lawrence	12 Sept. 1817	_____	Warren Co., Ky.

Name	Date	Item	County
Graham, Alexander	15 Sept. 1817	meal	Warren Co., Ky.
Cunningham, Bracket C.	16 Sept. 1817	flour	Warren Co., Ky.
_____	16 Sept. 1817	flour	Warren Co., Ky.
Stuart, A(lexander)	16 Sept. 1817	_____	Warren Co., Ky.
King, Ed(ward)	18 Sept. 1817	flour	Warren Co., Ky.
Cook, John W.	18 Sept. 1817	meal	Warren Co., Ky.
Powell, John	18 Sept. 1817	meal	Warren Co., Ky.
Lindsey, John	22 Sept. 1817	meal	Warren Co., Ky.
Graham, Alexander	23 Sept. 1817	meal	Warren Co., Ky.
Howarth, Lawrence	25 Sept. 1817	flour	Warren Co., Ky.
Cunningham, Bracket C.	26 Sept. 1817	flour	Warren Co., Ky.
Graham, Alexander	26 Sept. 1817	meal	Warren Co, Ky.
Cunningham, Bracket C.	30 Sept. 1817	meal	Warren Co., Ky.
Nash, William	06 Oct. 1817	meal	Warren Co., Ky.
_____, John	06 Oct. 1817	_____	Warren Co., Ky.
Davis, John	06 Oct. 1817	wheat, bran	Warren Co., Ky.
Middleston, Math	01 Jan. 1818	flour	Warren Co., Ky.
Ellsworth, Mathew	02 Jan. 1818	corn	Warren Co., Ky.
Clark, William	03 Jan. 1818	flour	Warren Co., Ky.
Claspy, Glasfy, John	06 Jan. 1818	draw. Chns	Warren Co., Ky.
Ellsworth, John	08 Jan. 1818	corn	Warren Co., Ky.
Howarth, Lawrence	13 Jan. 1818	meal	Warren Co., Ky.
Lewis, James	13 Jan. 1818	flour	Warren Co., Ky.
Ellsworth, James	13 Jan. 1818	corn	Warren Co., Ky.
Davis, William	15 Jan. 1818	bran, shorts	Warren Co., Ky.
Ellsworth, William	15 Jan. 1818	meal, flour	Warren Co., Ky.
Blakey, James	15 Jan. 1818	flour	Warren Co., Ky.
Gossom, William	16 Jan. 1818	flour	Warren Co., Ky.
Baker, Jonathan	17 Jan. 1818	salt	Warren Co., Ky.
Howarth, Lawrence	21 Jan. 1818	flour	Warren Co., Ky.
Ellsworth, John	22 Jan. 1818	meal	Warren Co., Ky.
Srader, Nick	22 Jan. 1818	flour	Warren Co., Ky.
Stuart, Mary	23 Jan. 1818	flour	Warren Co., Ky.
Ellsworth, John	24 Jan. 1818	meal	Warren Co., Ky.
Mitchell, William	24 Jan. 1818	flour	Warren Co., Ky.
Magness, Betsy	28 Jan. 1818	flour	Warren Co., Ky.
Cunningham, Bracket C.	18 Feb. 1818	bran	Warren Co., Ky.
King, Edmund	29 April 1818	flour	Warren Co., Ky.
Ellsworth, John	25 May 1818	meal	Warren Co., Ky.
Anderson, David	29 May 1818	meal	Warren Co., Ky.
Cook, John W.	29 May 1818	meal	Warren Co., Ky.
Cunningham, Bracket C.	26 May 1818	meal, flour	Warren Co., Ky.
Tindle, Ben	03 June 1818	meal	Warren Co., Ky.

Name	Date	Item	County
Ford, Ben	03 June 1818	meal	Warren Co., Ky.
Mitchell, Asa T.	04 June 1818	meal	Warren Co., Ky.
Stephens, G. W.	04 June 1818	meal	Warren Co., Ky.
Butcher, Henry	05 June 1818	meal	Warren Co., Ky.
Maxwell, James	05 June 1818	flour	Warren Co., Ky.
Cook, John W.	05 June 1818	meal	Warren Co., Ky.
Middleton, Math	06 June 1818	meal	Warren Co., Ky.
Ellsworth, John	06 June 1818	meal	Warren Co., Ky.
King, Edmund	08 June 1818	flour	Warren Co., Ky.
Lucas, B	08 June 1818	flour	Warren Co., Ky.
Haron, Able	10 June 1818	flour	Warren Co., Ky.
Rood, Isaac	16 June 1818	meal	Warren Co., Ky.
Cunningham, B. C.	16 June 1818	meal	Warren Co., Ky.
Cook, John W.	16 June 1818	meal	Warren Co., Ky.
Davis, William	17 June 1818	flour	Warren Co., Ky.
Ellsworth, John	18 June 1818	meal	Warren Co., Ky.
King, Edmund	18 June 1818	meal	Warren Co., Ky.
Lorton, F.	18 June 1818	meal, shorts	Warren Co., Ky.
Ward, T.	19 June 1818	meal	Warren Co., Ky.
Cunningham, B.C.	19 June 1818	meal	Warren Co., Ky.
Mitchell, A. T.	19 June 1818	meal	Warren Co., Ky.
Cook, John W.	25 June 1818	meal	Warren Co., Ky.
Butcher, H.	25 June 1818	meal	Warren Co., Ky.
Good, Robert, Sen.	26 June 1818	flour	Warren Co., Ky.
Ellsworth, John	27 June 1818	meal	Warren Co., Ky.
Magness, Joseph	27 June 1818	flour	Warren Co., Ky.
Middleton, Robert	27 June 1818	flour	Warren Co., Ky.
Lorton, Robert	27 June 1818	meal, shorts	Warren Co., Ky.
Rood, Isaac	29 June 1818	meal	Warren Co., Ky.
Ford, Ben	29 June 1818	meal	Warren Co., Ky.
Butcher, Henry	30 June 1818	flour	Warren Co., Ky.
Mitchell, Asa T.	30 June 1818	flour	Warren Co., Ky.
Hay, James S.	01 July 1818	meal	Warren Co., Ky.
Ward, Thomas	02 July 1818	meal	Warren Co., Ky.
Davis, John	02 July 1818	flour	Warren Co., Ky.
Ellsworth, John	02 July 1818	flour	Warren Co., Ky.
Cook, John W.	03 July 1818	meal	Warren Co., Ky.
Miller, James W.	03 July 1818	flour	Warren Co., Ky.
Cunningham, B. C.	03 July 1818	meal	Warren Co., Ky.
Simpson, Asel	07 July 1818	meal	Warren Co., Ky.
Cook, John W.	07 July 1818	flour	Warren Co., Ky.
Vanlandingham, Wm.	08 July 1818	meal	Warren Co., Ky.
Lawless, B.	08 July 1818	meal	Warren Co., Ky.

Name	Date	Item	County
Ellsworth, John	10 July 1818	meal	Warren Co., Ky.
Cunningham, B. C.	10 July 1818	meal	Warren Co., Ky.
Cook, John W.	13 July 1818	meal	Warren Co., Ky.
Tindle, Ben	13 July 1818	meal	Warren Co., Ky.
Easton, Nicholas	15 July 1818	meal	Warren Co., Ky.
Ellsworth, John	15 July 1818	bacon	Warren Co., Ky.
Ward, Thos.	16 July 1818	meal, corn	Warren Co., Ky.
Mitchell, Asa T.	16 July 1818	meal	Warren Co., Ky.
Ford, Benjamin	16 July 1818	meal	Warren Co., Ky.
_____, Meshek	17 July 1818	meal	Warren Co., Ky.
Miller, James W.	17 July 1818	meal	Warren Co., Ky.
Edwards, Ben	17 July 1818	meal	Warren Co., Ky.
Cunningham, B. C.	20 July 1818	meal	Warren Co., Ky.
Ellsworth, John	20 July 1818	meal	Warren Co., Ky.
Easton, Nicholas	20 July 1818	meal	Warren Co., Ky.
Vance, John	24 July 1818	flour	Warren Co., Ky.
Vanlandingham, Wm.	24 July 1818	meal	Warren Co., Ky.
Butcher, H.	25 July 1818	meal	Warren Co., Ky.
Ward, Thomas	27 July 1818	meal	Warren Co., Ky.
Hay, James	27 July 1818	bran	Warren Co., Ky.
Easton, Nicholas	27 July 1818	meal	Warren Co., Ky.
Mitchell, Asa T.	27 July 1818	corn	Warren Co., Ky.
Ellsworth, John	06 Aug. 1818	meal	Warren Co., Ky.
Vanlandingham, B.	06 Aug. 1818	meal	Warren Co., Ky.
Davis, Wm.	06 Aug. 1818	bran	Warren Co., Ky.
Vanlandingham, B.	07 Aug. 1818	meal	Warren Co., Ky.
Easton, Nicholas	07 Aug. 1818	meal	Warren Co., Ky.
Roland, Archibald	08 Aug. 1818	meal	Warren Co., Ky.
Cunningham, B. C.	08 Aug. 1818	meal	Warren Co., Ky.
Mitchell, Asa T.	11 Aug. 1818	meal	Warren Co., Ky.
Middleton, Mathew	11 Aug. 1818	meal	Warren Co., Ky.
Vanlandingham, Wm.	12 Aug. 1818	meal	Warren Co., Ky.
Ellsworth, John	13 Aug. 1818	meal	Warren Co., Ky.
McPheeters, Wm.	17 Aug. 1818	flour	Warren Co., Ky.
Davis, Wm.	17 Aug. 1818	bran	Warren Co., Ky.
Miller, Benj.	18 Aug. 1818	meal	Warren Co., Ky.
Cunningham, B. C.	21 Aug. 1818	meal	Warren Co., Ky.
Butcher, H.	21 Aug. 1818	meal	Warren Co., Ky.
Vanlandingham, Wm.	26 Aug. 1818	meal	Warren Co., Ky.
Easton, Nicholas	27 Aug. 1818	meal	Warren Co., Ky.
Roland, Archibald	31 Aug. 1818	meal	Warren Co., Ky.
Cunningham, B. C.	02 Sept. 1818	meal	Warren Co., Ky.
Ellsworth, John	02 Sept. 1818	meal	Warren Co., Ky.

Name	Date	Item	County
Roberts, Mark	02 Sept. 1818	meal	Warren Co., Ky.
Berry, J.	02 Sept. 1818	meal	Warren Co., Ky.
Cook, John W.	04 Sept. 1818	meal	Warren Co., Ky.
Lemon, Philip	05 Sept. 1818	meal	Warren Co., Ky.
Vanlandingham, Wm.	14 Sept. 1818	meal	Warren Co., Ky.
Lawless, Benj.	15 Sept. 1818	meal	Warren Co., Ky.
Miller, James W.	17 Sept. 1818	meal	Warren Co., Ky.
Easton, Nicholas	18 Sept. 1818	meal	Warren Co., Ky.
Cook, John W.	19 Sept. 1818	meal	Warren Co., Ky.
Butcher, H.	19 Sept. 1818	rye	Warren Co., Ky
Butcher, H.	19 Sept. 1818	meal	Warren Co., Ky.
Anderson, David	19 Sept. 1818	flour	Warren Co., Ky.
Cunningham, B. C.	19 Sept. 1818	meal	Warren Co., Ky.
Mitchell, Asa T.	19 Sept. 1818	meal	Warren Co., Ky.
Butcher, H.	23 Sept. 1818	corn	Warren Co., Ky.
Butcher, H.	23 Sept. 1818	barrels	Warren Co., Ky.
Cook, John W.	25 Sept. 1818	meal	Warren Co., Ky.
Anderson, David	25 Sept. 1818	meal	Warren Co., Ky.
Nash, Wm.	25 Sept. 1818	meal	Warren Co., Ky.
Davis, Wm.	02 Oct. 1818	bran	Warren Co., Ky.
Mitchell, Asa T.	10 Oct. 1818	whiskey	Warren Co., Ky.
Mitchell, Asa T.	13 Oct. 1818	whiskey	Warren Co., Ky.
Stuart, Alexander	13 Oct. 1818	corn	Warren Co., Ky.
Mitchell, Asa T.	17 Oct. 1818	whiskey	Warren Co., Ky.
Spalding, Charles	17 Oct. 1818	whiskey	Warren Co., Ky.

On the same sheet, it jumps to one entry in November and several in December written by William Bratton. The next sheet begins on October 21st, 1818 with the initials D.C. written after the date. The writing is different and often the writer ran the patrons first and last name together without capitalizing the last name. My educated guess is that William hired David C. Maxwell, his future brother-in-law to help him at his mill. Business had been pretty steady and recent purchases indicate that Bratton might have added a distillery to his services. Those entries by D.C. will be indicated in italicized print.

Name	Date	Item	County
Butcher, Henry	*21 Oct. 1818*	*meal*	*Warren Co., Ky.*
Butcher, Henry	*22 Oct. 1818*	*flour*	*Warren Co., Ky.*
Anderson, David	*22 Oct. 1818*	*whiskey*	*Warren Co., Ky.*
Simpson, William	*22 Oct. 1818*	*whiskey*	*Warren Co., Ky.*
Simpson, William	*23 Oct. 1818*	*whiskey*	*Warren Co., Ky.*

Name	Date	Item	County
Mitchell, Asa T.	23 Oct. 1818	whiskey	Warren Co., Ky.
Anderson, David	23 Oct. 1818	whiskey	Warren Co., Ky.
Middleton, Ben	24 Oct. 1818	whiskey	Warren Co., Ky.
Collett, James	24 Oct. 1818	whiskey	Warren Co., Ky.
Simpson, Little William	26 Oct. 1818	whiskey	Warren Co., Ky.
Mack, William	24 Oct. 1818	meal	Warren Co., Ky.
Mitchell, John	27 Oct. 1818	flour	Warren Co., Ky.
McFadden, John	26 Oct. 1818	whiskey	Warren Co., Ky.
Mitchell, Asa T.	28 Oct. 1818	bran	Warren Co., Ky.
Mitchell, Asa T.	29 Oct. 1818	meal	Warren Co., Ky.
Burd, Knight	29 Oct. 1818	meal	Warren Co., Ky.
Cunningham, Bracket	30 Oct. 1818	meal	Warren Co., Ky.
Maxey, James	30 Oct. 1818	meal	Warren Co., Ky.
Mitchell, John	30 Oct. 1818	meal	Warren Co., Ky.
Davis, John	30 Oct. 1818	bran	Warren Co., Ky.
Caloway, James	31 Oct. 1818	flour	Warren Co., Ky.
Mitchell, John	02 Nov. 1818	meal	Warren Co., Ky.
Mitchell, Asa T.	02 Nov. 1818	bran	Warren Co., Ky.
Spalding, Charles	03 Nov. 1818	whiskey	Warren Co., Ky.
Nash, William	04 Nov. 1818	meal, flour	Warren Co., Ky.
Anderson, David	04 Nov. 1818	flour	Warren Co., Ky.
Collett, James	04 Nov. 1818	whiskey	Warren Co., Ky.
Bratton, Arch	06 Nov. 1818	whiskey	Warren Co., Ky.
Maxey, James	07 Nov. 1818	meal	Warren Co., Ky.
Davis, James	07 Nov. 1818	whiskey	Warren Co., Ky.
Cook, John	07 Nov. 1818	meal	Warren Co., Ky.
Anderson, David	09 Nov. 1818	flour	Warren Co., Ky.
McFadden, John	10 Nov. 1818	whiskey	Warren Co., Ky.
Grider, Jesse	13 Nov. 1818	flour	Warren Co., Ky.
Stone, Daniel	15 Nov. 1818	bran	Warren Co., Ky.
Mitchell, A. T.	16 Nov. 1818	bran	Warren Co., Ky.
Cook, John	16 Nov. 1818	meal	Warren Co., Ky.
Mitchell, Asa T.	17 Nov. 1818	bran	Warren Co., Ky.
Davis, William	18 Nov. 1818	bran	Warren Co., Ky.
Caloway, James	18 Nov. 1818	flour	Warren Co., Ky.
Lawless, Ben	18 Nov. 1818	whiskey	Warren Co., Ky.
Middleton, Math	19 Nov. 1818	whiskey	Warren Co., Ky.
Vance, Benjamin	20 Nov. 1818	flour	Warren Co., Ky.
Maxey, James	20 Nov. 1818	meal	Warren Co., Ky.
Jenkins, Ezekiel	21 Nov. 1818	whiskey	Warren Co., Ky.
Collett, James	21 Nov. 1818	whiskey	Warren Co., Ky.
Anderson, David	21 Nov. 1818	flour	Warren Co., Ky.
Nash, William	21 Nov. 1818	meal	Warren Co., Ky.

Name	Date	Item	County
Vance, Ben	21 Nov. 1818	meal	Warren Co., Ky.
Grubbs, Moody	24 Nov. 1818	meal	Warren Co., Ky.
Collett, James	24 Nov. 1818	whiskey	Warren Co., Ky.
Cook, John	25 Nov. 1818	meal	Warren Co., Ky.
Mitchell, Asa T.	25 Nov. 1818	bran	Warren Co., Ky.
Vance, Ben	25 Nov. 1818	meal, flour	Warren Co., Ky.
Davis, William	25 Nov. 1818	bran	Warren Co., Ky.
Cunningham, Bracket	25 Nov. 1818	meal	Warren Co., Ky.
Baker, Jonathan	29 Nov. 1818	meal	Warren Co., Ky.
Lewis, James A	01 Dec. 1818	pork	Warren Co., Ky.
Mitchell, Asa T.	01 Dec. 1818	whiskey	Warren Co., Ky.
Caloway, James	01 Dec. 1818	flour	Warren Co., Ky.
Lawless, Benjamin	01 Dec. 1818	meal	Warren Co., Ky.
Quisenberry, Nichoas	01 Dec. 1818	whiskey	Warren Co., Ky.
Nash, William	02 Dec. 1818	meal	Warren Co., Ky.
Melton (Negro)	02 Dec. 1818	flour	Warren Co., Ky.
Cunningham, Bracket	02 Dec. 1818	meal	Warren Co., Ky.
Mitchell, Asa T.	03 Dec. 1818	bran	Warren Co., Ky.
Grubbs, Moody	03 Dec. 1818	meal	Warren Co., Ky.
Anderson, David	03 Dec. 1818	flour	Warren Co., Ky.
Vance, James	04 Dec. 1818	meal	Warren Co., Ky.
Humphry, John	04 Dec. 1818	meal	Warren Co., Ky.
Cook, John	04 Dec. 1818	meal	Warren Co., Ky.
Mitchell, Asa T.	5 Dec. 1818	whiskey, bran	Warren Co., Ky.
Vance, Benjamin	05 Dec. 1818	flour	Warren Co., Ky.
Roberts, Mark	07 Dec. 1818	flour	Warren Co., Ky.
Nash, William	09 Dec. 1818	meal	Warren Co., Ky.
McFadden, John	10 Dec. 1818	whiskey	Warren Co., Ky.
Davis, William	10 Dec. 1818	bran	Warren Co., Ky.
Grider, Martin	10 Dec. 1818	flour	Warren Co., Ky.
Magness, Joseph	10 Dec. 1818	whiskey	Warren Co., Ky.
Watson, Geoffrey	10 Dec. 1818	whiskey	Warren Co., Ky.
Anderson, David	10 Dec. 1818	flour	Warren Co., Ky.
Caloway, John	14 Dec. 1818	flour	Warren Co., Ky.
Mitchell, Asa T.	15 Dec. 1818	meal, rye	Warren Co., Ky.
Roland, Archibald	15 Dec. 1818	flour	Warren Co., Ky.
Caloway, James	17 Dec. 1818	flour	Warren Co., Ky.
Cunningham, Bracket	18 Dec. 1818	meal	Warren Co., Ky.
Ware, William	18 Dec. 1818	flour	Warren Co., Ky.
Davis, William	20 Dec. 1818	bran	Warren Co., Ky.
Lucas, Bennet	20 Dec. 1818	bran	Warren Co., Ky.
Tolbert, Tom	20 Dec. 1818	flour	Warren Co., Ky.
Titus	20 Dec. 1818	flour	Warren Co., Ky.

Name	Date	Item	County
Lawless, Benjamin	23 Dec. 1818	meal	Warren Co., Ky.
Roberts, Mark	28 Dec. 1818	flour	Warren Co., Ky.
Mitchell, Asa T.	29 Dec. 1818	meal	Warren Co., Ky.
Mitchell, Asa T.	31 Dec. 1818	meal	Warren Co., Ky.
Davis, William	02 Jan. 1919	bran	Warren Co., Ky.
King, Edmund	02 Jan. 1919	flour	Warren Co., Ky.
Bratton, William	05 Jan. 1919	flour	Warren Co., Ky.
Mitchell, Asa T.	06 Jan. 1919	meal, rye	Warren Co., Ky.
Davis	17 June 1819	tallow	Warren Co., Ky.
Bratton, Adam	17 June 1819	tole dish	Warren Co., Ky.
Bratton, Archibald	18 June 1819	bacon	Warren Co., Ky.
Baker, Jonathan	18 June 1819	wheat	Warren Co., Ky.
Davis, William	24 June 1819	meal	Warren Co., Ky.
Lewis, James A.	06 July 1819	flour	Warren Co., Ky.
Ware, William	08 July 1819	corn	Warren Co., Ky.
Middleton, Mathias A.	08 July 1819	meal	Warren Co., Ky.
Cunningham, Bracket C.	10 July 1819	meal	Warren Co., Ky.
Cunningham, Bracket C.	12 July 1819	meal	Warren Co., Ky.

William and Polly, his wife, moved to Indiana in 1822 and settled in Montgomery County, Indiana in 1823. His brothers-in-law and sisters-in-law moved to there as well by 1825. The rest of the book reflects William's personal business with them and his neighbors.

Name	Date	Item	County
Maxwell, David	22 July 1827	cash, postage	Mont. Co., In.
Maxwell, David	22 July 1827	coffee, tea	Mont. Co., In.
Maxwell, Martha	22 July 1827	cash, postage	Mont. Co., In.
Maxwell, John	22 July 1827	postage	Mont. Co., In.
Maxwell, David	Aug. 1827	bacon, cash	Mont. Co., In.
Maxwell, David	Aug. 1827	coffee	Mont. Co., In.
Maxwell, Martha	Aug. 1827	bacon	Mont. Co., In.
Maxwell, Malinda	1827	cash	Mont. Co., In.
Tabett, William	28 Oct. 1827	hemp	Mont. Co., In.
Maxwell, John	13 Dec. 1827	beef	Mont. Co., In.
Heath, William	13 Dec. 1827	beef	Mont. Co., In.
Sumner, James	13 Dec. 1827	beef	Mont. Co., In.
Bunnell, Bazilla	13 Dec. 1827	beef	Mont. Co., In.
Miller, Charles	13 Dec. 1827	beef	Mont. Co., In.
Donahue, Henry	13 Dec. 1827	beef	Mont. Co., In.
Maxwell, Martha	03 Jan. 1828	pd acct.	Mont. Co., In.
Maxwell, John	05 Mar. 1828	postage	Mont. Co., In.

Name	Date	Item	County
Bratton, Archibald	1828	cash	Mont. Co., In.
Bratton, Archibald	1828	postage	Mont. Co., In.
Donahue, Michael	04 June 1828		Mont. Co., In.

APPENDIX B
Petition, Samuel Fields case, Montgomery County, Indiana

To his Excellency James B. Ray,
Acting Governor of the State of Indiana

We the undersigned citizens of Montgomery County would recommend to your mercy and compassion Samuel Fields who has lately been convicted of murder and sentenced to bear the penalties thereof by the Franklin Circuit Court – We are unacquainted with the facts respecting this transaction and would not dare to say that the truth has not been told or that the law has not been faithfully administered, But we do believe that He is an objection which you may according to the power vested in you by the constitution exercise with the greatest propriety, that power in granting a pardon to this unfortunate man, A Soldier of the Revolution, who partook largely in the toils, dangers and difficulties in that glorious struggle by which we are emancipated from the yoke of tyranny and oppression and by which we now enjoy our independence. Citizens, will you not have compassion and extend mercy to one who at the Battle of Brandywine and that of Trenton with others so gloriously defended the rights and liberties of our country: He is now old and his head is as white as the driven snow which on that memorable morning covered the fields of Trenton. On that day, he was a man but now a child, the infirmities of old age no doubt has brought on this difficulty. As old age approaches, reason fails, harshness, fretfulness and jealousies commonly take their place, and he has done an act in his second childhood which he would not have done had not reason left its seat. The probability of this fact is strong having been near one hundred years and no crime of the kind having been before charged. We would now call forth your sympathies for his distressed family, several of those live amongst us. Respectable and industrious citizens, save them, we entreat you, from that disgrace which will fall on them and their posterity should his execution take place. There is no good reason to believe that by pardoning this man you will turn loose on society a wretch who will commit a like offence. We admit the possibility but there is not the most remote probability that such would be the fact. We now ask how much good would society derive from his execution, a man already dead to all the enjoyments of life whom God has spared to the great age of 85 years. Whose heart would not bleed to see a soldier of the Revolution, a man whose family is respectable, whose head is whitened by 85 winters, expiring under the gallows for a crime committed in his dotage? In your hands in a certain sense, are the issues of life and death. We hope you will take this matter into serious consideration, weigh all the circumstances and the intention of the framers of the constitution in placing in your hands this power and we trust you will determine that this is a case which will justify a reprieve.

Joseph Cox
William Burbridge
John Beard
John McCullough
James Rolston
John Dewey
Jacob Bush
John Brandenburg
Thomas Roby
John Rayburn
John Killin
Isaac _____
Thomas M. Curry
Abner Cox
Henry Ristine
William W. Gayley
Jacob Miller
Townsend Griffith
James Scott

Samuel Dollarwill
Winston M. Neal
Samuel Scott
Wm. Carpenter
David Gray
William Wilhite
Prov. M. Curry
Robert Johnston
Henry K. Nutt
Henry Bostwick

Shelby _____
Richd Phelan
John Tolliver
John Miller
Alfred Smith
Burwell Daniel
George Miller
Williamson Dunn

Wm. Symmes – Ohio
Ephraim Catterlin
David Vance
John Ristine
James D. Brockman
Hezh Robinson
Sinnet Ramey
Lanny Elder
John Trahan
William Phelan
Lewis Graham
Simon Roqefort
Wm. Nicholson
John C Symmes
Caleb Brown
Josephus Robinson
Joseph Scott
John Mack
Enoch Thompson
Daniel L. Hultz – Hendricks Co.
Benj. Patison – Hendricks Co.
Nathaniel Hultz – Hendricks Co.
John Carpenter
John Patterson
James Brown
Wm. Gladden
Isaac Williamson
Reed Satchwill

Amos Mack
A. Whitlock
Irvin B. Maxwell
John Wilson
Abraham Griffith
John Smith
Thomas Smith
B. T. Ristine
John Warren
James O. Laughlin
Jacob Sleepen?
Jonathan Crouch
E McConnell - Ohio

Joseph Thompson
Reub. Claypool – Hendricks Co.
William Martin
James L. Givan
Joseph Griffin
George Bullock
Joseph Patterson
James McClelling
William L. Merrell
Miles Martindale – Marion Co.
James Logan – Marion Co.
William Dodd – Marion Co.
Daniel McCain – Marion Co.
Thomas McCain – Marion Co.

ACKNOWLEDGEMENTS

I would like to recognize and thank the numerous people and institutions that aided me in my research efforts. First and foremost, I would like to thank Dellie Craig, the long-time local history archivist at the Crawfordsville District Public Library. She always went above and beyond to show me primary documents. I also appreciate her consistent encouragement and interest over the years, and her patience and kindness towards me no matter how many times I showed up to research. I would like to thank the Iota chapter of Delta Kappa Gamma in Indiana for their support in chasing down primary documents in Bowling Green. I would like to thank Jim Mallory with the Lewis and Clark Trust for his interest and encouragement, and for teaming up with the Gilder Lehrman Institute of American History in getting me out West to pick up Bratton's trail at Travelers Rest. I would like to thank the Lilly Endowment, Inc. for allowing me to trace William Bratton's footsteps through the Battle of River Raisin landscape and to chase William Bratton's POW parole record in Canada, and to also thank them for their never-ending support of Indiana teachers. I would to thank Vicki Casteel at the Indiana State Archives for her help in digging into the Samuel Fields petitions. I would like to thank my sister-in-law Amy Cox Smith for opening up her beautiful home in Madison, Indiana so that I could efficiently but economically research in Kentucky. I would also like to thank the staff at the Kentucky Historical Society for being extremely welcoming and helpful, and for granting me a fellowship that was essential to my research. I would also like to thank them for sending me to Gibby's for lunch where I was introduced to their state sandwich, the Kentucky Hot Brown. My life will never be the same! I also want to thank the staff at the following Kentucky institutions for always being so courteous and helpful over the years – the Kentucky Department of Library and Archives, the Special Collections at the University of Kentucky, the WKU Library Special Collections, and The Filson Historical Society. I would also like to thank the staff at the Oregon Historical Society for their help. Finally, I would like to thank my husband, my twin sister and my mom for keeping me company while tracing William Bratton's trail in Indiana, Kentucky, Michigan, Montana and Canada. Most of all, thank you for listening to me chatter on and on about history and genealogy.

BIBLIOGRAPHY

Aguirre, Adalbert. "Slave Executions in the United States." *The Social Science Journal*, 36, no. 1 (1999).

Augusta, Bedford, Botetourt, Culpeper, and Fincastle payrolls and public service claims, 1775. Fort Wayne, Indiana: Allen County Public Library.

Amos, Christine, "Pisgah Rural Historic District," National Register of Historic Places Nomination Form (Washington, DC: U.S. Department of the Interior, National Park Service, 1989), Section 7.

Appleman, Roy E. "Joseph and Reubin Field, Kentucky Frontiersman of the Lewis and Clark Expedition and their Father, Abraham." *Genealogies of Kentucky Families.* Filson Club History Quarterly, Baltimore, Maryland: Genealogical Publishing Company, 1981.

Ardery, Mrs. William Breckenridge. *Kentucky Court and Other Records: Wills, Deeds, Orders, Suits.* Staunton, Virginia: Genealogical Publishing Company, 1999.

Atherton, William. *Narrative of the Suffering and Defeat of the North-Western Army Under General Winchester.* Frankfort, Kentucky: A.G. Hodges, publisher, 1842.

Atkinson, George W. *History of Kanawha County.* Charleston: Printed at the Office of the West Virginia Journal, 1876.

Beatty, Erkuries. Diary (25 April 1787) New York Historical Society Library. New York, New York.

Beckwith, B. W. *History of Vigo and Parke Counties.* Chicago, Illinois: H. H. Hill and N. Iddings, Publishers, 1880.

Bowen, A.W. *History of Montgomery County, Indiana: with personal sketches of representative citizens.* Vol. 1. Indianapolis, Indiana: A.W. Bowen & Company, 1913.

Boyd, Gregory A. *Family Maps of Montgomery County, Indiana.* Plat Map. Norman, Oklahoma: Arphax Publishing Company, 2006.

Bradsby, Henry C. *History of Vigo County, Indiana.* Chicago, Illinois: S.B. Nelson & Company, 1891.

Bratton Historian, Vol. II, No. 1, Muskogee, Oklahoma. Bratton Association, 1979.

Brown, Orlando. "The Governors of Kentucky." *Register of the Kentucky Historical Society.* 1951.

Bruns, Jean Randolph. *Abstracts of the Wills and Inventories of Bath County, Virginia, 1791-1842.* Baltimore, Maryland: Clearfield Publishing Company, 1995.

Cemeteries in Montgomery County, Indiana. Vol. 11, Wayne Township. Crawfordsville, Indiana: Dorothy Q. Chapter, Daughters of the American Revolution. 1973.

Cerami, Charles A. *Jefferson's Great Gamble: the Remarkable Story of Jefferson, Napoleon and the Men Behind the Lousiana Purchase.* Chicago, Illinois: Sourcebooks, Incorporated, 2003.

Chalkley, Lyman. *Chronicles of the Scotch-Irish Settlement in Virginia: extracted from the Original Court Records of Augusta County, 1745-1800*. Vol. 1. Rosslyn, Virginia: Commonwealth Printing Company, 1912.

Chesterson, Maud J. Bratton. "William Bratton: His Service in the Lewis and Clark Expedition, 1804-1806 and in the War of 1812." Indiana Pamphlet-00000106839277, Indiana State Library.

Chuinar, Eldon G. *Only One Man Died: the Medical Aspects of the Lewis and Clark Expedition*. Fairfield, Washington: Ye Gallon Press, 2002.

Clark, Murtie June. *America Militia in the Frontier Wars, 1790-1796*. Baltimore, Maryland: Genealogical Publishing Company, 2009.

Clark, Thomas D. and Margaret Lane. *The People's House: Governor Mansions of Kentucky*. Lexington, Kentucky: University Press of Kentucky, 2002.

Cleek, George W. and Catherine Cleek Mann. *Early Western Augusta Pioneers*. Staunton, Virginia: Genealogical Publishing Company, 1957.

Clement, Eaton. "Slave-hiring in the Upper South: A Step toward Freedom." *The Mississippi Valley Historical Review* 46, no. 4 (March 1960).

Clift, G. Glenn. *Remember the Raisin!: Kentucky and Kentuckians in the Battles and Massacre at Frenchtown, Michigan Territory, in the War of 1812*. Frankfort, Kentucky: Kentucky Historical Society, 1961.

Conner, Roberta, speaker. *Lewis & Clark: An American Epic*. Gilder Lehrman Institute of History teacher seminar. Missoula, Montana. 15 July 2014.

Cox, Sandford C. *Recollections of the Early Settlement of the Wabash Valley*. Lafayette, Indiana: Courier Steam Book and Job Printing House, 1860.

Cruikshank, Ernest. "The Battle of Fort George." Niagara, New York: Niagara Historical Society. 1896. Reprint, Gutenberg, 2010.

Cuming, Fortescue. *Sketches of a Tour*. Pittsburg, Pennsylvania: Cramer, Spear & Kichbaum, 1810.

Darnall, Elias. "A Journal Containing An Accurate and Interesting Account of the Hardships, Sufferings, Battles, Defeat, and Captivity of Those Heroic Kentucky Volunteers and Regulars Commanded by General Winchester In the Years 1812-1813." Paris, Kentucky, 1813.

Darnell, Ermina Jett. *Filling in the Chinks*. Frankfort, Kentucky: Roberts Printing Company, 1966.

DeWitt, John H. "General James Winchester, 1752-1826." Tennessee Historical Magazine. Vol. 1, No. 2.

Dillard, R. T. "A Fragment of Kentucky History." *The Observer & Reporter*, Frankfort, Kentucky, November 14, 1843.

Downing, George C. "Early Marriage Bonds of Franklin County, Kentucky, 1803, 1804, 1805." The Register of the Kentucky Historical Society. Vol. 12, No. 36: 79.

Drake, Dr. Daniel. *Pioneer Life in Kentucky: A Series of Reminiscential Letters from Daniel Drake, M.D. of Cincinnati to His Children*. Cincinnati, Ohio: Robert Clarke & Company, 1870.

Dunbar, Seymour. *A History of Travel in America*. New York, New York: Tudor Publishing Company, 1937.

Dye, Ira. Introduction. Records Relating to America Prisoners of War, 1812-1815. British Records Relating to America in Microform (BRRAM) Series. London, England, 1980.

Eblen, Tom. "A Historic Icon, Kentucky Long Rifle Increasingly Seen as a Work of Art, too." Herald-Leader, 11 March 2014.

Eckert, Allan W. *A Sorrow in our Heart: the Life of Tecumseh*. New York, New York: Bantam Books, 1992.

Elmer, Josephine D. "The River Raisin Massacre and Dedication of Monuments." Historical Collections, Vol. 35. Michigan State Historical Society.

Eslinger, Ellen, ed. *Running Mad for Kentucky: Frontier Travel Accounts*. Lexington, Kentucky: The University Press of Kentucky, 2004.

Espy, Josiah. 1805. *A Tour in Ohio, Kentucky and Indiana Territory in 1805*. Robert Clarke & Company, 1871.

Falkenstein, George. *The German Baptist Brethren or Dunkers*. Lancaster, Pennsylvania: The Pennsylvania – German Society, 1900.

Fields, James T. to Eva Dye Letter. 18 November 1901. Eva Emery Dye Collection. Oregon Historical Society. Portland, Oregon.

Fogg, Ella Marea Meehan. Thesis titled "A Survey of the Schools of Honey Creek Township, Vigo County, Indiana. Indiana State Teachers College, 1931.

French, Brett. "Evidence Builds that Yellowstone Island was Clark's 1806 Canoe Camp." Billings, Montana: Billings Gazette: 27 April 2014.

Friend, Craig Thompson. *Kentucke's Frontiers*. Bloomington, Indiana: Indiana University Press, 2010.

Gorin, Sandra. *Warren County, Kentucky Order Book*. Book A. Glasgow, Kentucky: Gorin Genealogical Publishing, 1993.

Griffith, James Barton. *The Diary of Barton Griffith, Covington, Indiana, 1832-1834*. Crawfordsville, Indiana: R. E. Banta, 1932.

Hadley, John Vestal. *History of Hendricks County, Indiana: Her People, Industries, and Institutions*. Indianapolis, Indiana: B.F. Bowen & Co., Incorporated, 1914.

Hall, Daniel S. "Travelers Rest National Historic Landmark: Validation and Verification of a Lewis and Clark Campsite." Western Cultural, Inc.: June 2003.

Hall, James. *Sketches of History, Life and Manners in the West*. Vol. 2. Philadelphia, Pennsylvania: Harrison Hall, 1835.

Hamil, Lura Coolley. *A Story of Pioneering*. (The Illinois Company, 1955; Internet Archive, 2018.

Heiss, Willard, compiler. *The Honey Creek Monthly Meeting of Friends, Abstracts of Records Vigo County, Indiana. 1820*. Indianapolis, Indiana: John Woolman Press, 1961.

Hening, William Walter. *Hening's Statutes At Large*. Vol. 8. Richmond, Virginia: J. & G. Cochran, 1821.

Herndon, John Goodwin. "Colonel Alexander Dunlap (1743-1828): The Correction of an Identification." *The Virginia Magazine of History and Biography* 54, no. 4, (October 1946).

Indiana Historical Commission. *Governors Messages and Letters*, Vol. 3. Indiana Historical Collections, Vol. 12. Indianapolis, Indiana: Wm. B. Burford, 1924.

Jane Gay Stevenson Interview by Rev. John Dabney Shane. Draper Collection: Kentucky Papers, 1768-1892, 13CC:135-143, (microfilm) Wisconsin Historical Society, Madison, Wisconsin.

Jillson, Willard Rouse. *Early Frankfort and Franklin County: A Chronology of Historical Sketches Covering the Century 1750-1850*. Louisville, Kentucky: The Standard Printing Company, 1936.

Johnson, L. F. "Franklin County, Kentucky, Chapter VI: A.D. 1810-1820," The Register of the Kentucky Historical Society, Vol. 7.

Kelly, Walter H. "Arms, Arms Makers and Arms History in Kentucky," manuscript. University of Louisville, Kentucky, 1957.

Kentucky Historical Society, *Genealogies of Kentucky families: from the Register of the Kentucky Historical Society*. Frankfort, Kentucky: Kentucky: Genealogical Publishing Company, 1981.

Kindig, Joe. *Thoughts on the Kentucky Rifle in the Golden Age*. York, Pennsylvania: Trimmer Printing, Incorporated, 1960.

Knudsen, Susan L., "Cultural landscape report for the Lewis and Clark Expedition's Travelers Rest campsite near present-day Lolo, Montana" (2003). *Graduate Student Theses, Dissertations, & Professional Papers*. 1955. University of Montana. https://scholarworks.umt.edu/etd1955.

Kramer, Carl. *Capital on the Kentucky: A Two-Hundred* Year *History of Frankfort and Franklin County*. Frankfort, Kentucky: Historic Frankfort, 1986.

Kramer, Carl E. *The Corps of Discovery and the Falls of the Ohio*. Jeffersonville, Indiana: Sunnyside Press, 2003.

Lancaster, Clay. *Antebellum Architecture of Kentucky*. Lexington, Kentucky: University Press of Kentucky, 2014.

Lee, Patsy Ground. "Martinsville, Warren County's Lost City." *Smith's Grove Gazette*: 1-4. (submitted by Lee to The Kentucky Explorer as written by her great-great-uncle Victor Moulder, circa 1905.) The website address for the online article posted 16 October 2012 is defunct.

Lewis & Clark journals. University of Nebraska Lincoln. 20 Sept. 1806. (accessed 26 April 2015) https://lewisandclarkjournals.unl.edu/item/lc.jrn.1806-09-20.

Little, James Alexander. n.d. *History of the Little Family*. Plainfield, Indiana: Publishing Association of Friends.

Lossing, Benson John. *The Pictorial Field-book of the War of 1812*. New York, New York: Harper & Brothers, 1896.

Jefferson, Thomas. *Notes on the State of Virginia.* Philadelphia, Pennsylvania: H.C. Carey and I. Lea, printers, 1825.

Jones, Landon Y. *The Essential Lewis and Clark.* New York, New York: HarperCollins Publishers, 2000.

Mariner, Myrtle Fields. "William E. Bratton" *Heroes of 1812.* Nebraska Society of United States Daughters of 1812; (Omaha, Nebraska, 1930).

McAdams, Mrs. Harry Kennett. *Kentucky Pioneer and Court Records: Abstracts of Early Wills, Deeds and Marriages from Courthouses and Records of Old Bibles, Churches, Graveyards, and Cemeteries.* Berwyn Heights, Maryland: Heritage Press, 2007.

McCord, Shirley S. *Travel Accounts of Indiana, 1679-1961.* Indianapolis, Indiana: Indiana Historical Bureau, 1970.

McCormick, Ruth Glee and Essie Mae Potts. *Yountsville History*, n.p. Unpublished, 1968.

McKnight, William James. *A Pioneer Outline History of Northwestern Pennsylvania.* Philadelphia, Pennsylvania: J.B. Lippincott Company, 1905.

McRaven, Charles. *The Classic Hewn Log House: a Step-by-Step Guide to Building and Restoring.* East Peoria, Illinois: Versa Press, 2005.

McWilliams, James E. "The Panic of 1837." *The American Economy: a Historical Encyclopedia,* California: ABC-Clio, Incorporated, 2003.

Metheny, Constance Corley. *Bath County Marriage Bonds and Ministers' Returns, 1791-1853.* Warm Springs, Virginia: The Bath County Historical Society, 1978.

Michaux, Andre. *Travels to the West of the Alleghany Mountains.* London, England: D.N. Shury Publishers, 1802.

Miller, James M. "An Early Criminal Case – Samuel Fields." Indiana Quarterly Magazine of History. Vol. 1, No. 4, 1905.

Moore, Jr., Robert J. and Michael Haynes. *Lewis & Clark, Tailor Made, Travel Worn: Army Life, Clothing & Weapons of the Corp of Discovery.* Helena, Montana: Farcountry Press, 2003.

Morton, Oren Frederic. *A History of Rockbridge County, Virginia.* Staunton, Virginia: McClure Company, Incorporated, 1920.

Murray, Joyce Martin. Deed Abstracts of Warren County, Kentucky, 1812-1821. Ericson Books, Nacogdoches, Texas, 1986.

National Park Service, post. "Clark Canoe Camp on the Yellowstone." (accessed 25 April 2015). https://www.nps.gov/places/clark-s-canoe-camp-on-the-yellowstone.htm.

Naveaux, Ralph. *Invaded on all Sides: the Story of Michigan's Greatest Battlefield Scene of the Engagements of Frenchtown and the River Raisin War of 1812.* Marceline, Missouri: Walsworth Publishing Company, 2003.

Norwalk, Jay. *Johan Jost Zimmerman: and Related Genealogies of Roth, Yaggy, Schlunegger, Bratton, Cochlin, Elliott, Campbell and McCullough.* Newcastle, Maine: Axion Press, 1998.

Perry, Oran. *Indiana in the Mexican War*. Indianapolis, Indiana: Wm. B. Burford Printing and Binding, 1908.

Perkins, Elizabeth A. *Border Life: Experience and Memory in the Revolutionary Ohio Valley*. Chapel Hill, North Carolina: The University of North Carolina Press, 1998.

Petersen, William J. *Steamboating on the Upper Mississippi*. New York, New York: Dover Publications, Incorporated, 1995.

Pisgah Presbyterian Church and Academy, Louisville, Kentucky. Historic American Buildings Survey (photographs, measured drawings, written historical and descriptive data), National Park Service, U.S. Department of the Interior. Prints and Photographs Division, Library of Congress (HABS KY 120-PISG V, 1- and 2-).

Porter, William Arthur. *The Descendants of Peter Porter, an emigrant of 1621*. Minneapolis, Minnesota: Argus Publishing Company, 1937.

Railey, William E. *History of Woodford County*. Frankfort, Kentucky: Roberts Printing Company, 1928.

Ranck, George Washington. *History of Lexington, Kentucky: Its Early Annals and Recent Progress*. Cincinnati, Ohio: Robert Clarke & Company, 1872.

Remley, David. *Kit Carson: The Life of an American Border Man*. Norman, Oklahoma: University of Oklahoma Press, 2011.

Robinson, Dick. "Henry Crawford Was an Early Merchant." Montgomery County Magazine. Dec. 1977.

Ronda, James P. *Lewis & Clark Among the Indians*. Lincoln, Nebraska: University of Nebraska Press, 1984.

Rothert, Otto. *The Outlaws of Cave-in-Rock: historical accounts of the famous highwaymen and river pirates who operated in pioneer days upon the Ohio and Mississippi Rivers and over the Old Natchez Trace*. Cleveland, Ohio: Arthur H. Clark, Publisher, 1924.

Sarver, Bina Thompson. *Memories 1816-1819*, n. p, 1976.

Scott, B.V. *The Voice of Nature to the Invalid; or the Oxford Pioneer Medical Truth Versus Medical Mystery*. London, England: Job Caudwell, printer, 1863.

Scott, Calista. Letter. Eva Emery Dye Collection. Oregon Historical Society. 9 March 1903.

Shanklin, Mabel V. *Montgomery County, Indiana Will and Marriage Records*. Vol. 1. Danville, Illinois: Heritage House, Danville, Illinois. Vol. 1, 1971.

Shewmaker, William O. *Pisgah and her People: 1784-1934*. Woodford County, Kentucky: Pisgah Presbyterian Church, 1935.

Small Salmon, Steven, speaker. "Lewis & Clark: An American Epic." Gilder Lehrman Institute of History teacher seminar. Missoula, Montana. 16 July 2014.

Snyder, Marion Bratton. n.d. *History of William H. Bratton Family*. n.p.

Staples, Charles R. *The History of Pioneer Lexington*. Lexington, Kentucky: The University Press of Kentucky, 1996.

Stevens, Warder W. *Centennial History of Washington County, Indiana: Its*

People, Industries, and Institutions. Indianapolis, Indiana: B. F. Bowen and Company, Incorporated, 1916.

Stuart, John G. "A Journal, Remarks or Observations in a Voyage Down the Kentucky, Ohio, Mississippi Rivers." Frankfort, Kentucky: Kentucky Historical Society: 1806.

Thwaites, Reuben Gold, Ed. *Early Western Travels, 1748-1846*. Vol. 4. Cleveland, Ohio: The Arthur H. Clark Company, 1907.

Thwaites, Reuben Gold, Ed. "Meriwether Lewis letter to William Clark, 19 June 1803." *Original Journals of the Lewis and Clark Expedition, 1804-1806*. Vol. 7. New York, New York: Dodd, Mead & Company, 1905.

Tillson, Albert H. *Gentry and Common Folk: Political Culture on a Virginia Frontier, 1740-1780.* Lexington, Kentucky: University Press of Kentucky, 1991.

"Transylvania University Early Documents." TUA1, Special Collections, Transylvania University, Lexington, Kentucky.

Union Presbyterian Church. *Minutes of the Session of the Presbyterian Church of Union*. Vol. 1, 1834-1858: 17. The Marian Morrison Local History Collection. Crawfordsville District Public Library.

United States. Congress. U.S. Statutes at Large, Volume 6. Private Laws and Resolutions – 1845. United States, - 1845, 1789. Periodical. https://www.loc.gov/item/llsl-v6/.

Von Steuben, Baron Frederick William. 1794. *Revolutionary War Drill Manual*. New York, New York: Dover Publications, Inc.: reprint, 1985.

Waddell, Joseph A. *Annals of Augusta County, Virginia*. Richmond, Virginia. Wm. Ellis Jones, printer, 1886.

Walters, Pauline Randel. *The History of Churches in Montgomery County, Indiana, 1821-1975*. Wesley Methodist Church (formerly Wesley Chapel) Indiana: CPR Walters, 1975.

Waynetown Sesquicentennial, 1830-1980. Waynetown, Indiana: Waynetown Sesquicentennial Book Committee, 1980.

Wilds, John, Charles L. Dufour and Walter G. Cowan. *Louisiana, Yesterday and Today: A Historical Guide to the State*. Baton Rouge, Louisiana: Louisiana State University Press, 1996.

Willis, George L. *The History of Shelby County, Kentucky*. Louisville, Kentucky: C.T. Dearing Printing Company, 1929.

Wilson, Samuel M. "Kentucky's Part in the War of 1812." *Register of Kentucky State Historical Society*, Vol. 9, No. 27. 1911.

Wood, Russell G. The Bratton Home survey report. WPA Virginia Historical Inventory, Report 120. Library of Virginia.

Wood, Russell G. The Burger Home survey report. WPA Virginia Historical Inventory, Report 54. Library of Virginia.

Wood. Russell G. Slave Cottage survey report. WPA Virginia Historical Inventory, Report 130. Library of Virginia.

Works Progress Administration. 1939. *Military History of Kentucky*. State Journal, Frankfort, Kentucky.

Wright, Andrew. Pen name of Dudley Drewwright. Blog titled "200 Years Ago in Washington County." Blog entry, 14 Oct. 2014.

Yater, George H. *Two Hundred Years at the Falls of the Ohio: a history of Louisville and Jefferson County.* Louisville, Kentucky: The Heritage Corporation, 1979.

Young, Chester Raymond, Ed. *Westward into Kentucky: The Narrative of Daniel Trabue.* Lexington, Kentucky: The University Press of Kentucky, 1981.

INDEX

Adams, John, 31
    Martin, 169
    William Greer, 169
Agney, Peter, 178
Airhart, Polly, 232
Alexander, Jacob, 29
Allen, John, 124-125, 134-135
Anderson, 222
Arnold, John, 36, 63, 90-91, 93, 117
    Stephen, 36
Arnold's Station, 63
Ashton, Eliakim, 189
Austin, Tx., 179, 181-183
Baker, Jonathan, 165, App. A
Ball, Dennis, 209, 213, 217, 243
Ballard, Bland W., 131
    William, 45
Barclay, Samuel, 87
Barkley, James, Appendix A
Barnes, David, 223
Bates, Ephraim, 3, 24
    Thomas, 29
Battle of Fallen Timbers, 28-29
Battle of Point Pleasant, 4
Beauchamp, Dr., Appendix A
Bean, Elizabeth "Betty," 57-58
Beard, John, 190, Appendix B
Beatty, Erkuries, 18
Beeler, Isaac, 190
Bellair, Oliver, 138-139
Bereman, Thomas, 43-45
Berry, David Doak, 221, 225
    Elizabeth B. 228
    James, 221, 225
    Jane Doak, 221, 225
    John, 231
Big Barren River, 52, 155-158, 162-163
Bill, enslaved men, 23, 222
Bimson, Joseph, 34-36, 42, 51, 53-54,
    62, 90-91
    in Kentucky militia, 34-36

Blackburn, Julius, 24
Blackford, Stephen, 203
Blane, William Newnham, 167
Bledsoe, Richard, 146
Bloomfield, John, 198-199
Bob, enslaved man, 7
Bohannon, Richard, 24
Boone, Daniel, 33-34, 52, 99
    Samuel, 31-32
    Squire, 33, 99
Bostwick, Henry, Appendix B
Bowling Green, Ky., 89, 154
    157, 159, 163, 203, 217
Brandenburg, John, App. B
Brant, Henry, Appendix A
Bratton, Abel W., 235, 239
    Adam, 2, 6, 7, 15
    Adam, 7, 114, 156-157,
        161
    Adam, s/o W. E, 197, 205,
        246-247
    Agnes, 1, 7
    Andrew, 221, 223
    Andrew, s/o Wm R., 211
    Ann McFarland, 1, 7
    Anne, 1-2, 7, 17, 21-23,
        34-36, 42, 49-51, 89-91
    Annetta, 179
    Annie "Lady", 179
    Archibald, 9, 17, 21-23,
        34, 42, 50, 90, 149, 165,
        176-203, 247, 250
    Chas., s/o W. R., 223, 234
    Cynthia Moore, 248-252
    David, s/o W.R., 227-234
    Eliza Jane, 215-216
    Elizabeth, 1
    Eliz., d/o Rob. & N., 179
    Eliza. M., 149, 201, 247
    George, s/o R. & N., 164,
        168, 169-179-184

Bratton, George Sr.,
    in Virginia, 1-15
    in Ky., 17-36, 38, 40-54, 111-116
    George Jr., 9, 21, 43, 50, 90, 149-150
        154, 156-159, 208
    Geo., s/o W. E., 172, 245, 234, 248-249
    George Washington, 248
    Grizzilla Jane, 163, 250-252
    Grizzella Ann Berry, 199, 250-252
    Harriet Ann, 163
    James, s/o Wm R., 226, 227, 232
    James B., 2, 6, 7, 221
    James Maxwell, s/o Wm E., 163, 167,
        210, 219, 243
    James Maxwell, son of Archibald, 163
    Jane Frances, 168, 170, 177, 179
    Jane "Jenny," 3, 17, 42, 149, 164, 176
    Jean Elliott, 1, 2, 6, 9, 14-21
        in Kentucky, 42, 48
    John, 6-7, 29
    John, s/o Robert and Nancy, 168, 170,
        178-182
    John, s/o Wm E., 191, 245
    John, b/o Wm R., 231, 234-235, 239
    Joseph, 178-179
    Malissa, 248, 250
    Margaret, d/o Robert & Nancy, 178
    Margaret, d/o Wm R., 226-227
    Martha, d/o Wm R., 226-227
    Martha Jane Lane, 179
    Mary, 2, 7
    Mary Etta, 219, 246, 248
    Mary "Polly" Gambrel Berry, 221-225
    Mary "Polly" Hutton Maxwell, 167-174
        182-183, 186-198, 222-251
    Nancy A. G., 20
    Nancy Charlotte, 226, 230, 234
    Nancy Eunice, 179
    Nancy McCoskey, 117-118, 165, 168,
        173, 182-183
    Rachel, d/o Wm R., 226, 230, 234
    Rebecca Graham, 156
    Rebecca Hogshead, 221

Bratton, Robert, 1, 2, 7, 9
    in In., 153-154, 159-175
    in Ky.,16-21, 37-54, 91
        111, 114-115, 120
    in Ky militia, 27-28
  in Texas, 178-184
    Rob., s/o R, 177-178, 180
    Rob., s/o W., 204, 213
  Robert Pat., 1, 2, 7-9
    Susanna R. Ashley, 49-50
    Warren, 252
    Wm, s/o R,177-180
    Wm, s/o Wm E., 201, 245
    William E., 1, 15
        apprenticeship of, 31-33
        birth of, 1
        expedition, 55-87
        in In, 167-175, 185-194
        201-219, 241-244
        in Ky., 17-54, 89-120
        149-166
        War of 1812, 121-147
    William B., 163
    William H., 168-170, 177
    William R., 221-240
Brazell, James, 46
Briggs, Robert, 164
Brockman, Jas. D., Appendix B
Brooking, Samuel, Appendix A
Brookville, IN., 194-196
Brown, Caleb, Appendix B
    James, Appendix B
    Samuel, 41, 190
Bryan, Daniel, 31-32
Bryant, John, 158
    Randle D., 206
    Robert, 158-159
Bullock, George, Appendix B
Bunnell, Bazilla. Appendix A
Burbridge, Wm, 223, App. B
Burger, Joseph, 223
    Martha Crawford, 223
Burk, Patrick, 8

Burnsides, William, 217
Burr, Aaron, 31
Bush, Jacob, Appendix B
    Philip, 40
Caldwell, David, 35
Camp, John, Appendix A
canal, construction of, 233-234
Carpenter, John, Appendix B
Carpenter, William, Appendix B
Carter, Elihu, 156
Castilow, John, Appendix A
Catterlin, Ephraim, Appendix B
    T.N., 190
Chapline, William, 163
Charlotte, an enslaved woman, 222
Chesterson, Maud Mary, 186, 191, 253
Chinn, Francis, 131
    Thomas W., 146
Christian, Matthew, 46-47
Clark, Anne, 2, 63
    Elizabeth, 2
    Gen. George Rogers, 2, 56
    James, 2
    Jonathan, 67
    Joseph, 147
    Sarah, 2
    William, 2, 59-87, 185
    see also Lewis & Clark Expedition
Clarksville, Indiana, 56-57
Claypool, Reuben, Appendix B
Clifton, Nancy, 206-208
Clinch's Ford, 10
Coffey, Isaac, 46
Collier, Coleman, 146
Collins, Bartlett, 20-21
Colter, John, 65
    see also Lewis & Clark Expedition
Comstock, Lyndon, 146
Confederated Salish Kootenai tribe, 74
    see also Salish people
Cook, Abraham, 25
    Betsy Bohannon, 25
    Betsy Edrington, 25
    Hosea, 25

Cook, Jesse, 25
Cook's Station, 25
Cooley, James Maxwell, 251
    Jon., 203-211, 242-249
    S. M., 208, 242, App. A
Cornstalk, (Shawnee Chief) 4
Cox, Abner, Appendix B
    Joseph, 190, Appendix B
    Sandford C., 186-187
Craig, John W., 155
Crawford, Andrew, 223
    Henry, 218
    Rev. James, 20
    Marg. B., 222-228, 234
    Margaret Simpson, 224
    Nathan Sr., 223
    Nathan Jr., 222, 224, 234
    Wm, 223-224, 219, 234
Crawford Cemetery, 227
Crawfordsville, 174, 187-197
    202, 205-210, 218, 223-252
Crooks, William, 204
Crouch, Andrew, 192
    Jonathan, Appendix B
Cruft, John F., 177
Cumberland Gap, 10-11
Cuming, Fortescue, 91-116
Cunningham, Bracket, App. A
Curry, Prov. M., 189, App. B
    Thomas M., 189, App. B
Daniel, Burwell, Appendix B
Daphne, an enslaved woman, 7
Darnall, Allen, 137, 141
    Elias, 121-147
    Davis, Abigail, 215
    Isaac, 215
    Randolph, 215
    William, 24, Appendix A
Dewey, John, 190, Appendix B
Dickey, James, 24
Dickson, John, 161, 169-170
Digby, William, 193, 213
disease, 170-171
Dodd, William, Appendix B

Dollarwill, Samuel, Appendix B
Donahue, Henry, 204-205, Appendix A
    Michael, 205, Appendix A
Donaldson, Louis, Appendix A
Drake, Isaac, 21-22
    Daniel, 26
    William, 169
Dudley, Peter, 117, 147
Dudley, Thomas Parker, 140
Dunlap, Agnes Gay, 10
    Alexander Sr., 2
    Alexander Jr., 2, 10-15, 21, 30
    Elizabeth, 2
    John, 2, 3, 63
    Robert, 2
Dunmore, Lord, 4
Dunn, Bathsheba Cook, 26
    James, 38, 41
    William, 26
    Williamson, Appendix B
Durst, David, 29
Earl, William, 178
Elder, Laney, Appendix B
Elliott, Archibald, 2
    Jane Clark, 1-2
    John, 17, 20
    Margaret, 7
    Mildred Cleveland, 14
    Richard, 3
    Robert, 14
    William Sr., 1
    William Jr., 14
Ellis, James, 3
Espy, Josiah, 57
Evans, Margaret, 228
Ewing, Henry, 156
Farrar, Asa, 26
Faught, Paul, 24
Fennick, Lewis, 147
Field, Joseph, 60
    Reubin, 60
    see also Lewis & Clark Expedition
Fields, Abbie Jane, 250
    Eliza Ayers, 199
    Foster, 197-199

Fields, George Wash., 249-250
    James T., 117, 249, 252
    John, 249
    Lovia Forster, 196
    Mary, 249
    Samuel, 194-199, App. B
    Step., 199, 247, 249-250
    Stephen, 197
Findley, James, 70
Finney, John, 24
Fitch, John, 31-32
Floyd, Charles, 60
    see also L & C Expedition
Fort Clark, 32, 57
Fort Defiance, 127-128
Fort George, 141-144
Fort Harrison, 169-171
Fort Jefferson, 32
Fort Malden, 132, 137-138
Fort Nelson, 32, 35
Fort Niagara, 143-146
Fort Washington, 27-28
Fort Wayne, 124-127
Forster, Thomas, 194
Foster, John I., 190
    Mary Ann, 228
Fowler, John, 20
Franciscoe, Capt. John, 28
Frankfort, KY, 35-44, 47, 91-92
    111-117, 123, 146-147, 167
Frankfort Bridge Company, 47
Franklin, Benjamin, 75
Frenchtown, 129-139
Fry, Eliz. Julia Speed, 214
    Dr. Tom. Walker, 214, 236
Gapen, Zachariah, 190
Garrard, James, 38, 40-41, 50
Gass, Patrick, 70-87
    see also L & C Expedition
Gay, James, 10
    John, 10, 12
    Sarah Lockridge, 10, 12
Gayley, William W, App. B
Geeter, Bunnell, 159
George, enslaved man, 119-120

Gibson, George, 66
   see also Lewis & Clark Expedition
Girty, James, 125
   Simon, 125
Givan, James L., Appendix B
Givens, Robert, 7
   William, 7
Gladden, William, Appendix B
Goode, Samuel, 157, 161
gouging, 18
  see also hand-to-hand fighting
Graham, Alex., 155-156, 164-165, App. A
   Lewis, Appendix B
   Nancy Hubbard, 156
   Robert, 166
   William, 31-32
Graves, Benjamin, 140
Gray, David, Appendix B
   John, 119
   John Sanford, 244-246
Greenup, Christopher, 47, 112
Gregory, Samuel, 24
Gresham, William, 46
Grider, Henry, 114-115, Appendix A
   Martin, 116, 171
Griffin, Joseph, Appendix B
   Thomas, 232
Griffith, Abraham, Appendix B
   Barton, 211-212
   Townsend, Appendix B
grist mill, 33, 155-157, 162-166
  see also mill business
gunsmithing, 31-34, 38, 42, 51
Gwin, David, 3
Hahn, Ann, 197
   Dorcas Fields, 186-187
   Joseph, 197, 200, 204
   Michael, 204
hand-to-hand fighting, 18
  see also gouging
Hall, Horatio, 27
Hall, Daniel S., 74
   James, 24
Hambleton, Andrew, 25
Hardin, Martin D., 121, 146-147

Harlow, Garret, 246
Harpe brothers, 46
Harpe, Micajah, 46-47
   Wiley, 46-47
   see also Harpe brothers
Harriman, Moses, 203-203
Harrison, Wm H, 99, 124-128
   132-133, 137, 140, 146
Hart, Nathaniel, 133, 140
Harvey, John, 31
Hayden, Ezekiel, 28
Hayhurst, John, 226
Heath, William, Appendix A
Heaton, Baldon, 206
Henderson, Elizabeth, 228
   Hannah, 228
   Joseph, 228
   Matilda, 228
Henry, John, 122
Herndon, Elisha, 147
Hickman, P., 122-124, 128-131
Hobson, Jonathan, 155
Hoggatt, Moses, 173, 178
   Robert, 178
Hogsett, James, Appendix A
Holmes, Magnus, 189
Holton, John A., 147
Hopkins, Daniel, 204
   James, 193
Howarth, Lawrence, App. A
Hubbard, Ephraim, 165
   Harriet, 165
   Nancy Stuart, 165
   S. M., 155, 166
Hubble, William, 29
Hudspeth, David, 155
Hultz, Daniel L., Appendix B
   Nathaniel W., App. B
Hughes, John, 210
Humble, Michael, 31
Humphrey, Robert, 185-189
Hunter, William, 112
hunting, 22, 52, 61, 82-84,
  104, 188
Hutton, Grizella Maxwell, 209

Hutton, Jonathan, 54
    Joseph, 34
    Leonard, 209
    Martha "Patsy" Wilson, 209
    Mary Berry, 209-210
    Prudence Steele, 209-210
    Samuel, 34-35
    Sarah Dryden, 209
    Susannah Watkins, 54
Isaac, an enslaved man, 222
Isbell, Livingston, Appendix A
Jack, an enslaved man, 1, 3
James, Ann, 23
    Henry, 146
Jameson, Will, 8
Jamison, John, 29
Jefferson, Thomas, 55-56
    see also Lewis & Clark Expedition
Jennings, Gov. Jonathan, 171, 233
Jewell, Tabby, 3
John, Robert, 196
Johnson, Benjamin C., 155
    Cave, 27, 29
    Francis, 163
    Harvey, 217, 241
Johnston, Rob, 191-192, Appendix B
Jones, Matthew, 31-32
Judge, Hugh, 172
Keel, James, 155
Kelly, Samuel, 14
Kennedy, David, 35
Kentucky Academy, 30-31
Kentucky Gazette, 20, 27, 36
Kerr, John G., 242
Kesly, Jacob, 53
Key, George, 189
Killen, John, 190, Appendix B
King, Edward, Appendix A
Kinkead, William, 6
Kirk, James, 8-9
Kirkham, Michael, 29
Krout, Jacob, 215
    Jane, 215
    Mary Hannah Kennedy, 215
    Robert Kennedy, 199, 214, 242

Lambert, Isaac, 161, 169-170
Lasselle, Jocko, 134
    Nannette, 134
Laughlin, James O, Appendix B
Latta, Barbara Mewhinney, 183
    James, 179-180, 183
    John, 164
    Malinda Burrows, 183
    Mary J. McCoskey, 164
    William, 179-180, 183
    Sylvanus, 183
Leiper, John, 46-47
Lexington, Kentucky, 10-18
Lewis, an enslaved man, 241
Lewis, Aaron, 149, 164
    Archibald, Appendix A
    Andrew, 4
    Fanny, 157
    George, 176-177
    John, 3
    James A., Appendix A
    Isaac O., 157
    Isham, 119
    Lilburne, 119
    Meriwether, 55-87
      see also L & C Exp.
    William, 129, 136
    Zachariah B., 147
Lewis & Clark Exp., 53-84
Liggett, John, Appendix A
Lillard, Thomas, 37
Lilly, an enslaved woman, 222
Lindsey, Neville, 46
Liston, Edmund, 169
    Joseph, 169
Little, Alexander, 31, 151-152
    Thomas, 17, 31
Little Turtle, 28
Lockridge, Elizabeth C., 235
    Rachel, 235
Logan, James, Appendix B
Long, Henry, 230
    Ruben, Appendix A
Loop, Andrew, 237-238
Love, James, 38

Love, Thomas, 40
Lucas, Bennet, Appendix A
    Sary, Appendix A
Lyons, Henry, 156
Mack, Amos, Appendix B
    John, Appendix B
Madison, James, 122
Magness, Joseph, Appendix A
Mann, Christopher, 206-208
    Elizabeth Rusk, 206
    John, 206
    Samuel, 216
    William, 206
Manual Labor College, 212
Mariner, Myrtle Fields, 186, 252
Martin, William, Appendix B
    Hut, 51
Mary, an enslaved woman, 222
Mastin, Lewis, 26
    Margaret Cook, 26
Martindale, Miles, Appendix B
Maxey, John, Appendix A
Maxwell, Betsy, 201
    David C., 165, 201-202, 217
    Grisal Berry, 163, 202, 209
    Harriet, 163, 165
    James, 163, 165, 203, Appendix A
    John, 163, 201-203, Appendix A
    Malinda, 163, 201-203, 208
    Martha, 163, 202-203, Appendix A
    Martha, d/o David C., 201
    Prudence, 163, 202-203
May, an enslaved woman, 222
Mayhall, Francis, 146
    John, 146
McBee, Silas, 46
McBrayer, Jane Montgomery, 46
McCabe, David, 224
McCain, Daniel, Appendix B
    Thomas, Appendix B
McCallester, James, Appendix A
McClelland, Dr. Albert, 244
McClelling, James, Appendix B
McClung, Samuel, 191-192, 204
    Rebecca Bratton, 222

McConnell, E., Appendix B
    Francis, 11
McConnell's Station, 10-12
McCoskey, John, 117, 151
    Joseph, 164, 176
    Nancy Little, 151, 164
    Robert, 164
    Thomas C., 164, 176
McCullough, John, Appendix B
McCutcheon, William G., 228
McDaniel, Joshua, 228
McFarland, Duncan, 3
McFarling, Alexander, 46
    John, 46
McGraw, John, 156
McIllvain, Moses, 14
McIntire, James, 250
McKinney, John, 10
McMurtry's Station, 34
McQuidey, James, 31-32
McWilliams, Charlotte, 238
Mendenhall, Absalom, 191-192
Merrell, William, Appendix B
Michaux, Andre, 52-53
Middleton, Mathias A., App. A
    Thomas, 90
mill business, 33, 155, 162-166
    see also grist mill
Miller, Abe, 190
    Charles, Appendix A
    George, 190, Appendix B
    George Davidson, 209
    Grisal Maxwell, 209-210
    Jacob, 190, Appendix B
    John, 190, Appendix B
Mitchell, Asa T., Appendix A
Moore, Elias. Appendix A
    Lawson, 215
    Reuben, 169
    Samuel, 176
    William, 192
Morris, Jacob, 154
    Miriam Bogue, 154
Morehead, James, 157
Mosburger, Daniel, 205

Mose, an enslaved man, 1, 3
Mt. Olivet Cumberland Presby. Ch., 163
Mt. Pisgah, 14, 19, 67
   see also Pisgah Presbyterian Church
Mt. Zion Presbyterian Church, 19
Munger, Laura, 208
      Reuben, 208
Murray, William, 18
Murphy, Robert, 194-195
Nail, Thomas, 3
Nall, Martin, 24
      William, 24
Napper, Fanny Alley, 10
Nash, William, 154, 157
Nat, an enslaved man, 241
Neal, Richard D, Appendix A
      Winston M., Appendix B
Neale, Thomas M., 164
Ned, an enslaved man, 58
New Madrid, 107, 117-118
Nez Perce, 77
   see also Lewis & Clark Expedition
Nicholson, Henry, 190
      Robert, 190
      William, 190, Appendix B
Nutt, Henry K., Appendix B
O'Bannon, William, 29
O'Dowland, Bridget, 8
Ogamorpenance, Chief, 135
Old Pioneer Cemetery, 244, 247-248, 252
Ordway, John, 55-87, 118
   see also Lewis & Clark Expedition
Orville, an enslaved man, 222
Page, J.R., 249
Palladium, 58, 44, 57-58, 64
Parker, William, 208
Patterson, Benjamin, Appendix B
      John, Appendix B
      Joseph, Appendix B
Paxton, James, 91
Payne, William R. 159
Pemberton, Bennet, 38
Peggy, an enslaved woman, 222
Perry, Lewis, 29
Phelan, Richard, Appendix B

Phelan, William, Appendix B
Philips, Arch. Bratton, 250-251
      George, 250-253
      Minnie, 251
Pinkston, Daniel T., 175
Pisgah, comm. of, 14-15, 67
Pisgah Presbyt. Ch, 14, 19, 67
   see also Mt. Pisgah
Poage, George, 3
Pogue, Elizabeth, 228
      Cynthia Ann, 228
      Hannah, 228
      Jane, 228
      John H., 228
      Silas, 228
Porter, Delilah, 227-228
      John, 225-228, 234-235
      John Reason, 226
      Margaret, 234-235
      Mary Elizabeth, 225
      Nancy A Bratton, 225-226
      Nancy Jane, 234-235
      R. B., 225-226, 234-235
      Rebecca, 228
      William Arthur, 226
Pottawatomies, 126-127
Pound, Daniel, 179
Powers, Jonathan, 189
      Lovia Fields, 197
Preston, William, 8
Prevost, Sir George, 143
Price, Maj. William, 28
      William, 31-32
POW parole, 144-146
Pryor, Nathaniel, 66
   see also L & C Expedition
Quick, Edwin, 206
Quisenberry, Jane, 163
      Nicholas, 163, Appendix A
Ramey, Sinnet, Appendix B
      W. P., 190
Ramsey, William, 24
Rankin, A., 12-14, 19-20, 67
Rariden, Elizabeth, 194
Ray, Gov. James, 195

Rayburn, John, Appendix B
Reed, Moses B., 70
    see also Lewis & Clark Expedition
Remley, David, 253
Renick, Alexander, 147
Republic of Texas, 179-181
Revolutionary War, 5-6, 75
Rice, David, 30
Richardson, Jesse, 191-192
    John, 147
    Nathaniel, 44-45
Ristine, Ben T., 189, 212, App. B
    Henry, Appendix B
Ristine, John. Appendix B
River Raisin Massacre, 139-141, 47
Robertson, Alexander, 147
Robinson, Hezekiah, Appendix B
    Josephus, Appendix B
    William, 91
Roby, Thomas, Appendix B
Robey, Mary, 184
Rolf, Walter, 196
Rolston, James, Appendix B
Roosevelt, Nicholas, 94, 118-119
Roquefort, Simon, Appendix B
Roundhead, 135
Rude, Isaac, 159
Rusk, David, 206
Rust, Tom, 84
Sal, an enslaved woman, 1, 3
Salish people, 74
    see also Conf. Salish Kootenai tribe
Sam, an enslaved man, 222
Sarver, Bina Thompson, 171, 213
Satchwill, Reed, Appendix B
Saunders, Ralph, 84-85
Scott, Gen. Charles, 28, 113, 123
    James, Appendix B
    Joseph, Appendix B
    Lucius H., 170
    Robert Wilmot, 40
    Samuel, Appendix B
Scruggs, William, 27, 29-30
Sebree, Uriel, 146
Seceder Cemetery, 199

Sellers, Isaac, 38
Settle, William, 31
Shane, Rev. John Dabney, 10
Shanklin, James, 226
Shannon, George, 65
    see also L & C Expedition
Sharp, Solomon P., 162
Shelby, Gov. Isaac, 27, 34, 146
Sheldon, Charles. Appendix A
Shields, John, 66
    see also L & C Expedition
Simpson, Thomas, 31
    William, 162
Slevin, William, 3
Small, Mrs., Appendix A
smallpox, 43-44, 239
Smith, Alfred, Appendix B
    Andrew, 223-224
    Charles, 29
    Jacob, 156
    John, Appendix B
    Mary Speed, 214
    Mrs. Stephen, 57
    Thomas, Appendix B
    William, 214
Soesbe, Anna M, 164, 175
    Daniel Jr., 164, 175, 177
    Daniel Sr., 177
Spalding, Charles, Appendix A
Spear, R. W., 175
Speed, Judge John, 214
St. Clair, Gen. Arthur, 28
Steele, Andrew, 30
    Prudence Berry, 209
    William, 24, 27, 29
Stegall, Moses, 46
Stephens, Thomas L., App. A
    Warner, 155
Sterrett, Thomas, Appendix A
Stevenson, Samuel, 10-15
    Jane Gay, 10-15
Steward, William, 158
Stitt, John, 190
    Judge, 190
Stoddard, Amos, 63

Stone, Daniel, 163
    Samuel, 155
Stuart, Alexander, 150, 157, 165, App. A
    Ann Mariah, 213, 217
    Charles, 165, 213, 217, 241-242
    Harriet Amanda, 213-214, 217
    James Alexander, 213-214, 217
    James, 157, 166
    John G., 86-114
    Mary, 90
    Mary Elizabeth, 213-214, 217
    Sarah Berry, 165, 213-219, 241-244
    Sarah Jane, 213-214, 217, 241
Stucker, Philip, 1114-115
Sumner, James, Appendix A
Sutton, David, 29
Swearingen, John, 204
Switzer, Milton J., 248
    William, 216
Symmes, John C., Appendix
    William, Appendix B
Talbert, William, 205
Tarleton, Gen. Banastre, 5-6
Taylor, Fanny, 205
Tecumseh, 121
Telford, Robert, 154
    Sarah Ann McCoskey, 154
Temple, Benjamin, 67
Terre Haute, In., 166, 159-168-183
Thompson, Enoch. Appendix B
    Isabella, 196
    John, 194, 196, 199
    Joseph, Appendix B
    Sarah, 194, 196, 199
Thompson Cemetery, 199
Todd, Levi, 21
    Thomas, 45
Tolliver, John, Appendix B
Tompkins, James, 46
Trabue, John, 46
Trahan, John, Appendix B
Transylvania Seminary, 18, 30
Trigg, William, 38
Tully, John, 46
Turner, James C., 175

Umatilla people, 77-78
    see also L & C Expedition
Union Hill Cemetery, 240
Union Hill Presbyt. Ch, 228
Vance, D., 209, 223, App. B
Vanlandingham, Benj., App. A
Varswell, Jones, 36
Voorhies, Peter G., 124
Von Steuben, Baron, 75-77
Vredenburg, Hackaliah, 189
Wabash College, 209, 212
Wabash Courier, 178
Walker, Elizabeth Forster, 196
    James Forster, 196
    Rachel Fields, 196
Walkup, John, 228
Wallace, Rev. Matthew G., 198
Walnut Hill Presby. Ch, 19
Ward, John, 34
Ware, Isaac, 29
    William, Appendix A
Warren, John, Appendix B
Washburn, Cornelius, App. A
    John W., 205, App. A
    Joseph, 205
    William, Appendix A
Washington, Geo., 6, 27-28, 75
Watkins, Isaac, 223
Watts, John, 208
Wayne, Gen. Anthony, 28, 56
Waynetown, IN., 198, 213, 216, 218, 242-244, 247-248, 252
Weir, James, 117
Weisinger, Dan., 38-39, 40, 42
Wesley, community of, 216
West, Edward, 31-32
White, Robert, 46
Whitlock, Maj. A., 188, App. B
Wilderness Road, 10-14
Wilhite, William, Appendix B
Willard, Alexander, 63, 67
    see also L & C Expedition
William, an enslaved man, 222
Williams, Jane, 206
    John, 29

Williams, Samuel, 126
    Samuel L., 146
Williamson, Isaac, Appendix B
Wilson, David, 91
    James, 24, 147
    William, Appendix A
    Thomas, 42, 44
Winchester, James, 126-134, 137
Wise, Michael, 229-230, 234, 239
Wisehart, John, 232
Work, Samuel, Appendix A
Wright, Elizabeth, 3
    Jane E., 232
Youel, Jane Berry, 225-226, 228, 230-231
Youel, Mary Margaret, 225
    William Nelson, 225, 228-229
York, 74, 77-78, 82, 84-85
    see also Lewis & Clark Expedition
Young, Margaret "Peggy" McCoskey, 164
    Richard, 24
    Samuel, 164
Zimmerman, William, 228
Zuck, Abraham, 241, 243

www.ingramcontent.com/pod-product-compliance
Lightning Source LLC
Chambersburg PA
CBHW020655060526
44119CB00068B/23